BREAD AND JUSTICE

BREAD AND JUSTICE

Toward a New International Economic Order

JAMES B. McGINNIS

PAULIST PRESS
New York / Ramsey

Cover Design: Gloria Ortíz

Library of Congress
Catalog Card Number: 79-90224

ISBN: 0-8091-9537-2

Published by Paulist Press
Editorial Office: 1865 Broadway, N.Y., N.Y. 10023
Business Office: 545 Island Road, Ramsey, N.J. 07446

Printed and bound in the
United States of America

Acknowledgements

We wish to acknowledge material taken from the following works:

"Development and Underdevelopment: Two Sides of the Same Coin":
Reprinted by permission of *Development Education Viewpoint*, the
Development Education Centre, Toronto, 1975 #1.

"Price Stabilization for Whom?": Reprinted by permission of *Bread
for the World*, New York, September 1977.

Food First by Joseph Collins and Frances Moore Lappe: Reprinted
with permission. Copyright © 1977, Boston, Houghton-Mifflin, Inc.

"The Limitations of the Trade Issue" by John Dillon: Reprinted by
permission of GATT-Fly, Toronto, 1973.

"Export Agriculture and Economic Development" by Peter Dorner:
Reprinted by permission of the Interfaith Center for Corporate Responsibility, New York, 1976.

"Jute, Not Plastic" by Rudolf H. Strahm: Reprinted by permission of
Ideas and Action, Food and Agricultural Organization, Freedom from
Hunger Campaign/Action for Development Program, Rome, Novem-
ber 1976.

Graph of the National Land for People Program: Reprinted by permission of NLP, California.

Ad for Allis-Chalmer Corporation: Reprinted by permission of Allis-Chalmer.

Charts from the Del Monte Working Group: Reprinted by permission.

Bill Mauldin cartoon: Copyright © 1973, The Chicago Sun-Times. Reproduced by courtesy of Wil-Jo Associates, Inc. and Bill Mauldin.

Nestlé boycott emblem: Reprinted by permission of INFACT.

Contents

Acknowledgements

This book has been truly a cooperative venture. It is dedicated to those people whose struggles for justice are described inside and whose contributions to both the text and to my own commitment to justice are greatly appreciated. Special thanks are due to Mary Evelyn Jegen, SND, of Bread for the World's Education Fund, who originally commissioned the work and whose faith in me is a real gift. Those who helped me with Part II include Jack Nelson (Clergy and Laity Concerned), Joe Collins and Toby Stewart (Institute for Food and Development Policy), Dave Nesmith (National Land for People), Brennon Jones (Bread for the World), Frank Quinlivan, CSC (Justice and Peace Office, South Bend), and Philip Land, SJ (Center of Concern). I was helped in Part III by Doug Johnson and others working with the Infant Formula Action Coalition, Mike Crosby, OFM Cap (National Catholic Coalition for Responsible Investment), Mary Roodkowsky (Boston Industrial Mission), Harris Gleckman (United Nations Commission on Transnational Corporations), Robin Jurs (Del Monte Working Group), Richard Barnet (Transnational Institute), Al Gedicks (Community Action on Latin America), Jim Phillips (American Friends Service Committee, Cambridge). In Part IV, Sheldon Gellar (Indiana University) and Akumar Kumar (Gandhi Peace Foundation) were quite helpful. Earl Pike (Shakertown Pledge Group) and Don Foran, SJ (Seattle University) contributed to Part V. Other members of both the International Coalition for Development Action and the National Coalition for Development Action made valuable contributions, especially Steve Commins, Jane Blewett, Roy

Laishley, Bill Davis, SJ, and Viki Oshiro. I also appreciate the suggestions from the many teachers who reviewed the manuscript, especially Tony Cernera at Bread for the World. Present and former staff members of our Institute for Education in Peace and Justice helped greatly. Kathy McGinnis was invaluable as an editor. Most of the graphics originated with Beth Druhe Gorman. Greg Stevens and Mary Ann McGivern, SL, offered numerous suggestions throughout the text. Chris Henderson, Duane Jager, and Marilyn Lorenz did important research, especially in Part III. To all of you, thanks.

Why don't those poor countries help themselves? Why are some people saying that poverty overseas is caused by the policies of rich countries? Aren't the causes within poor countries themselves? With food production increasing and with the Green Revolution, why does world hunger persist? Why are some people so upset with multinational corporations? Why is trade so important for Third World countries (that is, the countries of Latin America, Asia, and Africa)? What's behind the high oil prices imposed by the oil-producing countries? Does foreign aid do any good? Is capitalism the answer or is socialism? What about population control? What is this "new" international economic order all about? What can be done about any of these things? The issues seem so complex, what should I do? Besides, what does any of this have to do with a person's religious faith?

Have you ever found yourself asking any of these questions? If so, then you should find *Bread and Justice* a helpful tool in trying to answer them. *Bread and Justice* is written especially for three groups of people:

(1) People concerned about world hunger: what are its underlying causes, what changes in the international economic order have to happen if hunger is to be overcome, and what can we do to help bring about these changes?

(2) People concerned about justice: what does justice mean, what are the major justice issues in the world today, how do these issues relate to us, and what can we do about them?

(3) People looking for a way to understand, evaluate, and act on global economic issues, particularly the "New International Economic Order" (hereafter referred to as the NIEO).

Bread and Justice is addressed in a special way to people professing the Christian faith. As the World Council of Churches put it in the documents of their Fifth Assembly

(Nairobi, Kenya, 1975), individual Christians and the Christian churches have a vital role to play in these issues.* Specifically, in "Human Development: Ambiguities of Power, Technology, and Quality of Life," we Christians are challenged to do three things:

"1. joining hands with all who are engaged in the task of organizing the poor in their fight against poverty and injustice;
"2. educating the more privileged to co-operate in the establishment of new socio-economic orders with changed wealth and income distributions enabling a production pattern and use of technology favouring the needy;
"3. searching for new structures for human beings to live together in justice, freedom, and peace." (section #12)

The "new socio-economic orders" and "new structures" referred to by the World Council of Churches include in a special way the NIEO. In the next paragraphs, the document urges Christians to study the NIEO carefully:

"As an effort to restructure patterns of international trade, transfer of resources, and technology, to bring about monetary reforms, and to change patterns of decision-making in international economic affairs, all geared to ensure that the poorest countries of the world have a fairer share in these matters, the NIEO deserves to be studied carefully. However, we must not forget that at the international level there are yet no political processes to implement any radical change in the economic order and that changes in *international* economic orders alone do not go to the roots of the problems of poverty and underdevelopment. The question is: Can a new (i.e., a more just) international economic order really be built on the basis of the present one or should it at the same time be accompanied by changes at the national level?" (section #14)

It is clear from this World Council of Churches statement that a new *international* economic order will need to be coupled by basic changes within countries—new national or *inter-*

nal economic orders. That is why this book is entitled *Bread and Justice*. If our concern is the poor of this world, then we should judge the proposals for change in the international economic order by how well they help the poor to achieve "bread" and "justice." "Bread" stands for or is a shorthand expression for the overcoming of world hunger by increasing peoples' opportunity to feed themselves. "Bread," then, means helping people get the means (land, irrigation, etc.) to produce their own food more than it means shipping our surplus food overseas. "Justice" means the right of each person to basic human necessities, to dignity, to control over their own lives, and the corresponding duty to promote these rights with and for others.

But what about the subtitle of this book—*Toward a New International Economic Order*? What is this NIEO and in what ways is it "new"? Basically, the NIEO is a set of principles and a series of proposals for change in the institutions and rules governing the international economic order. It is "new" in at least three senses.

First, while the principles and many of the proposals for change have been urged at the United Nations and elsewhere since at least 1964, they were formulated and approved only in 1974 and 1975—at the Sixth and Seventh Special Sessions of United Nations General Assembly.

Secondly, the NIEO is "new" in that it calls for a "restructuring" of the international economic order. Despite the efforts of many First World (the industrialized capitalist countries—U.S., Canada, Japan, and Western Europe) countries to limit the changes to a modest reform of the present or "old" international economic order, the United Nations documents and most versions or perspectives on the NIEO go much further. They see the necessity of changing the basic international institutions and the basic "rules of the game" that regulate the international economic order. This is what the

World Council of Churches means when it says in the same document referred to earlier that

> "Poverty, we are learning, is caused primarily by unjust structures that leave resources and the power to make decisions about the utilization of resources in the hands of a few within nations and among nations, and that therefore one of the main tasks of the Church when it expresses its solidarity with the poor is to oppose these structures at all levels." (section #11).

Bread and Justice focuses specifically on some of these structures: what they are and how they relate to world hunger, some ways in which these structures need to be changed, and some ways in which we can help bring about these changes. *Bread and Justice* downplays other factors in world hunger—such as population and the impact of oil price increases on Third World countries—not because these factors are unimportant, but in order to highlight those structural factors not adequately treated in most popular discussions of hunger.

Thirdly, the NIEO is "new" in that it embodies a new—or at least different—vision or model of development than the one pursued during the UN's first two "Decades of Development" (1960s and 1970s). Not all interpretations of the NIEO agree on this. Many Third World countries, as well as First World and Second World (the USSR and the communist countries of Eastern Europe) countries, still think of "development" primarily in terms of higher Gross National Product, increased rates of growth, larger scale technology, modern buildings, greater production and consumption of modern conveniences (cars, TVs, air conditioners, etc.).

Others, however, are challenging the economic growth models and the affluent life-styles of the West. They (and I) see economic development as a part of, but secondary to, human development. If we view development in human terms—as many of the versions or perspectives on the NIEO do—then we get a little different picture. The traditional values and culture of a people become more important than the rate of technological advancement or the modernization of buildings. An increase in peoples' participation in decision-making and in control over their own lives becomes more important than an increase in the Gross National Product.

The term being used to describe this "new" vision or model of development is "self-reliant development." In this book, self-reliant development is defined as

> a model of development that emphasizes meeting the basic human needs of the masses of people in a country— through strategies geared to the particular human and natural resources, values, and traditions of the country, and through strategies maximizing the collective efforts of people within each country and among Third World countries as a whole.

Out of all this come four basic statements or positions around which *Bread and Justice* revolves:

(1) Hunger is a *scandal, not a scourge*; that is, it is the result of specific human decisions, not natural calamities.

(2) These decisions are made through institutions, especially global economic and political institutions, and thus it is these *institutions or structures that must be changed.*

(3) The NIEO represents a major attempt to make some of the necessary changes in global economic institutions, but a new *internal* economic order (a redistribution of wealth and power within countries) is equally important for Third World countries, if "bread and justice" are to be achieved for the whole human family.

(4) It is both possible and necessary for us to promote such changes, difficult as they are.

---

*The excerpts from the Fifth Assembly of the World Council of Churches are taken from the documents printed in *Breaking Barriers, Nairobi 1975,* edited by David Paton and published by Wm. Eerdmans Publishing Co., Grand Rapids, MI, 1977.

Thus, *Bread and Justice* takes a position on the issues. It is important to realize from the outset that there are different positions on each of the issues presented in this book. At least one of these positions is included in each Part, along with my own. Several times this is done in a "point-counterpoint" format. Within the space limitations of this book, I try to develop and document my position as thoroughly as possible. Particularly in Chapter 12, where a specific corporation is singled out as a case study, I have tried to get the company's position and data, as well as its critics'. Where there is conflicting data, I have generally used the most conservative figures, so as not to overstate my positions. Finally, while I clearly draw conclusions and take stands throughout the book, I try to acknowledge the extent of the evidence for my conclusions and stands. That is, if the evidence seems to support a position, then I use the word "seems."

A word about the organization of *Bread and Justice*. Part I establishes basic principles—of "justice", of "bread", and of the New International Economic Order. The other four Parts examine different aspects of the NIEO in light of the basic principles of "bread and justice." Each of these four Parts examines four questions: what is the problem, what changes does the NIEO propose with regard to that problem, how adequate are these proposals, and what can we do to promote the necessary changes.

This will not be easy reading. Economics is a complex subject. But hopefully the organization of the book, the glossary of terms with each chapter and the use of "lay" terms whenever possible, the examples and case studies, the point-counterpoint selections, and the concreteness of the action suggestions will help simplify the concepts and data. It is important that you get beyond the concepts and data to the real point of the book—to decide how to become an agent for global economic justice. In other words, "bread and justice" need to be struggled for and not just studied.

Part I

AN OVERVIEW

Introduction

As Christians, we are called to hunger and thirst for justice. Action on behalf of justice, we are told, is a "constitutive dimension" of the preaching of the Gospel.[1] "Constitutive" means absolutely essential, of the very constitution of something. Thus, action for justice is an essential part of our lives as individual Christians, as well as of the mission of our Church.

But concretely, what does it mean to do justice? Further, in light of our call to justice, how are we to think about and act on hunger and the global economic issues embodied in the "New International Economic Order"? Chapter 1 will outline four components which are crucial to a Christian vision of justice. Chapter 2 will elaborate four basic principles for dealing with hunger in light of the four components of justice. Finally, Chapter 3 will examine the New International Economic Order (NIEO) according to these same components. Thus, a Christian understanding of justice will form the framework for evaluating and acting on the specific aspects of the hunger and NIEO issues.

Chapter One

FOUR COMPONENTS OF JUSTICE

This chapter explains the meaning of justice and shows that justice requires us to work to change not only our own lives but also those institutions and rules that produce injustice.

In simple terms, justice has long been understood as giving each person his or her due. And what is due to each person is the fundamental right to live a fully human life. But what does it mean to live a fully human life? I see four major categories of rights and duties that spell out the meaning of justice. Each of these four is closely paralleled by four stages of human development. All four components of justice are deeply rooted in the Christian understanding of the human person, reflected not only in the Jewish scriptures and in the New Testament, but also in the social teaching of the Christian churches. This is especially true as that teaching has developed in the last fifteen years. In diagram, it looks like this:

Components of Justice	Their Christian Basis	Stages of Human Development
SUFFICIENT LIFE-GOODS—food, shelter, clothing, health care, skills development, work (economic rights)	The earth is the Lord's; it is for the use of all; stewardship	Security (concern for survival)
DIGNITY/ESTEEM—recognizing, affirming & calling forth the value/uniqueness of each person and each people (cultural rights)	Each person is created in the image and likeness of God	Self-worth (concern for personal recognition)
PARTICIPATION—the right of individuals & peoples to shape their own destinies (political rights)	Each person is called by Jesus to help build His Kingdom in our world	Self-determination (concern for control over one's life)
SOLIDARITY—the corresponding duty to promote these rights with & for others (duties as well as rights)	We are created in the image of a God Who is a (community) Trinity of persons	Interdependence (concern for others)

Sufficient Life-Goods

The first component of justice is the right of each person to those basic goods without which human life would be impossible. These involve three categories of goods. Food, clothing and shelter are all items people need for their individual use. Health care and skills development are essential services that are provided by and to the community as a whole. Lastly, the right and need for work—for creative worthwhile labor—is a special life-good. It serves both as a means to fulfilling other needs and as an end in itself. These are the economic rights of persons and parallel the stage of human development sometimes called security, where the concern is basically survival.

That these life-goods are matters of justice is clear from
the very first chapters of Genesis. God created the earth and
its fullness for all the people of the earth. The earth is the
Lord's, says the psalmist. Its resources are not meant just for
those with the economic, political or military power to take
them for themselves. The Scriptures are definite about this.
Economic sharing is part of the Judeo-Christian way of life. In
the Acts of the Apostles, we read about the early Christian
community: "The faithful all lived together and owned everything on common; they sold their goods and possessions and
shared out the proceeds among themselves according to what
each one needed" (2:44–45).

God's wrath toward those who refused to recognize this
fundamental human right has troubled Jews and Christians
for centuries—from the harsh condemnations of the prophets
to St. Matthew's description of the Final Judgment (25:31–46).
Amos, for instance, writes:

> For the three crimes, the four crimes, of Israel, I have
> made my decree and will not relent: because they have
> sold the virtuous man for silver and the poor man for a
> pair of sandals, because they trample on the heads of
> ordinary people and push the poor out of their path, ...
> See then how I am going to crush you into the ground as
> the threshing sledge crushes when clogged by straw; flight
> will not save even the swift, the strong man will find his
> strength useless, the mighty man will be powerless to save
> himself (2:6–16).

The notion of stewardship has been the core of Christian
teaching and practice about property or goods for twenty
centuries, in clear continuity with the Jewish tradition of
responsibility for the world's resources. The early Christian
fathers were equally explicit. To quote St. Ambrose—with
regard to the attitude of persons with possessions toward those
in need:

You are not making a gift of your possessions to the poor person. You are handing over to them what is theirs. For what has been given in common for the use of all, you have arrogated to [taken for] yourself. The world is given to all, and not only to the rich.[2]

But this is very difficult for most of us to hear. We live in a society where "more is better," where private property means private property in an exclusive sense. That is, we can do with it pretty much what we want. This is true about our national wealth as well as about our personal possessions. The Church's teaching on property—that it must always be used for the common good—is foreign to us. Many of us resist the idea that our national wealth—grain, for instance—is not ours to do with as we please, but belongs to all.

Dignity or Esteem

The second component of justice is the right to human dignity. Each person and each people (society or culture) must have their personhood—their uniqueness, values, etc.—recognized, affirmed and called forth. This component embraces what might be called the cultural rights of persons and parallels the self-worth stage of human development. As expressed by the American Baptist Churches, USA, there is both

The right to human dignity, to be respected and treated as a person, and to be protected against discrimination without regard to age, sex, race, class, marital status, income, national origin, legal status, culture or condition in society; (and)
The right of ethnic or racial groups to maintain their cultural identity and to develop institutions and structures through which that identity can be maintained.[3]

This second component of justice tells us two things. First, no one is expendable. People with physical or emotional disabilities, people in prison, people half-dead from hunger—all are equal in the sight of God. It may cost us a lot of money, time and emotional energy to respond to their special needs. But Matthew 25:31–46 will not allow us to conclude that some people are not worth it. "Whatever you do to the least of My brothers and sisters, you do unto Me."

Secondly, to do justice to another person is not to *do for* them. Rather, it is to work to enable them to develop and contribute their unique gifts to the human family. This holds true for any classroom, home, community. It also holds true for national and global development. "Helping" means *doing with* and calling forth.

For instance, in working with older people, our purpose should not be just to do for them what they cannot do for themselves. We should also try to identify what their talents, insights and interests are and seek out opportunities for these to be shared with others. Inviting older persons into our schools as resources to be learned from, rather than needy persons to be cared for, is one step in the right direction. This is equally true of poor people, especially people of different races and cultures.

Each people or culture, just as each individual person, mirrors the infinite truth, beauty, and richness of God. Each is unique. All persons have a dignity and an irreplaceability rooted in their being created in the image and likeness of God. So central is this notion that it forms the basis of the Christian Churches' teaching on human rights. Pope John XXIII's *Pacem in Terris* is echoed eloquently by the 1974 Catholic bishops Synodal statement on "Evangelization":

> Human dignity is rooted in the image and reflection of God in each of us. It is this which makes all persons essentially equal. The integral development of persons makes more clear the divine image in them. In our time the Church has grown more deeply aware of this truth; hence she believes firmly that the promotion of human rights is required by the Gospel and is central to her ministry.[4]

Participation

This third component of justice means the right of each person and each people to shape their own destinies. That is, we are all entitled to exercise some meaningful control over the political, economic and cultural forces shaping our lives. In this category come the political rights of persons, like free speech and assembly. Parallel to this component of justice is the self-determination stage of human development.

Doing justice to others, then, means working to empower them to be the *agents* of their own development and not just the beneficiaries of someone else's efforts. No one likes to be always cared for. How much greater is our satisfaction when we help design, build or create something, rather than just being allowed to enjoy it. This is as true of our childhood clubhouses as it is of our adult neighborhood community centers. It is also true in our classrooms. Students invited to help shape what happens there (some of the content of the course, ways of learning that content, and rules of classroom behavior) can develop much more than those who are just the beneficiaries of someone else's knowledge or who have to operate within someone else's rules.

Thus, *how* sufficient life-goods are provided often becomes more important than *that* they are provided. A redistribution of goods often happens only because the poor begin to organize themselves and discover their power.

A redistribution of goods without a redistribution of power is what people mean by "paternalism." "We don't want your hand-outs—we want to be represented on the city council" has a familiar ring. If it is the wealthy and influential who make the rules and who run the economic and political institutions of a society, no matter how well-meaning they may be, the poor cannot expect those rules and institutions to adequately respond to their needs. Those who make the rules get the goods. Thus, it is a redistribution of power even more than a redistribution of goods that justice demands.

In the U.S., we have experienced this demand especially in the past two decades. Black Power, La Raza, Navajo Nation, Mohawk Nation, women's groups, the United Farm Workers and other union struggles all express this fundamental right of peoples to shape their own destinies. Globally, this same expression has been felt in the various unions of Third World nations—"the Group of 77", "the Nonaligned Nations",. the Organization of Petroleum Exporting Countries (OPEC). In each case, the issue is less dependence and greater control, greater participation in shaping the economic rules of the game. Black people in southern Africa, like the farm workers in the U.S., struggle for more than better wages and working conditions. They struggle to participate fully in the political and economic institutions of their society and to develop themselves and their society according to their own values and traditions. They neither need nor want to copy anybody.

The Scriptural basis for this basic right is again the image of God. We are made in the likeness of a God Who invites us to share in the creative and redemptive work of Jesus—to recreate the earth. We are to be, in Jesus' words, "the salt of the earth" and "the light of the world" (Matthew 5:13–16). We do this not as servants but as friends of Jesus—chosen by Him to go into the world, to bear witness to the truth, and to bear fruit (John 15:12–20). Indeed, we have both a right and a duty to participate in the development of ourselves and of our society. The recent social teaching of the Christian churches strongly emphasizes this participation dimension of justice. A passage from the pastoral letter of the Catholic bishops of Appalachia—*This Land Is Home to Me*—poetically captures this theme:

> Throughout this whole process of listening to the people, the goal which underlies our concern is fundamental in the justice struggle, namely, citizen control, or community control. The people themselves must shape their own destiny. Despite the theme of powerlessness, we know that Appalachia is already rich here in the cooperative power of its own people.[5]

Interdependence or Solidarity

This fourth component of justice—and the final stage of human development—involves duties as well as rights. Because we are social beings by nature, we have a responsibility to exercise our own rights and avoid frustrating the rights of others. But even more, we have a duty to actively promote these rights with and for others. This component is best expressed in my own religious tradition in Pope Paul VI's encyclical, *On the Development of Peoples*:

> But each person is a member of society. Each is part of the whole of humankind. It is not just certain individuals, but all persons, who are called to this fullness of development. Civilizations are born, develop and die. But humanity is advancing along the path of history like the waves of a rising tide encroaching gradually on the shore. We have inherited from past generations, and we have benefitted from the work of our contemporaries; for this reason we have obligations toward all, and we cannot refuse to interest ourselves in those who will come after us to enlarge the human family. The reality of human solidarity, which is a benefit for us, also imposes a duty.[6]

Human solidarity demands action. It is action on behalf of justice, not just studying about justice, that the Gospel requires of us. Matthew's account of the Final Judgment is echoed in Jesus' parable of the Good Samaritan. The letters of John and James repeat this theme again and again—faith demands works of love:

> If one of the brothers or one of the sisters is in need of clothes and has not enough food to live on, and one of you says to them, "I wish you well; keep yourself warm and eat plenty," without giving them these bare necessities of life, then what good is that? Faith is like that: if good works do not go with it, it is quite dead (James 2:15–17).

Like Matthew, Isaias is more detailed about the kinds of works we are to do:

Is this not the sort of fast that pleases me—it is the Lord Yahweh who speaks—to break unjust fetters and undo the thongs of the yoke, to let the oppressed go free, and break every yoke, to share your bread with the hungry, and shelter the homeless poor, to clothe the person you see to be naked and not turn from your own kin? Then will your light shine like the dawn and your wound be quickly healed over. . . . If you do away with the yoke, the clenched fist, the wicked word, if you give your bread to the hungry, and relief to the oppressed, your light will rise in the darkness, and your shadows become like noon . . . . (Isaias 58:6–12)

Three kinds of action are called for in this passage and all are essential today: the works of mercy, the works of justice, and changes in our lifestyles. Solidarity expresses itself in working side-by-side with the victims of injustice, whether it be the hungry, the unemployed, the imprisoned. Isaias speaks of sharing bread with the hungry and sheltering the homeless poor. Such direct service—the traditional corporal works of mercy—can deepen our commitment to work for justice. Nothing motivates most of us quite as much as being directly touched by victims of injustice.

But solidarity means more than caring for the victims. It also means working with people to change the political, economic and cultural situations and structures that victimize them in the first place. These are the works of justice. Such works are implied in the language of liberation in Isaias— "break unjust fetters", "undo the thongs of the yoke", "break every yoke", etc.

As important as they are, the works of mercy are not enough, if we really want to love our neighbor. Racial minorities in the U.S. need more than the friendship and hospitality of their white neighbors. They need white people to work with them to change the policies of businesses, unions, banks, real estate agencies, and school systems that deprive them of their rights. Prisoners need more than our letters. They need us to help change the attitudes and practices of employers and others that often make their return to society very difficult. The hungry need more than our food distribution centers. They need us to help change laws and regulations so that jobs and decent wages are available. That way they can get their own food. "Participation" as well as "sufficient life-goods" is essential.

But there is a third kind of action that is also important. The works of mercy and the works of justice need to flow out of a growing realization of our oneness as a human family, especially our oneness with the often voiceless victims of injustice. Changing our lives toward greater simplicity can help us identify more fully with the victims of injustice, especially the poor. It is not a matter of "playing at being poor." Rather, it is a matter of beginning to let go of some of the privileges that many of us have *at the expense of* those who are economically poor. This process of relinquishing our privileges may begin with eating and drinking less, buying fewer gadgets, etc.[7] But it moves beyond these first steps to a more radical letting go, which is examined in Chapter 17. What is important to realize here is that it is difficult for materially comfortable people to hunger and thirst for justice. Comfort can dull our sense of urgency and passion and prevent us from ever really identifying with those with whom we want to struggle. Thus, the vision and strategies for action in this book incorporate all three kinds of action.

Because so many of us feel powerless and are frequently asking what can we do, a significant portion of this book is devoted to these action suggestions. This is not just another book about how bad the problems are. It is meant to suggest possible solutions. It is to help you feel less overwhelmed by your growing awareness of economic injustice, by providing a variety of "action handles" and challenging you to generate other possibilities. Thus, if you are willing to consider *action* on behalf of justice, then you are ready to read this book.

Discussion Questions

1. Do the Scriptures really want us to share goods according to each person's need?
2. What would this mean for our lives today?
3. What does St. Ambrose mean by his statement? How is this Christian view of possessions different from how most people regard possessions in our country?
4. What does St. Matthew's Gospel (25:31-46) have to say about our attitude and actions toward people that society tends to discount, neglect, discard?
5. Why is it important for us to understand "helping" as "doing with and calling forth", rather than as "doing for"?
6. Why is it important to be an *agent* as well as a beneficiary of development?
7. Why is a redistribution of power more central to justice than a redistribution of goods?
8. What is the difference between the works of mercy and the works of justice?
9. Why are the works of justice absolutely essential today?
10. How can a "comfortable life" make the works of justice even more difficult?

Resources

On the Four Components in General
   —Denis Goulet, *The Cruel Choice* (New York: Atheneum, 1968) and many of his articles spell out this vision of justice in some detail. He is probably the best resource for "the ethics of development."
   —*Reshaping the International Order*, Jan Tinbergen's report to the Club of Rome (New York: E. P. Dutton, 1976), pp. 61–63, identifies six "guiding elements which serve to shape our development efforts", which closely parallel my four components of justice.

—Jurgen Moltmann, "A Christian Declaration on Human Rights," in *Network Quarterly*, Vol 5, #2, Spring 1977, is the best short exposition of the Christian basis for these human rights. Available from Network, 224 "D" Street SE, Washington, DC 20003. Moltmann's essay is also contained in Allen Miller, ed., *A Christian Declaration on Human Rights* (Grand Rapids: Eerdmans, 1977), a collection of essays on the Christian response to human rights.

On Sufficient Life-Goods and Stewardship
—The "basic needs" strategy is developed in the 1976 World Employment Conference of the International Labor Organization and is available in *Employment, Growth and Basic Needs: A One-World Problem* (New York: Praeger, 1977) and is reaffirmed by such diverse groups as the Non-Aligned Conference of August 1976; by Robert McNamara in his address to the Board of Governors of the World Bank on October 4, 1976; in *Reshaping the International Order*; and by the Overseas Development Council in its *U.S. and World Development: Agenda 1977* (New York: Praeger, 1977).

—William Byron, *Toward Stewardship* (New York: Paulist Press, 1975), is a fine presentation of the basis for stewardship in the Scriptures, in Church teaching, and in the needs of the world today.

—*The Earth Is the Lord's: Essays on Stewardship*, edited by Mary Evelyn Jegen and Bruno V. Manno (New York: Paulist Press, 1978), contains a number of excellent essays on stewardship. Especially helpful is Ronald J. Sider, "A Biblical Perspective on Stewardship" in which he details the Scriptural basis for stewardship and for justice in general. This is a summary of his fine book, *Rich Christians in an Age of Hunger* (Downers Grove, IL: Intervarsity Press, 1977).

Chapter Two

HUNGER: FOUR PRINCIPLES

This chapter examines the attitudes and some of the economic and political policies that cause hunger. Then it shows what needs to be done in order for hungry people to feed themselves.

Chapter Four in Arthur Simon's excellent book, *Bread for the World*, begins with the statement that "people are hungry because they are poor."[1] This insight needs to be expanded in two ways. First, the hungry are more than poor. They are capable of feeding themselves if allowed to do so. Secondly, they have not been allowed to do so because of their relative powerlessness.

Thus, to overcome hunger requires addressing the underlying economic and political powerlessness of the hungry. The only long-term solution to hunger that is consistent with the Christian understanding of justice presented in Chapter 1 might be called "food self-reliance." All proposed measures—

short-term and long-term—need to be evaluated in terms of
this goal: How well do they further peoples' control over their
own lives, especially over their basic human needs like food.
Four principles for thinking about and acting on the hunger
issue flow from this view of hunger and from the four components of justice. Each principle has a number of policy or
strategy implications that are important for attacking hunger
effectively.

Justice Components	Principles for Thinking about and Acting on Hunger	Policy Implications for Combatting Hunger
Sufficient life-goods	Food is a basic human right, not a speculative commodity	Redistribution of food according to peoples' need to eat Redistribution of the means of producing food
Dignity or esteem	The poor are more than poor	
Participation	Poverty as essentially powerlessness Solving hunger/poverty means empowering the poor	Redistribution of power— (1) between rich and poor nations (2) between rich and poor within Third World nations
Interdependence	Working to overcome hunger is a matter of justice (duty) and not charity (option)	

Principle #1: Food Is a Right, Not a Speculative Commodity

We Christians regard the earth's resources as gifts from
God for the development of all peoples. We apply this notion

first to food, the most basic of life-goods. In testimony before Congress in 1974, the director of the National Catholic Rural Life Conference put it this way:

> Although much of America's farm productivity is due to the application of advanced technology and the hard work and dedication of our farmers, it also results from the fact that this country is uniquely blessed with highly productive soil, plentiful water resources and a moderate climate. These are blessings which we in the U.S. in no way earned or deserved. They rather are gifts of creation, part of the universal ecosystem provided by God to support all of humanity. Their stewardship and development, therefore, are responsibilities we bear to the rest of humankind. . .[2]

That food is a right has been reaffirmed by all Christian churches. Further, thanks to the efforts of Bread for the World members and others, this principle has now been established as the basis for U.S. food policy. This "Right to Food Resolution" declares that "the United States reaffirms the right of every person in this country and throughout the world to food and a nutritionally adequate diet."[3] It was not easy, however. Some Congresspersons tried to substitute the phrase "urgent need" for "right". To call food an urgent need is not the same as calling it a right. "Right" implies obligation or duty. With a *right* to food, individuals can make a *claim* to have that right fulfilled. Human rights are matters of justice. On the other hand, *need*—even urgent need—does not imply obligation.

A major implication of this principle is that food ought to be distributed more according to peoples' need to eat than their ability to pay. In most countries, including the U.S., if you have money you can get food. How much you get and how good the food is depend primarily on how much money you have. The "Food Stamp Program" modifies this somewhat. But it is still our ability to pay that determines the food we get.

In the market ("free enterprise") economies of both First and Third World countries, food unfortunately is treated primarily as a speculative commodity, as a source of profit. Some examples are helpful:[4]

—The giant grain companies—Cargill, Continental, Bunge, Cook—thrive on speculation in "grain futures." That is, they buy a title, as it were, to future crops when the prices are relatively lower and sell these titles when the prices go up. They also buy, store, and sell actual grain in the same way. The result is hunger for those who cannot pay the high prices. In 1970–1974, for instance, U.S. Government policy drained all grain reserves in this country. As crops failed in different parts of the world during that period, the price of grain soared. The grain companies were then able to cash in on these quadrupled prices. Countries like India were forced to come to them to buy grain at these prices, using up their much needed capital for food purchases, on top of quadrupled oil and fertilizer prices.

—Multinational corporations involved in foreign agriculture often refer to the large land holdings they control as their "export platforms" and "offshore production sites." Likewise, the large local landowners and the governments of many countries regard agricultural resources as a means of profit primarily. The land is devoted more and more to cash crops like coffee, sugar, bananas, and cotton—for export and foreign exchange earnings. This is a far cry from the view of the small farmers who once farmed these lands for food for local consumption. To them, food is more a basic life-good, to be distributed first according to peoples' need to eat.

—The U.S. Government has used its food aid and grain exports as a weapon for political and economic gain. Sometimes it has been to gain favorable votes in the United Nations. Other times it has been to bargain for oil and other strategic minerals. For years, food aid has been a way of locking its recipients into becoming future buyers of U.S. agricultural goods. In the early 1970s, food aid was used to underwrite the military establishment in South Vietnam. That is, the military budget was financed in part from government sales of food aid provided by the U.S. Such "food power policies", as they have been called, are hardly consistent with a view of food as a basic human right.

1. Redistribution of Food

The principle that food is a right has two major policy implications. The first calls for a redistribution of food itself. Short-term emergency measures like food aid are often necessary. If used as a stimulant for local production, such aid can be quite helpful. Middle-term measures like the creation of a world food reserve help to provide a cushion for times when the supply of grain dramatically decreases. Longer-term changes in the consumption patterns of the well-fed are also important strategies for a redistribution of food. Our need to eat, rather than how much we can afford to spend, should become more and more the determining factor for how much food we consume.

2. Redistribution of the Means of Producing Food

The second and more basic policy implication is the need to redistribute the means of producing food. This means making land, credit, technical assistance, etc. available to the landless and to millions of tenant farmers and farm workers, so that they can produce their own food. So long as they remain dependent on more (and more) costly food purchases, often with less nutritional value, the world's hungry are not going to be able effectively to exercise their right to food. Nor are they able to exercise their right to shape their own destiny. "Justice" as well as "bread" requires that people have the opportunity to feed themselves. But the more that the land and other agricultural resources are controlled by the wealthy few, the more this right will be denied. Chapter 6 on export cropping examines this carefully.

Principle #2: The Poor Are More Than Poor

Corresponding to the dignity component of justice is the hunger principle that the poor are more than their poverty. That is, their economic deprivation does not define their total being. Although economically deprived, the hungry are often rich in many other ways. This principle has important implications.

In terms of its importance for action, if policies for food self-reliance are to be advocated and adopted, then attitudes will have to change. Both policy-makers and the general public whose attitudes often shape policies must come to realize that the poor *can feed themselves* if allowed to do so. Generally, the economically well-off conclude that the economically deprived are incapable of helping themselves. This is especially true in societies where personal worth is largely equated with one's position and possessions. This kind of perception leads to a view that the only answer to world hunger is a combination of First World food aid and First World technology. But it is this combination of ingredients that is actually part of the problem, as will be seen in Chapters 6 and 9.

This principle is crucial. With all the visuals we see showing the ugliness of hunger, we rarely see the richness of hungry people. What is seen as ugly is generally seen as expendable. What value is there in several hundred million starving people? All they do is make life difficult for the rest of us. If the world is a "life-boat", as some would see it (see Chapter 16), then it is clearly better for us and for the world that we valuable people be the survivors in that life-boat.

All this only reinforces the prevailing attitudes that shape public policy and personal action. With predominantly negative images, few viewers would believe that the Africans, South Asians, and Latin Americans featured in many films of the early 1970s were formerly (and remain potentially) self-sufficient farmers. Their present hunger is due to a variety of reasons. High among these reasons is a set of policies that use agricultural resources as exports for profits and not as food for local consumption. But the incapacity of these former farmers is not one of the reasons for their hunger.

To counteract this general perception of the inability of the poor, we need to re-examine all the helping situations we find ourselves in. Do they reinforce this false perception? Some of the most popular hunger actions include Thanksgiving and Christmas food baskets, food collections for food distribution centers to fight local hunger, and funding of overseas efforts to do the same kind of thing. But to do justice to the poor requires some kind of *reciprocal* relationship. That is, both parties should benefit from and give to the relationship.

Thus, we should be asking the poor what they need. Further, we might agree ahead of time to provide what they say they need, not what we think they need. Similarly, we should consider organizing exchanges between groups. Instead of the economically well-off always being the giver, the tutor, the coach, whatever, we might arrange an exchange of skills and services or an exchange of things like dramatic performances between inner-city and suburban school or church groups. Or we might help develop a vegetable garden to be cultivated together. Some churches and colleges have done this on part of their land. Vacant city lots have also been used for community gardens.

Another effective action to counter the myth of the inability of the poor to help themselves revolves around the handicrafts of poor people. A number of people have organized a booth at their church or school that displays some of these handicrafts (with catalogues of more). This is especially appropriate at Christmas, when gift-giving is on peoples' mind. Numerous "Third World outlets" for such handicrafts are described in the excellent publication, the *Alternate Celebrations Catalogue.*[5]

Principle #3: Poverty as Powerlessness; The Need for a Redistribution of Power

Corresponding to the participation component of justice is a dual principle. Stated negatively, it says that hunger is primarily a matter of the relative powerlessness of the hungry. Stated positively, it says that solving hunger ultimately demands the empowerment of the hungry to feed themselves. The hungry are not poor or "underdeveloped" by nature. Nor are they poor primarily because of some deficiency of resources, either personal resources and character or the human and natural resources of their country.

A helpful and intriguing way of looking at this idea of the poor as "deficient" is through the concept of "illth" that was coined in 1860 by John Ruskin. As the flip side of "wealth", "illth" is defined as "consumer goods and services that are injurious to the individuals who consume them and to society as a whole." Poverty is not a lack of goods but the presence of evil—policies and practices that load the poor with a string of "d's": discriminations, debts, deadends, and diseases. As E. V. Walter writes in *Communities of the Poor*:

> The life space of the poor is not an empty vessel simply deprived of the good things that fill the lives of everyone else—on the contrary, it is filled with bad experiences. The familiar distinction between the "have's" and the "have-nots" is a bit of fancy perpetuated by an ideology of scarcity. The idea of scarcity is frequently used to mask the presence of active evil. The poor have plenty, but it is plenty of what nobody wants.[6]

Part of this "illth" and a major reason for poverty are the economic policies of the First World. These policies have been called both "colonialism" and "neo-colonialism." The difference between these two terms is primarily in time and in degree. Colonialism refers to the military, political and economic control of the Third World by the First World during the 19th and 20th Centuries. Neo-colonialism refers to the continuing, yet more subtle, economic control of the Third World by the First World, especially since 1950. But both terms are describing the same reality: the economic exploitation of the Third World by the First World as the main reason for poverty in the Third World.

A classic example of this, which I quote at length, is the case of Potosi, Bolivia. It appears in an excellent essay entitled "Development and Underdevelopment: Two Sides of the Same Coin", produced by the Development Education Centre in Toronto.[7]

If we as Canadians tried to imagine what an underdeveloped area looks like, we would probably conjure up a town like Potosi, Bolivia. At an altitude of 15,000 feet above sea level, Potosi is difficult to reach. The roads leading to it are bad. The native Indian people who live there eke out a meagre living from the poor soil. The only other major source of employment is a tin mine in the mountain which overlooks the town. Housing is poor, and running water and electricity are a luxury in the area.

At first glance, it might seem that this town needs to be drawn out of its isolation and backwardness into the mainstream of "modern" economic development. It might seem that the town needs an injection of foreign capital and technical "know-how" to pull it out of this state of underdevelopment.

However, a closer look at Potosi reveals to the traveller that it was once a part of the great Inca empire and later, a cornerstone of economic growth and political power in the Spanish empire. The ruins of this once thriving centre of development are still visible. Baroque church facades carved in stone show eroded but discernible images of splendor and abundance. In the 1600s, in the heyday of Potosi, they say that even the horses were shod with silver. At the height of its boom, the town had a population equal to that of London and larger than that of European centres like Madrid, Rome, or Paris. Potosi attracted silks and fabrics from Canada and Flanders, the latest fashions from Paris and London, diamonds from India, crystal from Venice, and perfumes from Arabia. Something really valuable in the 17th Century was referred to commonly as being "worth a Potosi."

... The entire economic and social life of Potosi was based on wealth from a single commodity—silver. This silver was mined by the native Indian population and shipped directly to Spain. Potosi silver financed, in large measure, the development of the Spanish empire in the 17th Century.

"Between 1503 and 1660, 185,000 kilograms of gold and 16,000,000 of silver arrived at the Spanish port of Sanlucar de Barrameda. Silver shipped to Spain in little more than a century and a half exceeded three times the total European reserves—and it must be remembered that these official figures are not complete." (Eduardo Galeano, *The Open Veins of Latin America*)

The wealth which was extracted from Potosi's Cerro Rico—the "Rich Hill"—was shipped to the mother country rather than being accumulated in the area. Thus, the development generated by the valuable mineral occurred in Europe, rather than in Bolivia. When the silver ran out, Potosi's boom ended and the area was left to "underdevelop."

... The underdevelopment of Potosi, then, began with the abuse of its people and resources through the European colonial system. The Latin American economy was geared by the Europeans to meet their own needs, not those of the local people. The underdevelopment which is characteristic of this "ghost" town today, has its roots in the history of military conquests. Underdeveloped countries today are full of "ghost" towns like Potosi, and nearly all were European colonies at one time.

The arrival of the Europeans in Asia, Africa, and Latin America—what is known today as the Third World—fundamentally altered the processes of development which were taking place at the time. In some cases, these societies were more advanced than others; and all, of course, had problems to surmount. But the people in these areas were constructing societies which, although not industrialized, were often highly sophisticated and complex. They were able to meet their physical and psychological needs through their own institutions. The military conquest of Third World people led to the plunder and destruction of some of the world's greatest civilizations.

The reasons the Europeans ventured across the seas were largely trade and profit. They needed spices, gold, silver, land, and markets in which to sell their processed goods. In this relentless quest, the Europeans disrupted the development processes which were going on in the societies they conquered. It was military force—not innate superiority—which enabled the invaders to subdue the native people and destroy the basic social units of entire peoples, i.e., families, culture, and religious institutions.

... The example of Potosi indicates how development in Europe generated underdevelopment in the colonies. But Potosi was no exception in this—the pattern is repeated throughout the history of military expansion into the Third World.

... Development and underdevelopment, then, are both integral parts of the same process. The development of some areas was accomplished at the expense of others. Wealth in some areas was accumulated because it was drained from others, in the form of human, natural, and financial resources.

The poor, then, are and remain poor or underdeveloped primarily because of their relative powerlessness in face of the economic, political, social and military forces that set up and sustain these colonial patterns. Thus, what needs to be done to overcome poverty and hunger is more a matter of a redistribution of power than it is a redistribution of goods or food. This redistribution of power needs to take place on at least two levels—between the rich and poor nations of the world and between the rich and the poor within Third World nations (and elsewhere).

1. Between the Industrialized World and the Third World

As will be seen in detail in Parts II and III, the economic "rules of the game" made by the industrialized world contribute significantly to hunger. To cite but one example, the "terms of trade" that continue to widen the gap on prices and profits between Third World exports of raw materials like coffee and their imports of manufactured goods from the industrialized world make it extremely difficult for Third World countries locked into agricultural exports to do anything but increase the volume of food leaving their countries. If Costa Rica, Colombia, or any of the other 40 coffee-producing na-

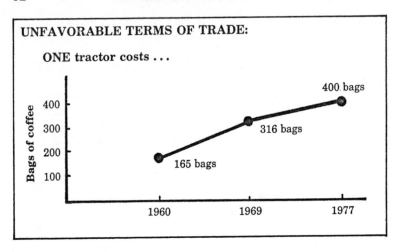

UNFAVORABLE TERMS OF TRADE:

ONE tractor costs ...

- 400 bags (1977)
- 316 bags (1969)
- 165 bags (1960)

Bags of coffee

tions wants manufactured goods like jeeps, it has to export. Because of long established colonial patterns, generally these exports are agricultural. So each year it takes more coffee to buy the same tractor. The result is either more land devoted to coffee (and thus less to food) or fewer tractors, at least according to the present rules.

So long as international decision-making about the terms of trade and other economic issues is in the hands of the industrialized world, hunger and poverty will continue in the Third World. Once again, those who make the rules get the goods. The New International Economic Order represents a concerted effort to redistribute such decision-making power, as will be seen.

2. Within Third World Countries

Secondly, it is crucial to redistribute power within Third World countries, from the rich few to the poor majority. Justice is concerned with the rights and needs of all people, not just a few. Changes in the international economic order must be designed to promote the development of all people in the Third World. Thus, there is an urgent need to re-examine some of the very policies designed to eliminate hunger that seem to have the opposite effect. Policies like the "Green Revolution," the expansion of export cash crops like coffee, and the concentration of agricultural resources in supposedly more efficient larger-scale farming enterprises actually seem to be extending hunger. As will be seen in Parts II and III, such measures have increased the wealth and power of a small percentage of the population at the expense of the majority.

The basic problem here centers on two very different views of hunger. Some see hunger as basically a technology problem that can be solved technologically. Others disagree strongly and see hunger as a social or political problem requiring social or political solutions. In an overly simplified way, the two views line up as follows:

Technological View

The Problem: inadequate production	The Solution: a technological revolution
Not enough food; not enough fertilizer, irrigation, modern equipment; not enough "know-how"	Produce more food: the Green Revolution More and better inputs (fertilizer, pesticides, etc.) More education A NIEO that redistributes technology

Social-Political View

The Problem: land ownership & use	The Solution: a social-political revolution
Land controlled by the few Producing non-essentials for profit	Land reform Land for local food needs first
Colonial patterns of trade: export crops for financial survival	A NIEO that redistributes decision-making power in international economic & political institutions, so that these institutions can be fundamentally changed.

As I see it, as long as hunger is viewed as a technological problem rather than a social-political one, the hungry will remain hungry. The answer to hunger offered in this book emphasizes a redistribution of power and a redistribution of the means of producing food, rather than an increase of production within present patterns of land ownership and use. As the chart indicates, when land is concentrated in the hands of a few, increasing production through more credit, fertilizer, extension services, seeds and irrigation for the large holders of land will fatten the few and leave the many small farmers worse off. Among other things, land needs to be redistributed to the many to feed themselves.

Currently, small farmers are being effectively driven from their land or forced to produce cash crops for export under marketing contracts with the multinational agribusiness companies. As more and more land that had been growing food for local consumption is devoted to export crops

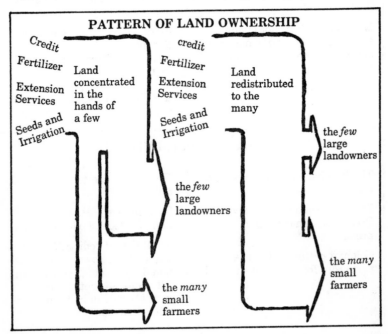

PATTERN OF LAND OWNERSHIP

Credit
Fertilizer
Extension Services
Seeds and Irrigation

Land concentrated in the hands of a few

credit
Fertilizer
Extension Services
Seeds and Irrigation

Land redistributed to the many

the *few* large landowners

the *many* small farmers

the *few* large landowners

the *many* small farmers

controlled by large land holders, the supply of local food staples (beans, rice, potatoes) dwindles, the prices of these staples go up, and the once adequately fed find themselves hungry (see Chapter 6 for a detailed view). To sustain a situation like this over a period of time requires increasingly repressive policies by the government. Thus, the hungry are victimized a second time. They are effectively denied their right to eat and then are imprisoned or killed if they resist. Measures to empower the hungry and to promote a "new internal economic order" to parallel the New International Economic Order will be considered in Part IV.

Principle #4: Action Is a Matter of Justice, Not Charity

Corresponding to the solidarity component of justice is the principle that, if food is a right, working to overcome hunger is a matter of justice rather than charity. That is, we have an obligation, not an option, to work with the hungry so that they can effectively exercise their right to food.

Since hunger is a scandal (resulting from acts of human institutions) and not a scourge (an act of God), the only adequate response are the works of justice. We have to attack the root causes of this persistent condition. Thus, Jesus' command—"when I was hungry you gave Me to eat"—needs to be interpreted today as more than just handing hungry people food. Efforts to evolve a New International Economic Order and to create new internal economic orders as well are essential to enabling the hungry to feed themselves. Finally, as part of these new economic orders, there is the need for those of us who are well-fed to evolve a just standard of living.

But to say that we have an obligation to do these things can seem threatening and risky to many of us. How do we attack root causes? And what are the root causes in the first place? And how can individuals do anything about institutionalized conditions and economic orders? Well, that is what this book is designed to do—to help us identify the economic causes of hunger and to help us begin to be a force for change in our world. Let's take a look, then, at this New International Economic Order and how it relates to justice and hunger.

Discussion Questions

1. Why is food a human *right*?
2. What is the difference between calling food a "right" and calling it a "need"? Why is this difference important?
3. Why is it more important to redistribute the means of producing food than it is to redistribute food directly?
4. Why is a *reciprocal* relationship with the poor important?
5. What are some other ways (besides those mentioned in the chapter) of helping others by "doing with and calling forth"?
6. How are "development" and "underdevelopment" related?
7. What is the difference between viewing hunger as a technological problem and viewing it as a social or political problem? Which kind of problem do you think hunger is? Why?
8. Why does hunger require acts of justice rather than acts of charity?

Resources

On Food as a Right
    —See the resources on "stewardship" in Chapter 1.
    —Besides *Food First*, the "basic human needs" model of development of the World Employment Conference of the International Labor Organization and the Dag Hammarskjold Foundation report, *What Now*, both describe development in terms of a redistribution of the means of producing food.

*On the Relationship between Development and
Underdevelopment*
    —See the resources on "What Self-Reliance Is Not," Chapter 14, especially Andre Gunder Frank, "The Development of Underdevelopment," in Robert Rhodes, Ed., *Imperialism and Underdevelopment: A Reader* (New York: Monthly Review Press, 1970).

On Technological vs. Social-Political Views of Hunger
    —Susan George, *How the Other Half Dies* (Montclair, NJ: Allanheld, Osmun & Co., 1977) and *Food First* both develop this contrast.
    —The best "point-counterpoint" example of these two different perspectives on hunger is a series of essays that appeared in *AgWorld* (a monthly newspaper-type magazine published by Ag World, 1186 W. Summer St., St. Paul, MN 55113). In the January and February 1978 issues, Peter Huessy of The Environmental Fund does a lengthy critique of *Food First*, entitled "Population Control or Food First?" His "technological" view of the problem is countered by Joseph Collins and Frances Moore Lappe in the April 1978 issue. Their "social-political" view of the problem is contained in an essay entitled "Food First Revisited."

*On Food and the New International Economic Order in
General*
    —Joseph Collins and Frances Moore Lappe, *World Hunger: 10 Myths* (San Francisco: Institute for Food and Development Policy, 1977) is a 50-page summary of *Food First* and is quite readable by high school students and adults.
    —The Institute for Food and Development Policy has also produced an audio-visual version of the "Food First" perspective, appropriately entitled "The Food First Slide Show." Besides addressing the basic hunger principles described in this

chapter, this slide show offers a variety of responses for promoting food self-reliance.

—*The New Internationalist*, September 1977, presents a cartoon version of each of the ten myths identified by Collins and Lappe.

Chapter Three

BASIC PRINCIPLES OF
THE NEW INTERNATIONAL
ECONOMIC ORDER (NIEO)

This chapter introduces the basic goals and some of the terminology of the New International Economic Order and shows why a "new"—a fundamental restructuring of the current—international economic order is necessary to overcome global poverty and hunger.

First World governments were moved to serious consideration of the NIEO more by the realization of their growing economic vulnerability or dependency on the Third World for strategic resources than by any other single cause. This realization was provided mostly by the oil power of the Organization of Petroleum Exporting Countries (OPEC). But citizen concern, to the extent that it exists, probably is due more to the growing awareness of the extent of world hunger than any other single cause. Increasingly, people are coming to see that hunger is more deeply rooted in the policies of governments, corporations, and international agencies than it is in the whims of the weather. Hunger is a scandal, not a scourge. It is the product of human decisions, not acts of God. And the longer hunger stays with us, despite abundant technological discoveries, the more people are looking to global economic arrangements for the causes. There is a growing realization of the need for both a New International Economic Order and for a new economic order within most Third World countries.

In 1974 and 1975, at the 6th and 7th Special Sessions of the United Nations, the UN formulated a New International Economic Order. This NIEO was spelled out in three basic documents. The basic principles or goals are described in *Principles for a New International Economic Order* and in the *Charter of Economic Rights and Duties of States.* The policy recommendations for achieving these goals are elaborated in the *Programme of Action.*

The four major goals into which all of the policy recommendations fall have as their ultimate objective to "correct inequalities and redress existing injustices, . . . eliminate the widening gap between the developed and the developing countries and ensure steadily accelerating economic and social development and peace and justice for present and future generations . . ." The basic means could only be "a fundamental restructuring of the world economic system."[1] As it stands now, the gap between rich and poor continues to widen. After World War II, the institutions and rules of the present or "old" international economic order were created by the First World to help mainly the First World. And they did! The per capita income (the average income per person) of people in the First World has increased over $2,000 the past 30 years. But the per capita income of people in the Third World has increased only about $120.[2] Clearly, justice demands a "new" international economic order.

There is a remarkable similarity between the four major goals of the NIEO and the justice components and hunger principles outlined in Chapters 1 and 2, as the following diagram indicates:

Justice Components	New International Economic Order Goals
Sufficient life-goods	Redistribution of wealth—by changing the mechanisms that distribute wealth (trade, monetary system, corporations)
Dignity or esteem	Development models and technology to be appropriate to local conditions and to the value systems and cultural traditions of Third World countries
Participation	Redistribution of power— (1) Third World sovereignty over their own resources (2) Decision-making power in international economic bodies (3) Collective self-reliance (4) Redistribution of power within Third World countries
Interdependence or solidarity	Interdependence— (1) Global approaches to global problems (2) "Vertical" (based on inequality) vs "horizontal" (based on sovereignty equality) interdependence

Goal #1: A Redistribution of Wealth

The first overriding goal of the NIEO could be described as a redistribution of wealth or a transfer of resources from the rich to the poor nations, so as to better meet basic human needs. There are different emphases placed on a basic human needs approach, with some calling for genuine redistribution within Third World countries as well.[3] But it is clear that all versions of a NIEO involve proposals for a direct transfer of resources. First priority is to the nations most seriously affected by hunger or mounting debts. This redistribution of wealth does not mean outright grants of money. Primarily it means changing the institutions or rules that produce and distribute wealth, as was noted in Chapter 2 (pp. 30-32).

One of the first changes needed and demanded by Third World countries is in trade structures. The *Principles for a NIEO* call for a

Just and equitable relationship between the prices of raw materials, primary products, manufactured and semi-manufactured goods exported by developing countries and the prices of raw materials, primary commodities, manufactures, capital goods and equipment imported by them with the aim of bringing about sustained improvement in their unsatisfactory terms of trade and the expansion of the world economy.[4]

As it stands now, Third World countries are on a treadmill. The graph in Chapter 2 on coffee showed how Third World raw materials buy fewer and fewer First World manu-

Permission of NARMIC
American Friends
Service Committee

factured goods each year. Their deficit in the balance of trade increases steadily. Part II examines this problem and a variety of solutions in detail.

With regard to the international monetary system, the *Principles of a NIEO* state that the NIEO is meant to ensure "that one of the main aims of the reformed international monetary system shall be the promotion of the development of the developing countries and the adequate flow of real resources to them."[5] Measures include greater access to international credit, debts moratoriums and debt renegotiations. As it stands now, a number of Third World countries have to divert 30% or more of all income from their exports to paying off their debts. They need loans to pay off previous loans. Again, the result is a finance treadmill quite similar to the trade treadmill we just saw.

Goal #2: Appropriate Models of Development and Technology

Paralleling the dignity component of justice—the cultural rights of persons and societies—is "the right of every country to adopt the economic and social system that it deems to be the most appropriate for its own development and not be subjected to discrimination of any kind as a result".[6] As Third World spokesperson and World Bank economist Mahbub ul Haq states it:

> We are not chasing the income levels of the rich nations. We do not wish to imitate their lifestyles. We are only suggesting that our societies must have a decent chance to develop, on an equal basis, without systematic discrimination against us, according to our own value systems, and in line with our own cultural traditions.[7]

Large-scale farm machinery may be appropriate for some First World agriculture. But that does not mean it is appropriate at all for Third World agriculture. Because precious energy resources are owned by private enterprise in many First World countries does not mean similar patterns of ownership are good for Third World countries. Bottle-feeding of infants may be the "modern" thing to do in the affluent world. But

that does not deny the wisdom of breast-feeding, especially for
economically poor women. Growing numbers of individuals
and countries are coming to see that "breast is best", rather
than "West is best." Chapter 12 takes up this last issue in
detail.

Among the more specific principles and proposals designed to accomplish this goal is one calling for the development of locally-developed technology geared to the abundance
of labor power in the Third World. But the implications of the
NIEO and particularly the more radical versions of the NIEO
go far beyond this call for "labor-intensive" technology. They
urge the pursuit of development models different from the
capitalist model that has been exported by the First World
during the 1960s and 1970s—often as the condition for receiving First World aid. The case studies in Chapter 13 point out
this diversity of development models.

Goal #3: A Redistribution of Power

A global redistribution of power is as vital to restructuring the world economic system as it is to the solving of hunger.
The right of participation or self-determination is expressed in
the UN version of the NIEO in four basic ways. While more
radical versions put greater emphasis on measures to empower the powerless sectors *within* Third World countries, the
UN version focuses primarily on the three ways of increasing
the power of Third World countries: 1) greater control over
their own resources, 2) greater share in the decision-making
power within international agencies, and 3) greater unity
through collective self-reliance.

1. *Economic Sovereignty*[8]

The NIEO calls, first, for the "full permanent sovereignty
of every State over its natural resources and all economic
activities." As it stands now, most Third World countries have

almost as little voice in the formulation of the economic rules of the game as they did during the colonial era. Although the following examples are amplified later in the book, they are mentioned here to illustrate this important point.

—The prices of the raw materials that Third World countries export are generally determined by their First World importers or the multinational corporations that control these exports in the first place. President Nyerere of Tanzania points out how the price of Tanzania's sisal (rope fiber) exports is determined by competition among the rich countries (see p. 67).

—The prices of the manufactured goods they import are likewise set by the rich. Nyerere mentions the tractors Tanzania imports. Their price is fixed according to two criteria: "first, those costs of its production which will enable its producers to enjoy a high standard of living; and second, what the market will bear—which is determined by competition among the rich" (p. 67).

—How land is used in Third World countries often is decided by multinational corporations. Even if Ghana, for instance, wanted to turn some of its massive cocoa bean lands to producing food for its own people, Nestlé would object. As the largest importer of cocoa beans in the world, Nestlé depends on (and effectively controls) Ghana's huge export crop. A second example is illustrated by the map of Jamaica (p. 168). It shows how much Jamaican land the aluminum companies control—land they sit on, so that their competitors do not have access to the bauxite below. Jamaica is now trying to renegotiate this control, so that the land can produce food for hungry Jamaicans.

In each of these and many other cases, like the value of Third World currencies, the amounts and conditions of the foreign aid they receive, the terms of investment contracts with the multinational corporations, and the kind of technology they use, the results are all mostly determined by forces on which the Third World has little influence.

This right to economic sovereignty is asserted first in relationship to the multinational corporations. The *Principles for a NIEO* say that countries have the "right of nationalization or transfer of ownership to its nationals." This means that countries can take over the operation and ownership of foreign corporations located in their country. One of the best examples was Chile's nationalization in 1971 of Kennecott and Anaconda, the multinational corporations that owned and operated Chile's copper mines (see pp. 185-187). The controversial issue in all this is primarily compensation. First World countries and their multinational corporations want compensation to be set by an international tribunal in which they have some voice. The NIEO, on the other hand, says that the host country can determine just compensation.

Next, the NIEO asserts the right to sovereignty in relationship to the forms of neocolonialism in the world, especially *apartheid*. South Africans have the right, this means, to overthrow such a racist regime by force. The NIEO further calls other nations to support liberation struggles against these forms of neo-colonialism.

2. *Decision-Making in Global Institutions*[9]

The second way in which power is to be redistributed in the NIEO is in relationship to decision-making power in the international economic bodies. According to the *Principles of a NIEO*, this means "full and effective participation on the basis of equality of all countries in the solving of world economic problems in the common interest of all countries ..." The *Programme of Action* makes this redistribution of power more specific. It calls for a redistribution of voting power in the International Monetary Fund and the World Bank. At present in the World Bank, the U.S. has 20.3% of the votes and five other First World countries (Japan, Canada, England, France, and West Germany) have another 29.4%. Thus, with 50% of the votes, six nations control an organization that is also supposed to be beneficial to over 100 Third World nations. Remember the insight in Chapter 1—those who make the rules get the goods.

3. *Collective Self-Reliance*[10]

The third expression of increased self-determination among Third World countries is called "collective self-reliance." This means countries with similar or complementary problems and/or resources band together, to better deal with their situations. One important expression of collective self-reliance is the strengthening of "producer associations" (called "cartels" by their critics). As noted at the beginning of this chapter, it has been this growing bargaining power of Third World producer associations that has made the First World take the NIEO somewhat seriously. It is clear that the restructuring of the world economic system that the NIEO envisions will depend on this bargaining power.

Before the Organization of Petroleum Exporting Countries (OPEC) was created, the oil resources of the Arab nations and of Indonesia, Nigeria, Venezuela and Ecuador were totally controlled by the seven giant multinational oil companies. The benefit to the countries whose oil it was was quite little compared to the benefit to the corporations. Thus, it seems that both economic sovereignty and a redistribution of goods depend more and more on collective self-reliance.

It should be becoming clear, then, that without such fundamental changes in the distribution of global economic power, poverty cannot be overcome. Higher prices, more trade, more credit, more technology—that is, a redistribution of wealth—will not suffice. As ul Haq correctly observes—

> There is much other evidence of instances in which unequal economic relationships have led to a denial of economic opportunities to the poorer nations, but the basic point already has been made: in the international order, just as much as within national orders, initial poverty itself becomes the most formidable handicap in the way of

redressing such poverty unless there is a fundamental change in the existing power structure.[11]

If you can imagine playing "Monopoly" against someone who starts the game with several hotels already in place, you have an idea of what ul Haq is saying. Reflect back on the example of Potosi, Bolivia, in the last chapter. We can all see how meaningless a gesture it would be for Spain, for instance, to send Potosi 1% of the silver wealth it extracted as foreign aid and expect that such aid would solve Bolivian poverty. How stupid, we would say, it is for those Spaniards who are urging the Bolivians to "work harder" and "pull yourselves up by your own bootstraps—if we could do it, so can you!" But First World people keep saying these things, even today. It is obvious that Potosi can never develop until the economic relationship between it and Spain is radically changed. That is what ul Haq is saying here and that is what the Third World keeps trying to say in the negotiations on the NIEO.

4. *Internal Redistribution of Power*

There is a slight acknowledgement in the NIEO of the need for a redistribution of power within Third World countries. Although not explicit in the *Principles for a NIEO* and definitely not central to the UN version of the NIEO as a whole, this goal nonetheless appears in Article 7 of the *Charter of the Economic Rights and Duties of States*, where it states:

> Every State has the primary responsibility to promote the economic, social and cultural development of its people. To this end, each State has the right and responsibility to choose its means and goals of development, fully to mobilize and use its resources, to implement progressive economic and social reforms and *to ensure the full participation of its people in the process* and benefits of development. All States have the duty, individually and collectively, to co-operate in order to eliminate obstacles that hinder such mobilization and use. (italics mine)

Unfortunately, the changes this principle implies do not seem to be part of the overall structural changes envisioned in the UN version of the NIEO. Part IV of this book focuses at length on this major shortcoming of the NIEO.

Goal #4: Interdependence[12]

The fourth goal of the NIEO is the same as the fourth component of justice. As the *Principles of a NIEO* state:

> Current events have brought into sharp focus the realization that the interests of the developed countries and those of the developing countries can no longer be isolated from each other, that there is close interrelationship between the prosperity of the developed countries and the growth and development of the developing countries, and that the prosperity of the international community as a whole depends upon the prosperity of its constituent parts.

It is basically self-interest on the part of the First World that has brought about this recent realization of the need for interdependence.

First, there is the growing awareness that the economies of First World countries are more and more dependent on Third World raw materials (and cheap labor and markets as well). As mentioned above, it has been primarily the economic power of OPEC that has brought the First World to the negotiation tables, willing to collaborate to some extent. Then there is the relative decrease in First World military power. The U.S. defeat in Southeast Asia and the spread of nuclear weapons technology to several Third World countries have strengthened the hand of the Third World. Furthermore, population trends show that the Third World's percentage of the world's population is increasing from today's 70% of the total to 80% in 2000 and 90% in 2050. Add these together and you get a real shift in the bargaining power of the Third World.

Thus, it is becoming clear that the long-term self-interest of the First World necessitates some accommodation to the Third World.[13]

Secondly, First World countries are talking interdependence because it is finally obvious that they are no longer able, if they ever were, to solve on their own a whole series of problems eroding their security and well-being. Gerry and Pat Mische's excellent book, *Toward a Human World Order*, puts these problems in three categories.

(1) Military insecurity—the balance-of-weapons competition. The arms race, the spread of nuclear weapons and nuclear power, and the arms trade are all mushrooming. Well over $400 billion was spent on the military worldwide in fiscal year 1980 and yet there is greater insecurity than ever!

(2) Monetary insecurity—the balance-of-payments competition. Nations are scrambling to get greater shares of world exports and to protect their own industries from cheaper imports. With the value of their currencies fluctuating, with inflation, with their deficits and debts growing, all nations wonder what their economic futures will be. First World countries are coming to see that the international economic system that they created is breaking down and that they are unable to stop the process.

(3) Resource insecurity—competition for scarce resources. Overfishing the world's oceans, gobbling up the world's energy resources, ever increasing production and consumption of goods, supporting dictatorships that promise us access to their country's resources all indicate insecurity as well as greed.

In face of these insecurities and others, interdependence seems to be a growing necessity.

But interdependence is a tricky term. It implies cooperation and mutual benefit. But there are really two types of interdependence, which we might call vertical interdependence and horizontal interdependence. Vertical interdependence is best described by Denis Goulet: "masters and slaves were bound to each other's interests as interdependent partners in a single enterprise, the plantation."[14] Vertical interdependence is a relationship of inequality—someone on top and others on the bottom. The current economic order is based on this kind of interdependence.

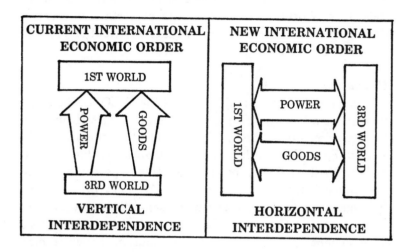

CURRENT INTERNATIONAL ECONOMIC ORDER	NEW INTERNATIONAL ECONOMIC ORDER
1ST WORLD — POWER / GOODS — 3RD WORLD	1ST WORLD — POWER / GOODS — 3RD WORLD
VERTICAL INTERDEPENDENCE	HORIZONTAL INTERDEPENDENCE

Any calls to increase this vertical interdependence—for instance, through increased trade—actually reinforces the privileged position of the few on top at the expense of the many on the bottom. Increasing the interaction between parties of unequal bargaining power only perpetuates the inequities of the current international economic system.

This is why the *Principles for a NIEO* calls for an interdependence that is based on equality. This horizontal interdependence is as concerned with future generations as it is with the present one. In the words of the UN document—

Thus, the political, economic and social well-being of present and future generations depends more than ever on cooperation between all members of the international community on the basis of sovereign equality and the removal of the disequilibrium [inequality] that exists between them.

As with the other basic goals of the NIEO, there are different views on how far to go in implementing an interdependence based on sovereign equality. The Third World, especially the more radical perspectives within it, are pushing hard for the horizontal interdependence pictured above. But most First World countries are back at vertical interdependence, which does not require any real redistribution of global economic and political power.

Conclusion

Each of these four major goals of the NIEO will be examined in detail in the chapters that follow. Part II on trade focuses primarily on the first NIEO goal—the redistribution of wealth. Part III on multinational corporations relates specifically to NIEO goal #3, the redistribution of power, especially the dimension of economic sovereignty. Part IV on a new internal economic order based on self-reliant development concentrates on the second NIEO goal—appropriate models of development—and the internal redistribution of power dimension of the third NIEO goal. Part V on global interdependence expands on this brief introduction to the fourth NIEO goal.

In each Part, the specific NIEO proposals for implementing changes in these four areas will be evaluated in terms of how well they promote bread and justice. That is, with the different perspectives on the NIEO and with the current state of uncertainty about what kind of NIEO will emerge from the lengthy negotiations, it is important to have a way of examining the NIEO—for both clear thinking and effective action. This means action on these issues designed always to promote justice and people's opportunity to feed themselves.

Discussion Questions

1. Explain the different ways in which the Third World is on an economic "treadmill."

2. What is the meaning of Mahbub ul Haq's statement and why is it so important for Third World countries?
3. Why is "economic sovereignty" such an important and emotional issue for Third World countries?
4. Do you agree that "those who make the rules get the goods"? Why or why not?
5. Why are "collective self-reliance" in general and "producer associations" in particular important for Third World countries?
6. What is the difference between "vertical interdependence" and "horizontal interdependence"?

Resources

On the New International Economic Order in General
(see Appendix for a more complete listing)

—Orlando Letelier and Michael Moffitt, *The International Economic Order* (Washington, DC: Transnational Institute, 1977). An excellent 60-page historical analysis of the NIEO, it provides a good summary of the various perspectives on the NIEO.

—Mahbub ul Haq, *The Third World and the International Economic Order* (Overseas Development Council, 1976, 54 pages) and his longer version in *The Poverty Curtain* (New York: Columbia University Press, 1976) are probably the most readable Third World perspectives on the NIEO.

—Thomas Fenton, *Coffee: The Rules of the Game and You* (New York: The Christophers, 1974) is a simple, concise presentation (20 pages) for high school students of the issues in the NIEO.

—*Development Education Viewpoints* (Development Education Center—see Appendix) is a series of six 1975 essays on development, international trade, foreign investment, aid and the food crisis. Although they contain no Christian references, they are outlined in a way to serve as a commentary on Pope Paul VI's *On the Development of Peoples.*

  —*Education/Action Kit on the NIEO* (American Friends Service Committee, 2161 Massachusetts Ave., Cambridge, MA 02140, November 1976) is a set of 25 articles organized into three categories—basic UN documents and commentaries on the NIEO, multinational corporations, and the need for nonviolent economics and social change.

  —*Creative Simplicity*, January 1977 is a 31-page issue of the Shakertown Pledge Group newsletter that puts together several excellent analyses of the NIEO, with an essay of Julius Nyerere, and classroom suggestions.

  —"Human Development: Ambiguities of Power, Technology, and Quality of Life", one of the official documents from the 5th Assembly of the World Council of Churches (in *Breaking Barriers, Nairobi 1975*; Eerdmans, 1976), reflects from a Christian perspective on the NIEO, on the need for a redistribution of power, appropriate technology, and multinationals.

  —*World Development Report, 1978* is the most recent World Bank publication detailing the statistics of global poverty and pointing to the need for a New International Economic Order.

Part II

TRADE, HUNGER, AND
THE NEW INTERNATIONAL
ECONOMIC ORDER

Introduction

As we saw in the example of Potosi, Bolivia (Chapter 2), the colonialization of the Third World was the beginning of its economic exploitation by the First World. This colonial pattern continues today—in the trading relationships between the First and Third Worlds. Chapter 4 in this Part II outlines the extent of the problem—the various ways in which trade inequities hurt economic development in the Third World. Chapter 5 examines the most important proposals for changes in trade relationships offered in the New International Economic Order. Chapter 6 evaluates the adequacy of these proposals by addressing the basic question of whether more trade on better terms is the answer to underdevelopment. Trade in agricultural products—export cropping—is the specific example used, because it is so critical to the issue of world hunger. Finally, Chapter 7 presents a variety of action possibilities to help us see how we can be part of the kinds of changes in the world trading system that will promote a fuller realization of bread and justice in the world.

Chapter Four

TRADE PROBLEMS CONFRONTING
THIRD WORLD COUNTRIES

In this chapter we will see why changes in the world trade system are far more important for the development of the Third World than foreign aid is. We will also consider the most basic inequities in the present system of world trade.

Trade, Not Aid

"Trade, not aid" has been the rallying cry of Third World countries since the first United Nations Conference on Trade and Development (UNCTAD I) in 1964. The Third World has come to see more and more clearly that aid creates a number of problems.

(1) Aid creates dependency on donor countries, for often it has strings attached. As we saw in Chapter 2 (p. 24), the recipients of U.S. "Food for Peace" aid are supposed to become purchasers of other U.S. agricultural products. U.S. aid loans

57

have generally required their recipients to buy U.S. goods with that money.

(2) Aid fluctuates with the changing political climate in donor countries. As Third World countries become more outspoken at the UN and elsewhere, First World countries seem to be less interested in "helping." "After all we've done for them, they're saying we're responsible for their poverty! Well, that's it! No more foreign aid giveaways!" sounds awfully familiar.

(3) Aid generates greater debts. Much of the aid to Third World countries has been in the form of loans, not grants. Loans must be repaid with interest. New foreign aid loans are often used to repay previous foreign aid loans.

(4) The amount of aid is relatively small. It represents less than ½ of 1% of the Gross National Product (GNP) of the First World donors. U.S. foreign aid in 1978 was less than ¼ of 1%. We spend as much or more as a nation on admission to sporting events, on barbershops and beauty parlors, and on watches and jewelry as we do on foreign aid. We spend more than twice as much on toys and sporting equipment, more than four times as much on tobacco products, and more than six times as much on liquor as we do on foreign aid.[1]

(5) The amount of aid is tiny in another sense. In fact, it represents a *negative* flow for Third World countries. Because Third World countries have been supplying First World countries for decades with cheap raw materials and have been buying their much more expensive manufactured goods, billions of dollars have actually been transferred to the First World, as the graph below indicates. By the mid-1970s, this trade deficit of the Third World, excluding OPEC countries, in relationship to the First World was *at least* $17.2 billion, less than the total of all First World government aid ("Official

Development Assistance"). And again, most of the $17.1 billion figure for Official Development Assistance for 1976 was loans, which must be repaid with interest. That adds the $18.1 billion figure for "Debt Servicing Payments" for 1976 to the equation. This means—in terms of trade vs. aid—that $18.2 billion ($17.2 billion minus $17.1 billion, plus $18.1 billion) is transferred from the Third World to the First World. "Aid," then, is a tricky term. It is really the Third World that has been aiding the First World, to the tune of about $21 billion in 1976, as the following graph indicates.[2]

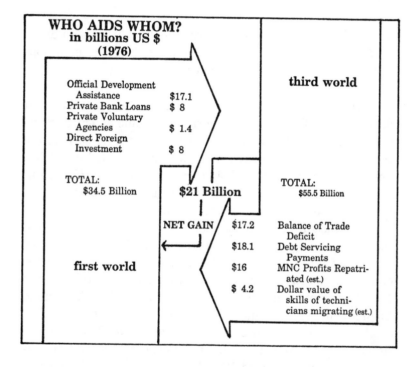

WHO AIDS WHOM?
in billions US $
(1976)

Official Development Assistance	$17.1	
Private Bank Loans	$ 8	
Private Voluntary Agencies	$ 1.4	
Direct Foreign Investment	$ 8	

third world

TOTAL: $34.5 Billion

$21 Billion

TOTAL: $55.5 Billion

NET GAIN

$17.2	Balance of Trade Deficit
$18.1	Debt Servicing Payments
$16	MNC Profits Repatriated (est.)
$ 4.2	Dollar value of skills of technicians migrating (est.)

first world

Thus, what Third World countries are demanding are "terms of trade"—that is, the relationship between spending for imports and income from exports—that are far more equitable than at present. In other words, if Third World countries can get better prices for their exports, especially in relationship to what they pay for the manufactured goods and oil they import, they will benefit in a variety of ways.

(1) It would promote greater independence. Third World countries would be generating the money they need for development by means of their own economic activities. Trading their goods rather than accepting loans from First World countries has an important psychological impact as well, especially for countries that had long been dependent on colonial rulers.

(2) Precisely because aid means loans which mean debts, more equitable terms of trade would reduce the enormous foreign debt of Third World countries.

(3) It would increase the amount of money available for development. Because the majority of income of Third World countries comes from their exports and because so much of this export income at present goes to paying off huge debts, not much is available for long-term development efforts. But more equitable terms of trade would increase export income, freeing at least some money for such development.

To illustrate this comparison between trade and aid—an increase of only 1¢ per pound in the price of raw coffee translates into more than $65 million a year for the coffee exporting countries. For Colombia, for instance, that 1¢ per pound adds up to the total amount of U.S. foreign aid loans to Colombia in 1976.[3] It should be no surprise, then, to learn that of all the one hundred or so proposals in the *Programme of Action* for the New International Economic Order, the primary focus of the Third World governments in the forums where the NIEO is being negotiated has been on trade.

The following excerpt from *On the Development of Peoples* not only indicates that Christian social teaching considers trade a key justice issue, but it also highlights its importance in relationship to foreign aid. Otherwise, what is given with one hand will continue to be taken away with the other hand.

"Equity in Trade Relations"

The efforts which are being made to assist developing nations on a financial and technical basis, though considerable, would be illusory if their benefits were to be partially nullified as a consequence of the trade relations existing between rich and poor countries. The confidence of these latter would be severely shaken if they had the impression that what was being given them with one hand was being taken away with the other.

Of course, highly industrialized nations export for the most part manufactured goods, while countries with less developed economies have only food, fibres and other raw materials to sell. As a result of technical progress the value of manufactured goods is rapidly increasing and they can always find an adequate market. On the other hand, raw materials produced by under-developed countries are subject to wide and sudden fluctuations in price, a state of affairs far removed from the progressively increasing value of industrial products. As a result, nations whose industrialization is limited are faced with serious difficulties when they have to rely on their exports to balance their economy and to carry out their plans for development. The poor nations remain ever poor while the rich ones become still richer.

In other words, the rule of free trade, taken by itself, is no longer able to govern international relations. Its advantages are certainly evident when the parties involved are not affected by any excessive inequalities of economic power: it is an incentive to progress and a reward for effort. That is why industrially developed countries see in it a law of justice. But the situation is no longer the same when economic conditions differ too widely from country to country: prices which are "freely" set in the market can produce unfair results. One must recognize that it is the fundamental principle of liberalism, as the rule for commercial exchange, which is questioned here.

The teaching of Leo XIII in *Rerum Novarum* is always valid: if the positions of the contracting parties are too unequal, the consent of the parties does not suffice to guarantee the justice of their contract, and the rule of free agreement remains subservient to the demands of the natural law. What was true of the just wage for the individual is also true of international contracts: an economy of exchange can no longer be based solely on the law of free competition, a law which, in its turn, too often creates an economic dictatorship. Freedom of trade is fair only if it is subject to the demands of social justice.

(On the Development of Peoples, #56–59)

Basic Trade Inequities

In 1960, Third World countries were facing a $5 billion deficit in their balance of trade. That is, the cost of their imports exceeded their income from exports by $5 billion. By 1973, that trade deficit had reached $9 billion. But only two years later, the deficit had reached a staggering $37 billion![4] Some of this deficit was due to the increase in prices of their oil imports. But as the graph on page 59 indicated, a conservative estimate of the Third World trade deficit with First World countries was $17.2 billion of the total $37 billion deficit.

There are a number of reasons for this trade deficit with the First World. To simplify the reasons as much as possible, they are grouped into three areas—the vulnerability of Third World exports, the spiral of debt, and the lack of Third World processing of their own raw materials.

1. The Vulnerability of Third World Exports

(A) *Single Export Economies.* Most Third World countries have what are called "single export economies." That is, they depend on one, or at most a few, commodities for the major portion of their exports. Industrialized countries that export thousands of different commodities can handle a drop in the price of a few of them. But single export economies are very vulnerable to changes in the prices of their exports. A drop of even 1¢ per pound in the price of raw coffee, as noted above, costs the coffee-producing countries—Colombia and forty others—about $65 million a year.

Ghana, for instance, depends on its cocoa beans for 56% of its export income. When the price of cocoa beans is low, as it generally has been in this century, Ghana has little chance to earn the dollars it needs to help its economic development. When the price of cocoa beans goes up, Nestlé and Hershey can always pass on this increased cost to the people who buy their chocolate products. Between October 1976 and August 1977, Hershey altered the size or price on its chocolate bars three times, because of higher cocoa bean prices, it claimed. In 1970, a Hershey Bar was 1½ ounces and cost 10¢. In 1977, the size was reduced to 1.05 ounces and the price raised to 20¢. A year later, the price jumped another 5¢. Ghana, however, has no such option. Generally, low cocoa prices have meant continuing poverty.

But single export economies are vulnerable in a second way. A country like Ghana is so dependent on its cocoa exports that it often feels impelled to sell at prices lower than the world market price. This is especially true when there are relatively few buyers, as with cocoa. Thus, we should not be too surprised to learn that Nestlé, *according to its own statistics,* paid Ghana only about 55% of the world market price for cocoa in 1974 when it paid much higher prices for cocoa to other countries that same year. The exact figures are:[5]

Nestle paid for 1974 cocoa	to Ghana	to all countries	world price
(1 metric ton 2200 lbs.)	$1135/ton 52¢/lb.	$1728/ton 79¢/lb.	$2163/ton 98¢/lb.

In terms of the Third World countries referred to in this chapter and elsewhere in the book, many of them are equally vulnerable as single export economies. The chart lists some of them.

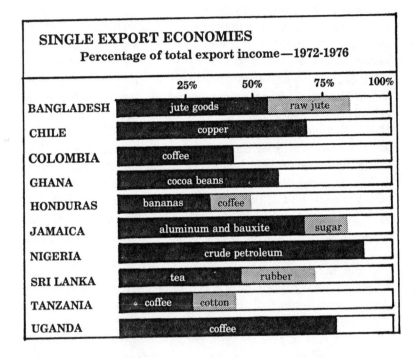

SINGLE EXPORT ECONOMIES
Percentage of total export income—1972-1976

	25%	50%	75%	100%
BANGLADESH	jute goods		raw jute	
CHILE	copper			
COLOMBIA	coffee			
GHANA	cocoa beans			
HONDURAS	bananas	coffee		
JAMAICA	aluminum and bauxite		sugar	
NIGERIA	crude petroleum			
SRI LANKA	tea	rubber		
TANZANIA	coffee	cotton		
UGANDA	coffee			

(B) *Wildly Fluctuating Commodity Prices.* Not only are prices on Third World raw material exports generally low, they are also subject to wild fluctuations. In less than ten years, the price of raw sugar varied from 3¢ per pound to about 60¢ per pound. Raw coffee prices jump around from 50¢ per pound to about $2.50 per pound.[6]

With unstable and usually very low prices, long-range economic planning becomes next to impossible for single export economies. We understand how impossible it would be for a family to plan its economic future if it did not know whether its yearly income would be $3,000 or $15,000. So too for Third World countries whose income in most cases is heavily based on its exports.

Ghana and cocoa is a good example.[7] As the chart indicates, the mid and late 1950s were good years for the price of cocoa beans—50¢ to 70¢ per pound. So Ghana decided to double its production of cocoa beans and base its development plans around this projected increase in its export income. More cocoa trees were planted, but they take about ten years to mature. By the late 1960s, when these new trees were yielding full harvests, the price of cocoa beans had dropped. In fact, it had been down during that whole period. Recently, the price of cocoa beans has risen dramatically, but Ghana certainly cannot count on it staying anywhere near the peak in 1976–1977. In fact, by mid-1978, the price had dropped to about $1.35 per pound. No wonder, then, some people describe this dependency on one or a few exports for the major source of national income as a "roller-coaster ride to development."

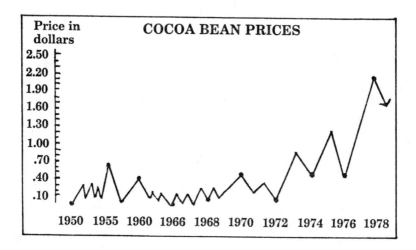

2. The Spiral of Debt

Most Third World countries are not only trapped on a roller-coaster, but they are also caught in a spiral of debt that is choking their efforts to develop. The spiral begins with the unfavorable terms of trade that have prevailed for most Third World countries since the colonial period.

(A) *Third World Exports Are Generally Cheap Raw Materials.* Eighty percent of Third World exports are raw materials. Ten Third World countries are fortunate enough to have a valuable item like oil for their primary export. A few others like Hong Kong, Taiwan, South Korea, India and Pakistan export sizable amounts of manufactured goods. But most Third World countries are limited to either non-fuel minerals like copper, bauxite and tin, or agricultural exports (export crops or cash crops) like cocoa, coffee, sugar, bananas, tea, cotton and jute. As we just saw with regard to cocoa beans, the prices on these export crops are generally quite low.

(B) *Third World Imports Are Generally Manufactured Goods.* In contrast with generally lower prices and profits on the raw material exports of Third World countries, most of what the Third World imports are manufactured goods. On these items, the prices and profit margins (rate of profit) are much higher. The graph in Chapter 2 (p. 32) showed how each year it takes more raw coffee to purchase a single tractor. So long as Third World countries want or need manufactured goods whose prices go up faster than the prices on their exports, these Third World countries will remain on that treadmill we saw in Chapter 3 (p. 42).

Even when the price on raw coffee skyrocketed in 1976 and 1977 and coffee drinkers were paying almost $5 a pound for ground coffee, the coffee producing nations did not get rich fast. They fared much better for that time period, but they still had ever increasing prices to pay for the manufactured goods and oil they had to import.

Sticking with the example of cocoa, its purchasing power continues to decline. In 1960, for instance, the Cameroon, the fifth largest cocoa exporting nation in the world, could buy 2700 meters of imported cloth for one ton of cocoa beans. Only five years later, that one ton could buy only 800 meters of the same cloth.[8] In 1977–1978, that same ton of cocoa beans could buy a lot more than 800 meters of cloth, but it may not have brought 2700 meters. Even if it had brought a little more than 2700 meters, that situation did not last long. As the graph on p. 65 shows, the price of cocoa beans has come down considerably.

Why do the prices of manufactured goods rise faster than those of raw materials? President Nyerere of Tanzania sees at least four reasons:

(1) Tanzania's sisal (rope fiber) exports have their prices kept low by the First World buyers who are what he calls "price-makers". With almost no economic leverage (no strategic item like oil), Tanzania is what he calls a "price-taker." It takes the price fixed by the buyers or it does not sell sisal.

(2) First World manufacturers add to the price of the manufactured goods they produce the higher price of oil they pay in order to run their plant.

(3) First World manufacturers add to the price the higher wages they pay because workers and owners need more income to compensate them for higher oil prices they pay to drive, to heat their homes, to buy goods that use oil.

(4) First World manufacturers add to the price the higher wages they pay because workers and owners expect more income to increase their standard of living.

(C) *The Resulting Spiral.* So what happens when sisal prices do not keep pace with the prices of capital goods (goods that produce other goods—machines) and manufactured goods? Nyerere mentions a timber production and paper mill project. If he planned to pay for these capital goods with 18 months worth of sisal, then he will have to borrow, because the price of the project has doubled. And taking out loans is the next step in the spiral of debt in which Third World countries find themselves trapped.

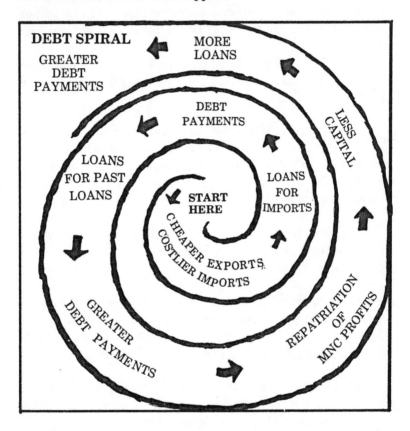

As this drawing indicates, loans mean debt payments, which mean further loans. Thus, even greater debt payments follow. This debt trap ties more and more of Third World resources in debt servicing payments. The amounts are staggering. From a total of about $20 billion in 1960, the total debt of Third World countries escalated to $80 billion in 1973 and passed the $250 billion mark by late 1978. While most of this debt had previously been owed to First World governments, the World Bank, and the International Monetary Fund, today close to half is owed to the giant banks based in the First World.[9]

Another way of imagining this spiral of debt is to picture a development aid bank and clients representing an Asian country, an African country, and a Latin American country. At one of the bank's windows clients receive their total share of aid for the year. This includes government loans, private bank loans, export credits, World Bank loans, etc. They then go to the other window to take care of payments due on previous loans. Tibor Mende, creator of this image, claims that by 1972, the Asian client paid back a little more than half of what was received. The African client paid back about 75%, and the Latin American client 87¢ for every $1.00 received.[10] And the situations continue to worsen. This is what Pope Paul VI meant in the selection quoted earlier: "what was being given them with one hand was being taken away with the others."

The consequences of this debt situation are equally staggering, as countries like Chile and Peru have found out. By 1976, Peru was in debt up to $3.7 billion, with interest payments at about $300 million a year. The price of copper, Peru's main source of export income, was down considerably. Peru, once the largest catcher of fish in the world, had seen its catches drop suddenly. Thus, its fishmeal exports were cut drastically. So Peru needed money badly.

It went to a group of giant banks and asked for a $240 million loan. This group of eight U.S. banks were willing to grant the loan, but only if Peru accepted a series of drastic economic changes. These included, as they usually do in such circumstances, a major reduction in government spending for social services like health care, education, welfare—including food subsidies and food programs for children. The banks demanded a reduction of government jobs and tight controls on wages. Imports would have to be reduced, while exports expanded. Finally, Peru would have to be willing to allow the multinational corporations to enter Peru much more easily.

This meant returning those corporations that Peru had previously nationalized and granting the multinational corporations special tax breaks.[11]

This was an expensive price to pay. The gradual social revolution that Peru was undergoing was quickly reversed. The poor majority of the country paid dearly in terms of higher food prices, less work, less pay, less services. But Peru was trapped. If it did not meet its debt payments, it might not be able to get a loan ever again. In one sense, it is similar to the bind that people get into when they deal with loan sharks. They are trapped.

A $400 million loan from the International Monetary Fund in 1977 extended the trap. The conditions became even tighter. The result was an escalation in both resistance from Peruvians and repression from the Peruvian Government. Riots over increased food prices forced on Peru were met with killings—May 1978. What is important to realize is that the banks and the IMF must at least share the blame for this repression. As Jeremiah Novak points out in a perceptive essay, "In Defense of the Third World," some "Third World dictators are creatures of the present international economic order."[12]

3. Little Processing Done by Third World Countries

As we have already seen, Third World countries import most of their manufactured goods. Most Third World countries do relatively little of the manufacturing or the processing of their raw materials. This represents a tremendous loss of income for these Third World countries. According to World Bank economist Mahbub ul Haq, only about $30 billion of the $200 billion that final consumers pay for products (excluding oil products) that involve the twelve key Third World raw materials goes to the Third World.[13] The remaining $170 billion goes to the processors, shippers, distributors, retailers, etc. In other words, on the average only 15% of the price we pay for manufactured goods goes to the Third World for their raw materials in the product.

This is borne out in the case of cocoa. The Food and Agriculture Organization of the UN reports that 75% of the cost of chocolate products goes to processing and marketing. 11% goes to taxes. Only 14% goes for raw materials, primarily cocoa beans.[14]

With regard to bananas costing 20¢ per pound in 1975, the breakdown looked like this:

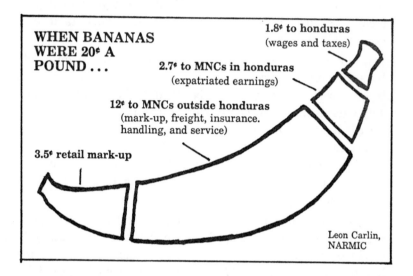

WHEN BANANAS WERE 20¢ A POUND . . .

1.8¢ to honduras (wages and taxes)

2.7¢ to MNCs in honduras (expatriated earnings)

12¢ to MNCs outside honduras (mark-up, freight, insurance. handling, and service)

3.5¢ retail mark-up

Leon Carlin, NARMIC

There are two main reasons why Third World countries do so little of their own processing. The first is First World tariffs. The second is that multinational corporations really control processing, even most of the processing that is actually done in Third World countries.

(A) *Tariff Barriers to Third World Manufacturing Exports.* Tariffs are import taxes or duties that people must pay to buy foreign products. Countries add tariffs and other measures like import quotas to protect their own products from foreign competition. In the case of First World–Third World relations, First World countries place much higher tariffs on Third World manufactured goods than on Third World raw materials. Such tariffs make these manufactured goods much more expensive and therefore less attractive to First World buyers. This makes it very difficult for Third World countries to develop the manufacturing (and most profitable) part of production. If you do not have a large market within your own country and are prevented by tariffs from exporting your product, then your manufacturing industry will never get off the ground. Mahbub ul Haq estimates that Third World countries today lose $20 billion to $25 billion a year in export income because they get frustrated by First World tariff and non-tariff barriers.[15]

For instance, U.S. tariffs are five times higher on candy bars than on raw cocoa beans. Ghana can export all the cocoa beans it wants to Hershey and Nestlé duty-free, but there is no way Ghana could sell candy bars in the U.S. or Switzerland. Tariffs have taken care of that. Japan has no tariffs on cocoa beans either, but it does have a 30% tariff on cocoa powder (semi-processed cocoa). Likewise, West Germany has only a 4% tariff on raw cocoa beans, but a sliding 12–22% tariff on chocolate.[16]

Jute (a strong fiber for making fabrics) is another good example. The chart on page 64 above shows that jute and jute products are almost the only source of export income for Bangladesh. Up until 1974, the jute products imported by Western European countries were subject to a 58% tariff, while raw jute was imported duty-free. Until 1972, the protective tariff on jute sacks imported into Switzerland came to about 33%. These high tariff barriers forced Bangladesh (and India) to export their jute in crude form and have it processed in the First World. The beneficiaries? First World processing industries, of course. Since the mid-1970s, these European countries have partially lowered their tariffs. So too in the U.S. Tariffs on manufactured jute products like pot hangers, coasters, place mats, belts and shoulder bags were about 20% until a three-year campaign succeeded in getting the U.S. Government in 1978 to allow jute handicraft items from Bangladesh to enter the U.S. duty-free[17] (see p. 121).

(B) *Most Third World Processing Is Controlled by Multi-national Corporations.* A large percentage of the processing operations that have been developed in Third World countries has been controlled by the multinational corporations. This should not be surprising. As we will see in detail in Chapters 8 and 9, multinational corporations control technology, capital (the money it takes to start), and marketing expertise (how to sell). These corporations are in the best position to take advantage of any profitable new possibility.

But if Honduras, for instance, could get some of the 2.7¢ and the 12¢ now going to the multinational corporations out of every 20¢ of bananas, as the graph on page 71 shows, then the price of bananas would not have to be raised in order to increase Third World incomes. As it stands now, most of us think that the only way to make trade more just for Third World countries and workers is to be willing to pay higher prices for our imports from Third World countries. That may be necessary. But it would not be as necessary if (1) the profits of the multinational corporations controlling bananas did not always "have to" increase, and (2) more of the profits to be made in the boxing, labelling, and shipping of bananas went to Honduras. Thus, the "enemy" of First World consumers like ourselves is not Honduras or Honduranian banana workers. If there is an "enemy", it is the multinational corporations in the middle who control the banana industry (United Brands—Chiquita; Castle & Cooke—Dole; and Del Monte). More on this in Part III.

Conclusion

So Third World countries are caught in a four-fold economic bind. First, they continue to be economically vulnerable because their exports are limited and their prices fluctuate wildly. Secondly, because of the unfavorable terms of trade, they are caught in an ever increasing spiral of debt. Thirdly, because of First World tariffs on manufactured goods, Third World manufacturing industries do not really have a chance to develop. Finally, those manufacturing industries that do develop in the Third World are generally controlled by multinational corporations.

This bind goes back to the colonial era when these patterns of trade were established. Thus, it is very difficult for Third World countries to break out of this bind. But the economic development of the Third World will not be achieved unless the bonds are broken. In Chapter 5, we will examine how the New International Economic Order proposes to break these bonds.

Discussion Questions

1. Why is First World foreign aid an unsatisfactory answer to Third World underdevelopment?
2. Why are changes in trade relationships much more important than increases in foreign aid?
3. Why are Third World economies much more vulnerable than First World economies?
4. What is meant by Third World countries having to ride a "roller coaster" to development?
5. Why is the debt situation of Third World countries described as a "spiral"?
6. What are the consequences of this spiral of debt?
7. Why don't Third World countries do their own processing, if it is so much more profitable than exporting raw materials?
8. Why is it inaccurate to say that the conflict over Third World demands for higher prices for their exports is between First World consumers and Third World workers?

Resources

On Trade and Aid in General

"Bread, Justice and Trade"—Part I of the filmstrips accompanying this project focuses specifically on trade and hunger—on the vulnerability of Third World economies, on the spiral of debt and on the lack of Third World processing of their own raw materials.

—Part I of "Sharing Global Resources" (NARMIC) also examines the trade aspect of the New International Economic Order. It presents Third World spokespersons describing the unfavorable terms of trade that Third World countries face.

—In addition to *Coffee: The Rules of the Game and You* (see Chapter 3 Resources), there are two good pamphlets on trade, both published by the Overseas Development Council: James W. Howe, "Protectionism, American Jobs, and the Poor Countries," *Communiqué #17*, October 1972; and Guy F. Erb, "U.S. Trade Goals and the Poor Countries," *Communiqué #20*, July 1973.

—George H. Dunne, *The Right to Development* (New York: Paulist Press, 1974) is an excellent short high school student text on justice and trade and aid issues in an explicitly Christian context. The emphasis is on the need to change sinful social structures. Unfortunately, there are not many action strategies presented.

—*The Trade Debate* (Washington: Government Printing Office, 1978) is the reflection of the U.S. Department of State on the variety of trade issues presented in this chapter, specifically as they relate to U.S. policy. It contains a good summary of the facts, some history of the trade issue, and excellent graphs.

—"US Foreign Aid: Its Impact and Our Responsibility" is the title of a pamphlet published by the Institute for Food and Development Policy in 1979. It presents a critical assessment of the policies of the World Bank, U.S. A.I.D., food aid, and the work of the voluntary agencies.

Chapter Five

TRADE AND THE NEW INTERNATIONAL ECONOMIC ORDER

In the Programme of Action *for the New International Economic Order, at least a quarter of the approximately 100 proposals for change in the present international economic order deal with trade. In this Chapter, we will examine the most important of these proposed changes in First World–Third World trade relations. Further, we will come to see that changes within Third World countries are also necessary if the changes in international trade are to promote justice for Third World peoples. The proposed changes in the world trade system will be considered in relationship to the three basic problem areas identified in Chapter 4.*

Basic Changes in Trade

1. Vulnerability of Third World Exports

    (A) *Diversification vs. Single Export Economies.* Individuals protect their economic interests by diversifying. People who invest in the stock market generally select a variety of stocks. They want to cover themselves in case one or two of the stocks turn out to be "losers." Corporations, as we will see in Chapter 8 (pp. 147-8), also protect themselves and expand by diversifying. They develop a variety of products and/or buy up companies producing such a variety. Likewise, countries must diversify their exports, especially those many Third World countries with single export economies that we saw in Chapter 4. It is risky to "put all your eggs in one basket," as the saying goes.

For many Third World countries to diversify their exports is easier said than done. They did not choose to be single export economies. They were forced into it by their First World colonial rulers who wanted an abundance of a particular raw material, so that they could process it and enjoy the higher profits that processed goods bring. Therefore, we can expect that breaking out of this bind will be a struggle.

Among the variety of means for promoting this diversification of exports is a NIEO proposal to establish a fund of about $500 million to finance diversification efforts over three years. The focus would be first on the commodities of tea, jute, bananas, rubber, and hard fibers like Tanzania's sisal. This proposal would help countries like Sri Lanka, Bangladesh, Honduras, Indonesia, and Tanzania—all major producers of these five commodities—in two ways. First, it would encourage them to diversify into different commodities, such as tea as well as coffee or rubber as well as tea. Secondly, the fund would help these countries move into the processing of these commodities. In other words, part of the money would be available to Indonesia, for instance, to help it begin to process its own raw rubber.

Further, this diversification fund would help protect these natural commodities from the growing number of First World synthetics. That is, part of the fund would be set aside for improving the quality and yields of these commodities, for reducing the costs of production, and for improving selling strategies. First World synthetics represent a real problem for Third World raw material exports. The more that Third World countries push for higher prices for their raw materials, the more that First World buyers look for synthetic alternatives to these raw materials.

Jute is a good example. Jute is mainly used for making sacks, carpet backing and twine. Since 1965, it has been faced with growing and deadly competition from plastics and synthetic fibers. Between 1960 and 1975, imports of synthetics into Switzerland, for example, increased ten times. During this period the consumption of jute goods dropped by 38%. This is more or less typical of the trend in other First World countries.[1]

Progress on this proposal for a diversification fund has been quite slow. As of late 1978, this fund was being resisted by the major First World countries who see it as an aid measure more appropriate for the World Bank, over which the First World has much greater control. This is another example of the basic problem in the NIEO proposals. Some First World countries are willing to settle for some redistribution of goods. But they are very reluctant to create any mechanism or institution that would lessen their control (redistribute power). A diversification fund over which Third World countries would have at least equal control with First World countries might benefit Third World countries too much, from a narrow First World perspective. Why? Because, as we have seen several times before, those who make the rules get the goods.

(B) *Commodity Agreements vs. Wildly Fluctuating Prices.* The basic means for replacing the roller-coaster ride to development (or underdevelopment, actually!) is something called "commodity agreements." In fact, the central focus of international negotiations since the NIEO was formulated has been the "Integrated Commodity Program" (ICP) put forth at the fourth United Nations Conference on Trade and Development (UNCTAD IV) in May 1976.

Basically, commodity agreements are designed to do three things:

(1) To stabilize the wildly fluctuating prices of Third World raw materials;

(2) To provide just prices for their Third World producers;

(3) And to guarantee adequate supplies at reasonable prices to consumers.

Commodity agreements achieve these three goals through two basic mechanisms: a "Common Fund" and "buffer stocks."

(1) *Common Fund.* Originally estimated by UNCTAD at approximately $6 billion, but now down to $1 billion, such a Fund would pay for the stockpiling of commodities like coffee, sugar, rubber, cocoa, tin, jute, and copper when there is a surplus of these commodities in the world. Buying up the surplus would keep the price of the commodities from falling disastrously. According to the "law of supply and demand," prices fall when the supply of a commodity is larger than the demand for the commodity, and prices rise when the supply is low (and demand remains high). This Fund is called a "Common" Fund because it would be for a wide range of commodities. Most of the initial $1 billion would come from First World countries.

(2) *Buffer Stocks.* The surpluses of the various commodities that are bought through the Common Fund become what are called "buffer stocks." That is, they provide a "buffer" or protection against times when the supply of a commodity would drop for some reason, like bad weather ruining Bangladesh's jute crop. Thus, buffer stocks help to guarantee an adequate supply of a commodity. This helps the consumer in two ways.

(a) Buffer stocks keep the price from rising to the point where consumers cannot afford to buy the amounts they need. If the supply of tin, for instance, would be low and demand remain high, then *without* a buffer stock of tin the price of tin would shoot up. *With* a buffer stock of tin, that would not happen because some of the buffer stock would be released once the price of tin reached a certain level. This level is called a "ceiling" or "trigger price" because it serves as a trigger for releasing some of the tin held in the buffer stock.

(b) Buffer stocks help the consumer know that there will always be a certain amount of tin available. Guaranteed supplies are important for long-term economic planning.

Thus, commodity agreements represent an attempt to modify the law of supply and demand to meet the demands of justice. As the excerpts from *On the Development of Peoples* in Chapter 4 pointed out:

> In other words, the rule of free trade, taken by itself, is no longer able to govern international relations.... Prices which are 'freely' set in the market can produce unfair results.... An economy of exchange can no longer be based solely on the law of free competition [or supply and demand], a law which, in its turn, too often creates an economic dictatorship. Freedom of trade is fair only if it is subject to the demands of social justice.

Commodity agreements modify the law of supply and demand in such a way as to bring the interests of producers and consumers more in line with each other. The law of supply and demand operates in a way that pits producers and consumers against each other. One benefits precisely when the other suffers. Higher prices help producers but hurt consumers. Conversely, lower prices help consumers but hurt producers.

On the other hand, with commodity agreements both benefit. Producers benefit because buffer stocks prevent the prices of their commodities from falling the way they have so often. The roller-coaster ride that Third World producers have traveled has a lot of low points, as the graph on cocoa prices in Chapter 4 (p. 65) revealed. More stable and somewhat higher prices on their raw materials mean greater ability to do long-range economic planning, additional income for diversification of their economies, and the possibility of freeing some land previously used for export crops to grow food for local consumption. If income from export crops is higher, then the quantity of export crops (and land used for this purpose) can be reduced and still break even. As we have already seen, consumers benefit from commodity agreements in two ways. They put a ceiling on prices and provide at least a limited guarantee of adequate supplies.

Two examples would help to make all this more concrete: a world food reserve and the International Cocoa Agreement.

(3) *A World Food Reserve.* Without a world food reserve (i.e., buffer stock of wheat) and with its own food production low in 1972–1974, India had to import large amounts of grain. At the same time, U.S. grain reserves had been deliberately depleted and worldwide shortages of grain were acute. Consequently, the price of wheat jumped four-fold to between $5 and $6 a bushel. This meant a pretty good year for U.S. farmers. But it also meant a terrible year for India. India had to transfer money it was using for long-term development to the First World to pay exorbitant prices for the grain it had to import. As we saw in Chapter 2 (p. 24), the real beneficiaries of this manipulated shortage of grain were the giant grain companies that had held onto wheat until the prices skyrocketed.[2]

With a world food reserve, on the other hand, much of the wheat in the reserve (buffer stock) would have been released before the price had reached $5 a bushel. This would have kept the price at a reasonable level. Thus, India would not had to have used up all its development money for grain imports.

(4) *The International Cocoa Agreement.*[3] The International Cocoa Agreement is one of about six international commodity agreements that have existed in some form during the past two decades. Coffee, wheat, tin and to some extent sugar and olive oil are the other five. Attempts to stabilize cocoa supplies and prices have been made since the 1920s. But it was not until 1972 that an International Cocoa Agreement was reached through the United Nations between cocoa producing and cocoa consuming nations.

There are four basic components in the Agreement. It

(1) established a minimum price of 23¢ (U.S.) and a maximum price of 32¢ per pound for cocoa beans. This was renegotiated in October 1975 to a range of 39¢ (minimum) and 55¢ (maximum);

(2) authorized a buffer stock of 250,000 tons of cocoa beans (about 17% of total world production in 1972);

(3) established a tax of 1¢ per pound on exports and imports of cocoa, to finance the building up of the buffer stock of cocoa beans;

(4) established export quotas for the producing countries. That is, at the beginning of the cocoa season, the Cocoa Council created by the Agreement meets to determine the amount of total world exports of cocoa beans to be permitted each cocoa producing country. These amounts are proportionate to the "basic quotas" assigned each country. The "basic quotas" are based on each country's highest production to date. The "basic quotas" for the top six producing countries for 1972 were:

Ghana	36.7%	Ivory Coast	14.2%	Cameroon	8.0%
Nigeria	19.5%	Brazil	12.7%	Dominican Republic	3.%

The way that the buffer stock works in the International Cocoa Agreement is that when the price of cocoa beans falls to 1¢ above the minimum price of 39¢, then each country is allowed to export only 90% of its quota for that year. Thus, each country is forced to hold on to 10% of its cocoa crop. This 10%, in effect, forms the buffer stock of cocoa beans. When prices go above the 55¢ ceiling, then the cocoa beans in the buffer stock can be released for sale.

Although the International Cocoa Agreement has been ratified and is in effect, it is really not operating yet. The price of cocoa beans rose dramatically in 1977 because supplies were short and no buffer stock had been built up. By October 1975, the 1¢ per pound tax (item #3 in the Agreement) had generated $85 million to purchase cocoa beans for the buffer stock. But no buffer stock was possible, as there was no surplus of cocoa beans to buy. Consequently, the effectiveness of the Agreement has yet to be tested.

Progress on the full "Integrated Commodity Program" proposed by the NIEO has likewise been slow. One important reason is control. The individual commodity agreements, like the International Cocoa Agreement, are largely controlled by First World participants. In contrast, the Integrated Commodity Program proposes to set up a single international authority in which producers (Third World) and consumers (First World) have roughly equal power. The responsibility of this international authority would be primarily to regulate the buffer stocks in all (reduced from 18 to 10) participating commodities. It would have a roughly $1 billion Common Fund with which to do this. Thus, the Integrated Commodity Program would incorporate all the individual commodity agreements and thereby reduce current First World control over these commodities.

UNCTAD IV set the end of 1978 as the target date for successful completion of a series of negotiations on all 18 commodities. Unfortunately, that target was not reached, and the future of the Integrated Commodity Program remains uncertain. Because this program represents a loss of power for First World countries, because the Common Fund would be largely financed by First World countries, and because commodity agreements are regarded as tampering with the "free market" system by some leaders, the Integrated Commodity Program has met resistance, especially from the U.S.[4] The U.S. has offered a counter-proposal—to locate the Common Fund within the World Bank. But this was rejected by Third World countries as a thinly veiled attempt to keep the Common Fund, and thus the whole Integrated Commodity Program, under the control of the First World.

2. The Spiral of Debt

(A) *Higher Prices on Third World Raw Materials.* As we saw in Chapter 4, the spiral of debt begins with Third World countries being exporters of cheaper raw materials and importers of more expensive manufactured goods. Thus, part of the answer to the spiral of debt is higher prices for Third World raw material exports. Although commodity agreements do tend to raise the price of these items, their goal is more to stabilize prices. To raise these prices and bring them into line with what Third World countries have to pay for their imports of manufactured goods, the NIEO calls for two basic measures: "indexation" and "producer associations."

(1) *Indexation.* Indexation means establishing an automatic link between the price of manufactured goods and the price of raw materials. Any increases in the prices of First World manufactured goods would automatically be matched by increases in the prices of Third World raw materials. For instance, going back to the coffee and tractor graph in Chapter 2 (p. 32), instead of always taking more bags of raw coffee to

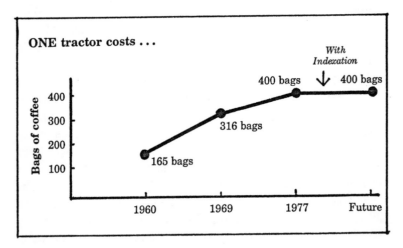

purchase a single tractor, there would be a constant ratio between the two. That ratio might be the 1977 figure of 1 tractor being the equivalent of 400 bags of coffee. Any increase in the price of the tractor would be matched with an increase in the price of coffee, so that it would still take *no more* than

400 bags of coffee to buy that tractor. This would be true no matter what the year—1987, 1997, etc. As the other chart shows, indexation would not close the gap between prices Third World countries get for their raw materials and the prices they pay for manufactured imports. But it would keep the gap from continuing to widen, as it does today without indexation.

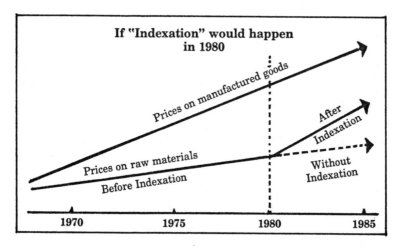

Although the term "indexation" is not used in the First World, it is definitely something that is done in the First World, in at least two ways. First, indexation is something like the automatic "cost of living" increases that are built into many wage agreements negotiated between labor and management. Workers are rightfully concerned about their wages being able to buy at least the same amount of goods as the year before. Secondly, indexation is something First World countries have been doing with regard to the costs of production. In other words, "the rich countries index their manufactured exports, so as to make sure that the relationship between their exports and their imports does not change to their detriment"(Nyerere). Interestingly, indexation for Third World raw materials has been strongly resisted by the U.S., West Germany, and a few other First World countries as tampering with the "free market." Thus, it has yet to be accepted or implemented.

(2) *Producer Associations*. In the absence of effective commodity agreements that are beneficial to the Third World as well as the First World, Third World countries have formed their own alliances or associations to get better prices for the raw materials they produce. The Organization of Petroleum Exporting Countries (OPEC) is only the most famous of these producer associations. An International Bauxite Association has effectively raised the price of bauxite (pages 188-189). Before the International Cocoa Agreement was reached, the top five cocoa producing countries formed the Cocoa Producers' Alliance Association to try to increase as well as stabilize the price of their cocoa bean exports.

In this way, some Third World countries are able to become "price-makers" as well as "price-takers." Unfortunately, the notion of more producer associations of Third World countries has produced even more resistance in the First World than indexation. First World countries are quite wary about the potential impact on their economies and especially on the present distribution of global economic power. "No more OPEC's!" comes through clear and strong.

(B) *Debt Relief.* In the long term, the staggering debt problems of Third World countries will be overcome only by a combination of all the measures described in this Chapter. For short-term relief, however, Third World countries are stressing the following points:

(1) cancellation of official debt (debt owed to First World governments) for the least economically developed countries. This would mean several billion dollars.

(2) debt relief for the 42 most seriously affected nations. This means extending the period of time in which to repay loans and lowering the interest rates on loans.

(3) consolidation of commercial debt (debt owed to commercial banks) and a rescheduling of payments over 25 years. This simplifies and eases repayment.

(4) convening a debtor-creditor conference to develop guidelines for renegotiating official and commercial debt, so that Third World countries can have some collective clout in those decisions.[5]

Bread for the World and others support these short-term measures and have suggested at least two additional items:

(5) an increase of grants, rather than loans. Grants do not require repayment and thus do not add to the debt burden of Third World countries.

(6) a sizable decrease in loans from commercial banks. As we saw in Chapter 4, bank terms and conditions are often quite devastating for Third World countries. The Third World does not need the banks' austerity measures, their higher interest rates, or their shorter repayment periods.

The response of the First World has generally been negative to these proposals. The U.S., West Germany, Japan and a few others have supported only "case-by-case" relief. That is, they reject the idea of "across-the-board" measures applying to whole groups of countries. However, there have been a few break-throughs in the First World's actions. In October 1977, Sweden and Canada took the bold step of cancelling $200 million and $254 million worth of debt owed them by a number of Third World countries. By the summer of 1978, the Netherlands, Switzerland and England had followed suit, cancelling partial debts for about 20 countries, totaling almost $2 billion.[6] But, as with commodity agreements and most of the other NIEO measures, the future of large-scale debt relief is an unknown.

3. Third World Processing of Its Own Raw Materials

(A) *Greater Access to Markets vs. Tariffs.* More important than commodity agreements and higher prices for Third World raw materials, according to economists like Mahbub ul Haq, is market access: increased exports. This applies especially to Third World manufactured goods. With regard to present First World trade barriers to Third World manufactured goods, the NIEO proposes several changes. Two of the most important are expansion of the "generalized system of preferences" and "collective self-reliance."

(1) *Expansion of the "Generalized System of Preferences".* First World countries grant preferences on most of the items they trade with one another. That is, the tariffs are lower for most goods coming from other First World countries than for goods coming from Third World countries. Nevertheless, the First World has extended these preferences to cover *some* (13% by 1976) of the exports coming from Third World countries. Now, what Third World countries want and what the NIEO calls for is an extension of these preferences to a much wider range of Third World exports.

This expansion of preferences (lowering of tariffs) would include Third World agricultural commodities, semi-manufactured goods, and fully manufactured goods. As ul Haq estimates, the elimination of tariff and non-tariff barriers on nine agricultural commodities alone would raise Third World export income by $7.1 billion or 36% by 1980. These nine commodities—beef, bananas, cocoa beans, coffee, tea, sugar, cotton, and wood products—account for one-half of the agricultural export income of the Third World.[7]

(2) *Collective Self-Reliance.* With regard to trade, collective self-reliance means increased trade among Third World countries by granting preferential treatment to each other's exports. A number of Third World trading alliances have sprung up in the last couple of decades. The Latin American Free Trade Association (LAFTA), for instance, was supposed to be South America's counterpart to Western Europe's Common Market (European Economic Community or EEC). At present, however, only about 21% of Third World exports go to other Third World countries.

On the surface, there does not seem to be any reason why Third World countries should not buy manufactured goods from one another. The most industrialized Third World countries, like Brazil, already export extensively to other Third

World countries. But there are a number of obstacles to this form of collective self-reliance.

(a) As we saw in Chapter 4, manufacturing industries are quite limited in Third World countries. They do not have nearly as many manufactured goods to export as industrialized countries do.

(b) As we will see in Chapter 9, multinational corporations charge very high prices for the technology they sell or allow Third World countries to use in the manufacturing of goods. This raises the prices of Third World manufactured goods, sometimes making them more expensive—and thus less attractive—than similar First World products.

(c) Similarly, multinational corporations place restrictions on the use of the technology they sell or allow Third World countries to use. Typically, as Chapter 9 also points out, accepting technology from First World multinational corporations prevents or limits Third World countries in exporting goods produced with this technology. The corporations want to limit their overseas competition.

(d) Some aid from First World countries is "tied" to the purchase of goods from those same First World countries. That is, loans from the U.S.—for instance, to Colombia for the purchase of agricultural equipment like tractors—often require that these tractors be purchased from U.S. companies. Since many Third World purchases are financed by First World loans, potential Third World suppliers are hurt by this loan restriction.

(3) *The Notion of Non-Reciprocity or Preferential Treatment.* These two measures to increase Third World exports of manufactured goods really ask for nothing more than First World countries grant themselves. Justice requires that the special restrictions First World countries have placed on Third World exports—like higher tariffs and import quotas—be removed.

But some NIEO measures go further and call for preferential and non-reciprocal treatment of Third World exports.

That is, First World countries are being asked to grant preferences to Third World exports that they do not grant even to other First World exports. Further, these measures do *not* require Third World countries to do the same in return.

Such non-reciprocal measures are the equivalent of "affirmative action programs" in the U.S. for the hiring of "minority" people and women. The point is to counteract the continuation of past injustices. "Equal Opportunity" is not really equal if the parties involved start from vastly different points. Because of past injustices and current restrictions such as we have seen here, many Third World manufactured goods cannot compete equally with First World manufactured goods. "Free trade" can be fair in its distribution of benefits only if the trading partners are roughly equal in power. But this is certainly not the case between the First World and the Third World.

Thus, non-reciprocal measures are essential if justice is to be combined with the so-called law (better, humanly established practice) of free trade. The passage from *On the Development of Peoples*, quoted in Chapter 4 (p. 61), reveals Christian teaching on this matter.

> In other words, the rule of free trade, taken by itself, is no longer able to govern international relations. Its advantages are certainly evident when the parties involved are not affected by any excessive inequalities of economic power.... But the situation is no longer the same when economic conditions differ too widely from country to country: prices which are "freely" set in the market can produce unfair results.... Freedom of trade is fair only if it is subject to the demands of social justice.

To make this more concrete, let's take a hypothetical example, but one not far from reality. Let's suppose that Ghana wants to develop a chocolate candy bar operation to process some of its own cocoa and get a share of the large profits that Nestlé and Hershey have been getting all these years.[8] Ghana would have a very hard time doing so, for at least four reasons.

a. Since the processes used to produce candy bars belong to Nestlé and Hershey (they have "patents" on them), these corporations will charge Ghana much more for the technology than they "charge" themselves.

b. As part of the contract that provides this technology, Nestlé and Hershey may also require Ghana to restrict its exports of candy bars to markets that the corporations are not interested in anyway.

c. Further, a $10 billion corporation like Nestlé might well use the profits it makes in other fields (infant formula, coffee, tea, vegetables, restaurants, hotels, etc.) to cover any losses in candy bars, should it choose to lower its prices in order to drive Ghana out of the candy bar business.

d. Nestlé and Hershey have sales forces all over the world. They have sophisticated advertising campaigns and access to bank loans on a scale far greater than Ghana. Nestlé's $10 billion figure for their total 1977 sales is at least twice the size as the entire Gross National Product of the country of Ghana.

Given this great imbalance of power and wealth and the great advantages Hershey and especially Nestlé have over Ghana as Ghana begins its candy bar production, how fair, adequate, and "equal" is it for the First World to limit its response to Ghana's situation to removing its tariffs on candy bars? Even without tariffs, Ghana will be hard pressed to sell candy bars at the same price as Nestlé and Hershey do. Without addressing past injustices and present inequalities of power and wealth, equal opportunity is not equal. Preferential, non-reciprocal measures are absolutely necessary if justice is to be done. And this principle holds true for many other NIEO proposals.

(4) *Increased Processing by the Third World of Their Own Raw Materials.* The gradual elimination of trade barriers to Third World manufactured goods would greatly encourage the

expansion of the Third World's share of profits from processing industries. As it stands now, the Third World's share of
the manufactured goods that the First World imports is only
about 6%. According to 1973 statistics, this 6% meant $14
billion of a total of $227 billion. Thus, at the Second General
Conference of the United Nations Industrial Development
Organization (UNIDO), First and Third World representatives
agreed to work for an increase of the Third World's share of
global industrial production to 25%.[9] The transfer of industrial technology on much better terms to the Third World is
put forth in the NIEO as one important way of reaching this
goal. Part III will examine this proposal in some detail.

(5) *Lessening the Control of Multinational Corporations
over Third World Processing.* Because of the tremendous advantages that Nestlé and Hershey have over Ghana, as we just
saw, if a candy bar operation were to thrive in Ghana, it would
probably have to be controlled and operated by Nestlé or
Hershey. So it is in most manufacturing industries in the
Third World. However, as Chapter 9 will point out, often it is
not until these industries are controlled by Third World countries and peoples themselves that they can truly benefit the
Third World. Part III, especially Chapter 10, examines a number of ways of increasing Third World control over its own
manufacturing industries.

NIEO Trade Proposals and Justice

The many changes in trade proposed in the New International Economic Order are clearly matters of justice. They are
ways of bringing the so-called law of "free trade" or "free
competition" or the "free market" into line with the fundamental goal of all human activity—namely, the well-being and
development of all persons.[10]

The primary force behind these changes has been a fairly
unified group of Third World countries. Just as workers in this
country and elsewhere had to organize trade unions to get
justice for themselves, so too Third World countries have

organized their own form of "trade unionism." As a united front, they increase their bargaining power with First World countries. And it is only as their bargaining power increases that agreements between them and First World countries can be expected to be more consistent with the demands of justice.

Nevertheless, increasing the Third World's portion of world trade and the benefits of trade creates a number of justice problems. A growing number of people whose vision of global economic justice is rooted in values of equity, dignity, participation and self-reliance are questioning these fundamental aspects of the New International Economic Order. Their main concerns are three:

1. Trade and Interdependence

Increased trade clearly means increased interdependence. But is this interdependence "horizontal" or "vertical"? That is, is this increased interdependence based on sovereign equality or is it based on continued exploitation? As Third World spokesperson Samuel Parmar points out in an excellent essay entitled "Self-Reliant Development in an 'Interdependent' World," ". . . in practice the history of trade has been one of domination by the strong and deprivation of the weak. It has been both an 'engine of growth' for developed nations and an instrument of exploitation of the developing."[11] In other words, examples like Potosi, Bolivia (see Chapter 2) are not all relics of the past. As this and the previous chapters have revealed, the exploitation continues today.

How willing is the First World to make the changes called for in this Chapter, so that increased trade might promote horizontal interdependence (and thereby justice)? Given the progress in NIEO negotiations to date, there is much basis for pessimism. First World countries seem reluctant to agree even to measures that remove some of the special barriers they have erected against Third World exports. And they have strongly resisted measures like the "Integrated Commodities Program" and producer associations. They do not want any reduction in First World control over world trade.

2. Trade and Workers

But the question of justice goes far beyond the claims of Third World *governments* to a fairer distribution of trade benefits—a bigger slice of the pie. Justice means justice for all, not just for some. The justice claim put forth in the selection from *On the Development of Peoples* (Ch. 4, pp. 61-62) was fundamentally on behalf of the poor within Third World countries.

Banana plantation workers are a good example. The graph in Chapter 4 (p. 71) showed that less than 2¢ on every 20¢ worth of bananas stays in Honduras as wages and taxes. In the Philippines, banana plantation workers get only 1% of the retail price for bananas in Japanese supermarkets.[12] But if a producer association of banana exporting countries or a commodity agreement for bananas would succeed in raising the price of bananas, would these banana workers be helped? Who would get the extra money from the higher prices? The workers? United Brands, Castle & Cooke, and Del Monte, who control the banana industry? Or President Marcos of the Philippines, from whom Del Monte leases some of the land it uses for bananas? As the next chapter and the whole of Part IV will show, the answer depends on the type of government and society in each Third World country.

At best, these changes in world trade policies and practices are a *necessary condition* for justice. President Nyerere is right when he says

> The truth is that however much we reorganize our economic system to serve the interest of the mass of the people, and however much our government tries to weight the income distribution in favor of the poorest people, we are merely redistributing poverty, and we remain subject to economic decisions and interests outside our control.[13]

But there is no guarantee that the majority of Third World people—the working poor and the non-working poor—will benefit from these changes in trade.

As Bread for the World points out, the benefits to the poor from commodity agreements, for instance, are somewhat tentative or conditional:

1. There is an immediate benefit to poor laborers employed in commodity production in that they would no longer suffer periodic layoffs and wage cuts when the price of their particular commodity bottomed out [dropped drastically].

2. No guarantee exists, however, that these same poor will share the benefits of stabilization in terms of fairer wages unless either they obtain it through strong cooperatives and unions or it is assured for them through strong political leadership.

3. The unemployed and the rural poor would benefit *if* increased earnings from stabilization were targeted towards sound national development plans that include land reform, major credit and extension services for small farmers, basic health and education services—all leading toward greater self-reliance.[14]

3. Trade and Bread

The final problem with trade and the New International Economic Order is bread. That is, will the changes proposed by the NIEO and examined in this chapter further Third World peoples' ability and opportunity to feed themselves? We saw earlier (pp. 87-88) Mahbub ul Haq's recommendation that Third World agricultural exports be included in the "generalized system of preferences." Will expanding these export crops decrease hunger in the Third World or will it actually increase hunger? In trying to answer this question, Chapter 6 serves as a more complete evaluation of the NIEO proposals in light of their impact on bread and justice.

Discussion Questions

1. Why is diversification of exports important for Third World countries?

2. How does a commodity agreement benefit both producers and consumers?
3. Why do Third World countries want commodity agreements to be combined in an "Integrated Commodity Program"?
4. What relief would be provided for Third World countries by the six short-term measures for dealing with their debt problems?
5. What is "indexation" and how would it benefit Third World countries?
6. Why is non-reciprocal, preferential treatment for Third World manufactured goods necessary?
7. Why are "free trade" and the "free market" (the law of supply and demand) sometimes inconsistent with the demands of justice?
8. How would the NIEO trade measures affect Third World workers?

Resources

On the NIEO Trade Measures in General
—The two filmstrips described in Chapter 4 Resources—"Bread, Justice and Trade," Part I of the Paulist series accompanying this book, and "Sharing Global Resources"—examine several of these trade measures as well as the problem areas to which these measures refer.
—For a commentary on these trade measures and for an exposition of others, see four of the major works on the NIEO—*Agenda 1977* (Overseas Development Council); *Reshaping the International Order* (Report to the Club of Rome); *Employment, Growth, and Basic Needs* (World Employment Conference); and Mahbub ul Haq, *The Third World and the International Economic Order* (Overseas Development Council).
—To keep up-to-date on developments in the trade issue and the NIEO in general, three newsletters/magazines would be most helpful—*The Interdependent*, an 8-page monthly pub-

lished by the United Nations Association of the USA; *Development Forum*, an 8-page monthly published by the UN Center for Economic and Social Information in Geneva; and *ICDA News*, an 8-page newsletter published irregularly by the International Coalition for Development Action.

—"US Trade Relations with Poor Nations: Suggested Reforms" (Interreligious Task Force for U.S. Food Policy, 110 Maryland Ave NE, Washington, DC 20002) is an excellent four-page summary of the major changes suggested in this chapter. Write for "Hunger Impact Statement No. 14".

On Commodity Agreements

—The United Nations NGO Conference on Commodities (December 1977) produced a series of 20-page studies of ten basic commodities (wheat, vegetable oils, jute, bauxite, bananas, cotton, sugar, copper, rubber, and coffee) that are excellent for initial research into any of these commodities.

—GATT-Fly in Toronto has published a number of case studies on specific commodities, including sugar, tin, and coffee, similar to the UN studies just mentioned.

—"Price Stabilization for Whom?" is an excellent 4-page analysis of commodity agreements by Bread for the World (September 1977), addressing especially the question of who benefits from these agreements.

On Tariff Barriers and Measures to Overcome Them

—"Tariff and Non-Tariff Barriers to Trade," *Development Issue Paper #9* (United Nations Development Program, 1975), is a good, though a little technical, 11-page presentation of the basic problems and NIEO solutions about tariffs.

On Trade and Justice

—*Statement of Proposed Reforms of U.S. Overseas Investment and Trade Policies for the 1970s* (Testimony of the U.S. Catholic Conference to the U.S. House of Representatives Ways and Means Committee, June 15, 1973) offers a number of proposed changes in trade from a Christian perspective (18 pages).

the people eat) received only 3%. The story is repeated throughout the Third World. Basic food crops in Brazil are receiving only 5% of government loans, with the bulk of credit going to coffee, soybeans, sugar, and beef exports.[4]

Eight Problems with Present Export Cropping

1. Less Food Produced for Local Consumption

When export cropping assumes the magnitude that it has today in many countries, the local food supply is usually undermined. Not only do export cropping operations get the bulk of government assistance, but they also get (take) the prime agricultural land. Through a variety of means, many small farmers are removed from their lands and forced to farm much less productive mountain slopes. As a result, these farmers are producing less food.

Prior to World War II, all three Third World continents were net exporters of grain. By 1969–1971, they were importing about 16 million tons of grain a year. Instead of being eaten at home, Philippine bananas are now being exported to Japan where United Brands, Castle & Cooke, and Del Monte can make sizable profits. United Nations estimates for 1985, based on present trends, project 85 million tons of grain needing to be imported by Third World countries, at a cost of about $18 billion.[5]

In Mexico, as cotton, coffee and vegetables for export replace rice and corn, the local food supply dwindles. The statistics that Collins and Lappe cite show that even with government-guaranteed price hikes of 112% between 1970 and 1975, the proportion of land growing basic foods declined. Between 1965 and 1975, the decline was 25% in wheat, corn, beans and rice. Simultaneously, Mexico was importing 15% of its corn, 25% of its wheat, and 45% of its soybeans. The results were two-fold—20 times the profits in exporting tomatoes than in raising wheat in the Sinaloa region, but a 10% increase in the childhood death rate due to malnutrition.[6]

In Colombia, it is carnations, marijuana, feed grains and chickens that have replaced wheat. Carnations are attractive in that they generate 80 times the income that wheat does per acre.[7] Marijuana is so profitable that it has become the country's second largest export crop (after coffee)—a $1 billion crop by 1979. According to the NACLA report cited earlier, marijuana producers are even experimenting with high-yield varieties of the plant.[8]

Brazil is another classic example. Its sugar, cattle, soybean and coffee exports are lucrative sources of income. As more and more land and government assistance are devoted to these export crops, malnutrition is increasing. The production of black beans, a staple of the diet of the Brazilian poor, declined 17% in 1976. Long lines have formed for the purchase of black beans, some of which are now being imported from Chile.[9]

2. Higher Prices for Local Food Staples

As black bean production decreases in Brazil, the prices go up—275% between December 1972 and August 1973, because of increased soybean production.[10] This is also true for Colombian and Mexican corn and wheat, since shortages always drive the prices up. Some corporate landowners like Ralston Purina and their local allies argue that their chickens produce protein-rich eggs, some of which are eaten locally. However, Ralston Purina's eggs are affordable only for the wealthy in Colombia. As Collins and Lappe put it, "for all the additional eggs that Ralston Purina can count on a national basis, there is evidence that Colombia's protein gap (between the well-fed and the poorly fed) is growing 8 times faster than the population."[11]

3. Agricultural Imports Cost More and There Is No Real "Natural Advantage"

One of the main defenses of export cropping is that it generates the foreign exchange to cover food imports and is a

Chapter Six

IS TRADE THE ANSWER?
EXPORT CROPPING

This chapter tries to answer the questions about the value of the NIEO trade measures by examining the impact of Third World exports of agricultural crops. Eight specific aspects of export cropping will be considered before the question is answered. Examples will be drawn primarily from Latin America, where a greater amount of land is devoted to export cropping than in Asia and Africa. But, as will be shown, it is not the amount of land devoted to export cropping or even export cropping itself that is the problem. It is primarily a question of who controls and who benefits from export cropping.

Introduction: The Extent of Export Cropping
The production of agricultural crops for export ("export cropping") is a critical issue for Third World countries. Agri-

culture is the largest source of employment, production, and export income for most Third World countries. In fact, discounting oil, about 75% of all Third World exports to the industrialized world are agricultural commodities, with coffee, sugar, cocoa, tea and bananas leading the way.[1] And this part of the economy—agriculture—continues to expand.

As Collins and Lappe point out, from 1955 to 1965, the growth rate of export cropping was more than twice as fast as the total agricultural growth rate in the Third World. In Mexico, between 1940 and 1962, cotton and coffee production grew almost three times faster than rice and corn (basic local foods). African coffee production has increased more than four times in the last 20 years, with tea up six times and sugar cane three times. In Nicaragua between 1952 and 1967, cotton acreage rose four times, while basic grains (wheat, corn) acreage was cut in half.[2]

In the 1970s, the trend has not changed. By 1973, 55% of agricultural land in the Philippines was devoted to export crops. Four years later, it was more. Bananas are a striking example. In 1960, bananas were as common to the diet of Filipinos as rice. Only $18,000 worth of bananas (less than 1%) were exported. By 1971, that total went up more than 300 times to about $5.4 million. In 1976, more than $79 million worth of bananas (more than 50%) were being exported, most to Japan. In their recent research trip to the Philippines, Lappe and Eleanor McCallie discovered that 57,000 acres of the most fertile land in southern Mindanao—land that used to produce rice, corn, and other staples—had been converted to banana production in only ten years.[3]

Finally, export agriculture receives the vast majority of government assistance. Government-financed irrigation, credit, government-financed research, and extension services to farmers all go to large export operations. As a North American Congress on Latin America (NACLA) study reports, 87% of government credit between 1964 and 1973 in Guatemala went to finance export crops, while rice, corn and beans (what more efficient use of Third World agricultural lands that have a "natural" or "comparative advantage" in producing export crops like coffee, tea and sugar. But this seems to be false in two ways.

(a) *No Economic Advantage.* In the overall picture, there seems to be no real economic advantage in exporting tea and importing rice, for instance. Income from export cropping has generally not kept pace with either industrial or agricultural imports. While over half of the 40 most seriously affected countries of the 1970s depend on agricultural exports for at least 80% of their export income, their agricultural imports cost them more. Between 1963 and 1973, the prices of their exports rose by only 19%, compared to a 26% increase in the prices they paid for their agricultural imports.[12]

Further, while their grain imports are increasing (page 100), the Third World's share of world agricultural trade is down from 40% of the total (1961–1963) to 30% (1970–1972). The First World's share is growing faster. Income from agricultural exports from the First World is twice that of agricultural exports from the Third World. In fact, $^2/_3$ of the benefits from the price increases on agricultural exports in the mid-1970s went to First World countries, especially to the U.S. and to a lesser degree to Canada and Australia.[13] These are the three countries that dominate grain exports worldwide.

Moreover, many export crops are quite vulnerable. They often mature slowly, thereby reducing flexibility. As we say in Chapter 4 (p. 65), cocoa trees take about ten years to mature. Coffee trees take five years. We also saw how prices on export crops tend to fluctuate wildly (Chapter 4, pp. 64-65).

(b) *Nothing "Natural" about Export Crops.* There is nothing natural about the situation of Sri Lankan lands, for instance, growing tea or Tanzanian lands growing cotton. Some land is clearly appropriate for tea. But often it is the choice land in fertile valleys that is given over to these cash crops.

This land could just as easily—though not as profitably—produce food for local consumption.

What "natural" really means is that certain economic forces have shaped practice over a long period of time. "Land use," as Collins and Lappe put it, "represents a choice by people, not by nature."[14] It is a myth that some countries can grow only tropical crops like bananas. The banana tree was not introduced into Latin America until the late 1830s. Corn, rice, and beans now grow on what were formerly banana lands of United Brands and Castle & Cooke in Central America.[15]

4. Export Cropping Can Disrupt the Ecological Balance of the Land

Despite the fact that basic food crops are now growing on some of United Brands' banana lands, export cropping often seems to disrupt the ecological balance of the land. This makes it difficult for farmers to grow other crops on that land in the future. The same export crop is often grown on the same land year after year. Continuous use of the land for the same crop decreases the amount of humus in the soil, causing the soil to erode easily. This, in turn, decreases the chances of future productive yields. Thus, because they are getting smaller yields on their current land, corporations often extend crop production to surrounding land, so that their total yield does not decrease.[16]

Especially as multinational corporations expand their control of export cropping, the use of chemical fertilizers and pesticides increases dramatically. Besides polluting surrounding water supplies and slowly working its way into human systems, heavy doses of pesticides and fertilizers eventually cause a decrease in crop yields. In Nicaragua, for instance, between 1950 and 1964, insecticides helped increase yields tremendously. Then, the trend reversed. By 1966, five times as much insecticides were being used. Yet yields continued to drop. In 1967 and 1968, over 500 cases of human poisoning and 80 deaths were reported because of exposure to insecticides.[17]

5. *Foreign Exchange Earnings Feed the Wealthy, Not the Hungry*

As we have seen in Chapters 4 and 5, most Third World countries have huge trade deficits. They have to increase exports to get foreign exchange (export income), if they want to continue to import goods and pay off past loans. However, the foreign exchange that export crops generate generally does not benefit the majority in most Third World countries. Why? Because the economic institutions and rules are controlled by the wealthy. Thus, the real problem is not so much export cropping and foreign exchange, but who controls them. Once again, those who make the rules get the goods.

For instance, if Senegal's increasing peanut exports during the famine in the Sahelian region of Africa (1968–1974) had meant more money to feed hungry Senegalese people, there might be a legitimate argument for such exports. But, with peanut exports accounting for $1/3$ of the entire national budget, 47% went to government salaries. In 1974, according to Collins and Lappe, at the height of the world's focus on African hunger, 23% of the foreign exchange from peanut exports went into luxury consumer imports.[18] Refrigerators, cars, and TVs do not feed hungry people.

6. *Agriculture Becomes Concentrated in Fewer and Fewer Hands*

Export cropping requires cheap and docile labor and control over large tracts of land. The sizable profits that United Brands, Castle & Cooke, and Del Monte get from banana exports in the Philippines, Honduras and elsewhere, are due in large part to the low cost of labor. As we saw in Chapter 5 (pp. 94-95), only 1% of the retail price for bananas goes to the banana workers in the Philippines.

In terms of land, profitable export cropping requires control over larger and larger tracts of land. This control used to mean outright ownership by foreign corporations. Now, for a number of reasons to be discussed in Chapter 9, corporations maintain control through what are called "marketing contracts." Corporations contract with local farmers to grow crops on their own land according to the corporation's specifications. In addition to selling ("marketing") the crop, the corporation provides seeds, fertilizer, and cash outlays to get the farmers started. These costs are then deducted from the payment for their crops at the end of the season. In this way, corporations maintain control without ownership.

Del Monte offers a good example. In Mexico, Del Monte has been making friends with the larger farmers at the expense of the smaller ones. Since its initial entrance into Mexico, Del Monte has used the contract farming system. This system has allowed most contract farmers to earn more. But this is primarily due to the fact that Del Monte has consistently contracted with the largest landowners. It is much easier for it to supervise production on a smaller number of large farms, than on a much greater number of smaller ones. Thus, it has been the wealthier farmers who have benefited from Del Monte's technology and investment.

As the large contract farmers become even wealthier, they have attempted to buy land from the smaller farmers at attractive prices (any cash offer is attractive in an area where credit is hard to get). By selling their land, small farmers become landless laborers. In 1964, Del Monte contracted with 21 growers in Mexico for a total of 413 acres—about 20 acres per grower. By 1974, 110 growers planted 5,000 acres for Del Monte—about 45 acres per grower. And in 1976, 150 farmers worked 7,500 acres—an average of 50 acres per farm.[19]

In the Philippines, the control is just as tight, but it is mostly smaller farmers who are involved with Del Monte. Not that they chose to be involved, though. Fr. Vince Cullen, who worked with these small farmers, cites two types of pressure exerted on small subsistence farmers to coerce them to lease their land to Del Monte. First, in some cases, Philpak (Del Monte's Philippine subsidiary) guards drove cattle onto the farmers' planted fields. They cut off access to roads, fenced farmers out of their own fields, and sprayed the fields with chemicals that killed crops and produced rashes on the farmers and their animals. It is not difficult to see why many farmers would soon lease their land. Secondly, in this region of the Philippines, there was a major dispute over land titles. Conveniently (at least for Del Monte), the Philippine Land Bureau was extremely helpful in securing the land titles for farmers who intended to lease to Del Monte. If they did not intend to lease to Del Monte, then a number of difficulties seemed to arise.[20]

Even in Colombia, where coffee production had been in the hands of smaller farmers for decades, control is more and more concentrated on a few large producers. The Colombian Coffee Institute has conducted a major public relations campaign for over 15 years, selling the image of the small producer. We have seen TV ads showing a Juan Valdez as the typical small coffee farmer—productive and proud. But Colombia's Juan Valdezes are fewer and poorer each year. Corporations and large local landowners are taking increasing control over coffee production.[21]

7. Export Cropping Means Less Work and Income for Small Farmers and Peasants

One of the main reasons why export cropping in general and corporate control over it in particular worries more and more people is precisely its effects on farm workers and small farmers like Juan Valdez and his Filipino counterparts. Besides less control over their land and higher prices for the food they now have to buy, small farmers under contract actually get less in income than they did as independent farmers.

Returning to Del Monte's operation in the Philippines, Fr. Ed Gerlock has estimated the financial cost to these small farmers because of their contract with Del Monte. As a person who worked closely with many of these dispossessed farmers, he calculates that a farmer on one hectare (about 2.5 acres), employing the crudest means of farming, and growing two crops per year, could earn about $600 a year. If this same farmer leases this hectare to the corporation at between $30 and $70 and works as a laborer for the going wage of $1.00 a day (see Chapter 8, page 143) he could only earn about $420 a year, even if he worked 350 days a year. Not only do these small farmers make less, but now they have to buy food staples which they used to grow themselves.[22]

Small farmers suffer sometimes even when the prices of the crops they grow for the corporations or others go up. Better sugar prices for Brazil, for example, could lead to increased removal of peasants from small land holdings, so that large landowners can plant more sugar. In fact, on July 4, 1973, right after the U.S. announced an embargo on soybean exports to Japan and others, the *Toronto Globe and Mail* reported that "when word of the (U.S.) controls reached Brazil, the price of land in soybean-growing areas shot up. In the town of Ribeirao Preto, big landowners raised tenant rents on soybean farms from an equivalent of $32 an acre to $65."[23]

As prices on export crops go up, the income that workers or peasant producers receive may not go up correspondingly or even at all. According to a UN report cited by Collins and Lappe, while international coffee prices increased 58% between 1968 and 1973, the prices received by small producers in the African country of Rwanda remained fixed. When the price of sugar on the world market increased 700% in 1974, the real wage of sugar cane cutters in the Dominican Republic fell below what it was in 1964.[24]

Thus, for farming families, there is less control over their own destiny (by not producing their own food) and tremendous insecurity. Their survival through the year becomes dependent on the cash received only once or twice a year at harvest time(s). This cash, as already noted, buys fewer staples because prices have risen, as greatly expanding export cropping creates shortages in these staples.

Thus, after detailing the examples of coffee operations in Guatemala, cotton in Nicaragua, and sugar cane in El Salvador, Peter Dorner concludes that export cropping is creating fewer and fewer jobs. In his words,

> ... the development of export agriculture along capital-intensive lines is reducing the capacity of this sector to absorb labor. While capital-intensity has diminished the need for permanent labor, increased yields and the present limited mechanization of most harvesting operations have intensified the need for seasonal labor. The increasing importance of temporary (as against permanent) labor represents a significant change in the nature of the labor market. Its overall impact is to reduce incomes and employment security of farm workers.[25]

Besides working only part-time, seasonal workers generally are not covered by minimum wage laws. Thus, in the Philippines, for instance, Del Monte's seasonal workers make about 75¢ a day (see Chapter 8, pp. 142-143).

8. *The Debt Spiral Locks the Third World into Export Cropping*

Export cropping continues to expand for two reasons. First, as we have seen, multinational corporations and large government and/or private plantation owners and farmers make sizable profits in carnations, tomatoes, and bananas. But there is a second reason—the spiraling debt of Third World countries.

Export cropping was forced on Third World countries by colonial powers through a combination of military force and the more subtle coercion of taxes.[26] Growing food for local consumption produced no cash income. Thus, Third World colonies had to shift to export crops to get cash to pay taxes to their colonial rulers. Now, they have a different sort of tax to pay—payments on massive loans taken out primarily to meet their balance-of-trade deficits. The colonial pattern of the Third World providing cheap raw materials for the First World has continued, as Chapter 4 discussed in detail.

The solution adopted by most Third World countries is to try to increase both the volume of their export crops and the prices on them. With their staggering debts, it is difficult for Third World countries to focus only on higher prices. The temptation to increase the volume of their export crops is great.

Finally, there is the same debt trap for small producers within the Third World. These producers may be obligated to earn a cash income to repay their loans for seeds, fertilizer, equipment, etc., or face the possibility of forfeiting their lands to a creditor. As in the colonial era, the only way for these small farmers to get a cash income is to produce cash (export) crops.

Conclusions

1. In deciding on the value of export cropping, social as well as economic costs of export cropping need to be evaluated. That is, what is the impact of export cropping on people as well as on the economy? Based on the four components of justice (Chapter 1), the following criteria are helpful—

—how does it affect peoples' diets and other basic needs (sufficient life-goods)?

—how does it affect their control over their own lives (participation)?

—how does it affect how they feel about themselves (self-worth/dignity)?

—how does it affect how they feel and act toward others (interdependence)?

This Chapter has provided a variety of data for answering these questions.

2. Export cropping generally benefits the few. According to a UN report cited by Collins and Lappe, "Gains from foreign trade ... and particularly from sharply increased export prices frequently tend to be concentrated among upper income groups to a much greater extent than is income from domestic production."[27] We saw how export income means

more luxury imports for the few. We saw how contract farming with Del Monte enriched the few large farmers at the expense of the many small farmers.

3. As a country's reliance on export cropping increases, its ability to pursue a self-reliance model of development decreases. More and more, it makes decisions about its resources according to conditions in foreign markets rather than to conditions, needs, values within its own country. Philippine bananas are exported not because Filipinos no longer want them. Rather, the reason is that Japanese people are willing to pay high prices.

4. The trade measures of the NIEO in general and export cropping in particular *could* promote justice and bread *if*—

—*if* Third World countries concentrate on food first. Once the basic food needs of the people are being met, then trade need not work against the welfare of the majority. The question is not so much trade, but trade by whom and for whom.[28]

—*if* export taxes on multinational corporation-controlled export operations are raised to ensure a greater Third World share in the income from export cropping.

—*if* this increase in government income (from increased taxes) is translated into meeting the basic needs of the general population, just as increases in the exporters' incomes must be translated into better wages for the workers.

—*if* diversification into manufacturing industries is actually achieved, both to increase the number of profitable exports and to reduce the country's need for manufactured imports. In this way, Third World countries can begin to unravel the spiral of debt.

—*if* the industrialization that is pursued is related to the agricultural base that is the country's primary asset. If industries are related to agriculture, then many of these new jobs will be in rural areas where most of the people live.

—*if* what these industries produce is designed at least in part for mass consumer goods, not luxury items for the relatively few, as is generally the case today.

IN FACT PEOPLE DO MAKE MONEY OUT OF COFFEE AND COCOA BUT THEY MAKE IT AT THE PROCESSING STAGE IN THE INDUSTRIAL COUNTRIES.

THEN WHY DON'T THE POOR ALSO PROCESS THEIR CROP? THEN THEIR ECONOMIES WON'T BE A FLOP.

BECAUSE TARIFFS MAKE THIS DIFFICULT

IN JAPAN WE LEVY NO DUTY ON IMPORTS OF COCOA BEANS.

...AND 35% IF IT'S CHOCOLATE BARS

BUT WE CHARGE 30% DUTY IF THEY WANT TO SELL US COCOA POWDER.

THEN WHY DON'T THEY STOP AND NOT GROW A CASH CROP? IF THEY'RE RIGHT IN THE HEAD THEY'LL GROW MORE FOOD INSTEAD

MMM... IT'S NOT THAT SIMPLE! YOU SEE, SELLING CROPS OVERSEAS BRINGS FOREIGN EXCHANGE. SELLING FOOD TO BE EATEN AT HOME DOESN'T

BUT A LOT OF THAT FOREIGN EXCHANGE IS WASTED ON LUXURY IMPORTS.

IN THE DOMINICAN REPUBLIC WE DEPEND ON SELLING SUGAR. IN 197_ THE WORLD PRICE WENT UP BY 40_ BUT THE INCOME WAS SQUANDERED ON FAST CARS AND WHISKY.

AND EVEN IF THE THIRD WORLD WANTS TO STOP GROWING AND SELLING CASH CROPS, IT'S DIFFICULT BECAUSE OF PAST DEBTS...

..BOTH OF INDIVIDUAL FARMERS

LOOK BWANA, WE CAN'T SWITCH TO GROWING FOOD FOR THE FAMILY EVEN IF THE PRICE OF COTTON GOES DOWN.

FOR WE'VE HAD TO BORROW TO PAY FOR THE FERTILIZER.

IF WE DON'T COME UP WITH THE CASH THEY'LL TAKE OUR LAND.

... AND OF GOVERNMENTS

OUR BALANCE OF PAYMENTS PROBLEM FORCED US TO TAKE OVERSEAS LOANS, WHICH HAD TO BE REPAID.

AND THE FOREIGN EXCHANGE CAN COME ONLY FROM EXPORTING CROPS.

SO:
* IT IS RISKY FOR THE DEVELOPMENT OF THIRD WORLD COUNTRIES TO BE BASED ON CASH CROPS
* FOREIGN EXCHANGE INVARIABLY BENEFITS ONLY THE SMALL ELITE
* AND ONCE COUNTRIES AND INDIVIDUALS ARE IN DEBT IT IS DIFFICULT TO STOP GROWING CASH CROPS

—*if* import needs are reduced, not only by providing more of one's own manufactured goods, but especially by reducing wasteful expenditures and pursuing a self-reliant agriculture that requires far less imported equipment, chemical fertilizers and pesticides, etc.

5. There is ample basis for pessimism about these seven conditions being met by any Third World country pursuing a model of development based on capitalist principles (private profit) or relying on multinational corporations to develop their agriculture and industry, at least as the multinational corporations presently operate. Capital (money) goes where the returns are the highest. Production of food for local consumption is not nearly as profitable as export cropping. As NACLA puts it, "it is a question of the inability of capitalism to allocate resources with a priority on meeting people's needs."[29] We will return to this question of capitalism and socialism in Chapter 13.

Discussion Questions

1. Why is export cropping a crucial issue for Third World countries?
2. Why does export cropping often result in increased hunger in Third World countries?
3. Why is there no real economic or "natural" advantage to export cropping for Third World countries?
4. How does export cropping affect the environment?
5. Why is it that export cropping benefits the rich much more than the poor?
6. How does export cropping increase control over agriculture by fewer and fewer people?
7. What is the relationship between export cropping and Third World debts?
8. Do you agree with the seven conditions listed as necessary for trade and export cropping to promote bread and justice? Why or why not?

9. In general, do you agree with the five conclusions to the
   Chapter? Why or why not?

Resources

Besides all the items referred to in the footnotes, there are
several resources that should be most helpful.

On Export Cropping in General
—The Food First perspective on export cropping is best
summarized in the April 1978 issue of *Ag World* (see Chapter 2
Resources) in an article by Joseph Collins and Frances Moore
Lappe entitled "Food First Revisited." It is their response to a
lengthy critique of *Food First* by Peter Huessy of the Environment Fund. The Huessy critique of the position taken in this
chapter appeared in the January and February 1978 issues
under the title "Population Control or Food First?"
—"Bitter Bananas" is a 1978 slide presentation produced
by the Del Monte Working Group and available through
Earthwork/Newsreel Media Center, 630 Natoma St., San
Francisco, CA 94103; rental $15. It examines Del Monte's role
in pineapple and banana production in the Philippines under
martial law. It is a visual translation of much of this chapter.
—On Del Monte Corporation, see the Resources listed in
Chapter 9.
—The Institute for Food and Development Policy (see
Appendix) has just released a slide presentation on the basic
themes of *Food First*. Write them for details and prices.
—NACLA's *Report on the Americas* often focuses on is-
sues of agriculture in Latin America. The whole January–
February 1978 issue, entitled "Agribusiness Targets Latin
America" is excellent on export cropping. Besides the "Agro-
Exports" article cited in this chapter, there are articles enti-
tled "Seeds of Hunger: Roots of Rebellion," "The Food Proces-
sors: Soft Drinks & Hard Profits," and an appendix on "U.S.
Food Processing Investments."

—The April 1978 issue of the Bread for the World newsletter contains an excellent four-page summary of the export cropping issue by Brennon Jones—"Export Cropping and Development: We Need to Know More."

Chapter Seven

WHAT CAN I DO?

Chapters four, five, and six have pointed out the need for trade on much better terms for Third World countries and the problems connected with export cropping. In this chapter we will examine what others are doing to promote bread and justice through changes in trade. This will help us see what we might do to promote these changes. First, though, it is important to see how much we are a part of present patterns of trade.

How Trade Relates to Us

There are a number of ways in which we are personally involved in or affected by the trade issues examined in the three previous chapters. In some cases, we are unintentionally part of the problems that Third World countries and peoples face. In other cases, we—as well as Third World people—are the victims of unjust trade practices of First World countries. Finally, many aspects of our lives are quite dependent on trade.

1. Jobs

First, trade is the source of one out of every eight jobs in U.S. manufacturing industries. One out of every three acres of U.S. farmland produces crops for export. Since 25% of all U.S. exports go to the Third World,[1] we encourage these countries to export their crops and other items so that they will buy our exports. The jobs of many people in the First World depend on Third World countries exporting and importing more.

But other jobs are threatened by Third World exports. In textiles, shoes, steel and electronics industries, especially, thousands of workers have been laid off because we can buy cheaper shoes, etc. from the Third World. Thus, tariffs are imposed on these items to try to protect the jobs of First World workers. Others encourage us to "Buy American." When we see this bumper sticker, we find ourselves in a dilemma. We do not want to put our fellow citizens out of work by buying a lot of imports. But we do not want to put our brothers and sisters in the Third World out of work either. Decisions in these matters are sometimes not simple.

2. Prices

While tariffs protect some jobs in this country, they hurt us as consumers because they raise the price on goods we buy from overseas.

Secondly, Chapter 5 stressed the need for higher prices for Third World raw materials. But these higher prices that First World corporations will pay for their raw materials will be passed on to us as consumers of the goods these corporations produce. Who will be hurt the most? Those least able to pay— low income consumers in this country. But this need not be the case, at least entirely. As Chapter 4 (page 71) showed in the banana graph, it is the multinational corporations in the "middle" that really benefit. If they can be regulated or if tax reform can assist low income consumers hurt by the higher prices, then these higher prices would be more helpful.

3. What We Buy

Until mid-1978, many of us were supporting the incredible repression of General Idi Amin, ruler of Uganda. We were not aware of it, probably, but when we bought Maxwell House coffee, Nescafe, or Tasters' Choice coffee, we were buying from the two largest importers of Ugandan coffee beans. General Foods and Nestlé accounted for at least 25% of all of Uganda's income in 1977—99% of it comes from coffee exports. As Franklin H. Williams, former U.S. Ambassador to Ghana, wrote recently in a *New York Times* editorial, the income generated through coffee exports "is used almost exclusively to maintain President Amin's mercenary army and his notorious State Research Bureau, the key agency responsible for liquidating his opponents."[2]

Fortunately in May 1978, this indirect support of Amin's inhumanities came to an end. The International Relations Committee of the U.S. House of Representatives unanimously adopted a resolution condemning Amin and calling on President Jimmy Carter to "support and where possible implement measures such as an embargo on trade with Uganda." Within a few days, the four major coffee roasters (processors)—General Foods, Procter & Gamble (Folgers), Hills Brothers, and Nestlé—agreed to discontinue all purchases of Ugandan coffee.

A second example relates to the "Jute Campaign" described later in this chapter. We do not realize it, but when we buy a lot of synthetic products, we put people out of work. Plastic bags, for instance, are everywhere. We use "Baggies" for wrapping our sandwiches and pick up plastic shopping bags in department stores. But many people in Bangladesh and India depend on the sale of the natural jute bags they make. Most of us, however, do not even know what jute is or have ever seen a jute bag. We will see shortly how to change this.

4. Export Cropping

Northern Mexico has been turned into the major source of the fruits and vegetables consumed in the U.S. during the winter. This massive transition from smaller farmers producing for local consumption to export cropping has impoverished unknown numbers of small Mexican farmers. Some of these dispossessed farmers are among the thousands of Mexican people immigrating to the U.S.—many illegally. This is a growing problem for the U.S. Government and for some workers whose jobs are threatened by the influx of Mexican people looking for work. However, the real issue and the source of the problem is unjust land ownership patterns and export cropping.

As we import more and more of our food from Central America, U.S. farmers, especially in states like Texas and Florida, are hurt. Further, we are becoming more and more dependent in our food needs. The Northeast particularly faces a serious problem in importing most of the food it needs.

5. The Image of Who We Are as a People

Many people around the world know us only by the products we trade. What do our exports say about us? Our major exports are grain (between $22 billion and $24 billion annually the past few years), weapons (more than $14 billion annually), and a whole host of manufactured goods. From cosmetics to computers, U.S. manufactured goods offer Third World countries a variety of ways to "modernize." What do our products say about us? Is this the picture we want people to have of us?

How Dependent Are We on Trade?

To discover how dependent all of us are on trade, do the following research—

1. Make a list of all the things you rely on each day that come from other countries. Many manufactured goods you buy from U.S. manufacturers use Third World raw materials, so be sure to consider that. To help you start, think about large categories like food, clothing, appliances, machinery, transportation.

2. Investigate your local supermarket (or family pantry, if well stocked) for food items that come from other countries. Of the food items that come from the Third World, make a list of those items that are processed in the Third World and a list of those items whose raw materials (e.g. cocoa beans) originate in the Third World but are processed in the First World (e.g. chocolate bars).

3. You might next investigate one food item in detail, to determine all that it takes to get that item to your table. With the graph in Chapter 4 (p. 71) and the information presented in Chapters 4–6, bananas might be an interesting example to use. You might call the produce manager of your grocery store and ask him or her where the store's bananas come from. Checking with this distributor and perhaps with local importers (see the Yellow Pages of your phone book) might generate further information.

What Are Others Doing?
Buying Directly from Third World Peoples

1. *Alternative Celebrations Catalogue*
This *Catalogue* (from Alternatives, 1924 E. 3rd, Bloomington, IN 47401) is a source of numerous "Third World outlets" in the U.S. for the handicrafts of Third World peoples. Buying from these distribution centers enables us to support poor people who are supporting themselves by the handicrafts.

2. The "Jute Works"

A similar possibility exists with regard to jute handicrafts. It exists because of the hard work of a number of people in the U.S. between 1975 and 1978. Fr. Frank Quinlivan, one of the key actors, describes the effort in this way—

Following the War of Independence in Bangladesh (early 1970s), Caritas Bangladesh undertook an innovative project of cottage industry (village-based industry) throughout the country. The economy had suffered greatly during the war and many women had been widowed. Capitalizing on Bangladesh's availability of jute (the country's one exportable crop), women were trained in their villages throughout the country to make jute handicraft items—mats, coasters, rugs, belts, pot hangers, shoulder bags.

An export-marketing operation—the Jute Works— was established in Dacca (the capital) to buy the items from the villages, provide for quality control, and export the items. 80% of the sale price goes to the village women. This project provided needed income, enhanced the position of women, provided them with skills and work that could be done socially and with their children. It also provided occasions for other education to go on, including literacy work.

The Jute Works was soon exporting $500,000 worth of items, mostly to a few Western European countries and to Australia and New Zealand. The U.S. was not a good place to export to because of very high tariffs [see Chapter 4, p. 72].

A long campaign was then launched in the U.S. to have these jute handicrafts listed in the Generalized System of Preferences [see Chapter 5, p. 88], so that they could come in duty-free . . . . Three years later, after much effort, on March 1, 1978, the order was signed by President Carter placing these items on the GSP. Despite mistakes, we did succeed and the most common jute items now come into the U.S. duty-free. This makes them, of course, much more attractive to import, should increase the sales here, and very directly benefit the women in the villages of Bangladesh.[3]

Public Education Campaigns around Specific Commodities

Western European groups have created a number of highly imaginative public education campaigns on trade and development issues by focusing on specific commodities. Few of these campaigns had a large organization behind them, so they may well be able to be duplicated or adapted by others. Here are three of the most creative.[4]

1. Chocolate Bar Campaign in West Germany

In October 1975, a Third World Action group in West Germany initiated an educational campaign around a chocolate bar wrapped in aluminum foil. Their purpose was to bring the world trade situation in cocoa and bauxite to the public's attention. With the chocolate bars were distributed educational materials and petitions urging the German Government to lower the tariff barriers that discouraged Ghana and others from manufacturing and exporting chocolate bars made from their own cocoa beans (recall Chapter 4, pp. 71-72). Write Aktion Dritte-Welt Handel, 6000 Frankfurt M.1, Fichardstr. 38, Stadtsparkasse Wuppertal, W. Germany, for further information.

2. Tea Campaign in England

The World Development Movement (Bedford Chambers, London WC2E 8HA) organized a campaign to increase the price of tea through an International Tea Agreement and to try to ensure that the increases get back to tea workers in the Third World. WDM's educational materials include a background briefing on tea, action ideas, petition forms, a leaflet on tea for distributing on the street, bumper stickers and posters. The advantage of this campaign for persons who only read English is that the materials are all in English. Similar action is being taken in Australia and New Zealand where groups have formed ANZTEA to import, process and distribute tea more cheaply than the multinational corporations and to do educational activities around the tea operation.

3. *"Jute, Not Plastic"—A Campaign to Educate Swiss Consumers*

While Fr. Quinlivan and others were working in the U.S. to remove the tariffs on jute handicrafts from Bangladesh, Third World Action in Switzerland designed a campaign to raise the consciousness of Swiss consumers, so that the same thing could happen in Western Europe. Rudolf H. Strahm describes the Swiss campaign in an article in *Ideas and Action.* Excerpts are included here because of the way in which he relates the trade issue with jobs, the environment, energy, and life-style questions.

"Jute, Not Plastic"[5]

The newest campaign is an attempt to create greater public awareness of a number of inter-related issues: development policy, ecology, life-styles, growth. The "posters" are 40,000 jute shopping bags, hand-made from women's cooperatives in Bangladesh. They bear the slogans "Jute, not plastic" (in German); "Jute—Solidarity—Ecology" (in French); and "Why Jute?" (in Italian). These handsome bags are of course a publicity device for introducing the main issues of the campaign. To help the local groups work out their educational programmes, a number of approaches are being suggested. They are as follows:

1. *"Jute, Not Plastic" means employment in Bangladesh*

Jute is Bangladesh's vital export commodity: over 80% of all export income is earned on jute and jute goods. For millions of poor Bengali farmers, there are only two crops that can be produced: jute and rice. For nearly 200,000 landless Bengalis, there is only one source of employment: jute products. 52% of the jute exported from Bangladesh is in its raw state, which is then processed abroad. This, too, is a heritage of colonialism and the existing international division of labor . . . .

Jute is mainly used for making sacking, carpet backing and twine. Over the last decade it has been faced with

124   BREAD AND JUSTICE

growing and deadly competition from plastics and synthetic fibres [see Chapter 4, p. 72]. Jute consumption has been stagnating for years, and even the increases in the prices of petroleum and plastics since the oil crisis have been powerless to check the downward trend of jute....

Jute and rice are competing crops on Bengali farms. High rice prices drive out jute crops and lucrative jute prices diminish rice production. Rice being the basic food staple of Bangladesh, it is certainly not desirable that rice-growing gives way to increased jute production. The idea of the jute campaign is not to encourage the growing of jute at the expense of rice production, but to promote the increased processing of jute in Bangladesh itself. There are only too many idle hands awaiting employment, while the existing jute weaving mills are operating at only 80% of their capacity, so that no new mills are needed.

2. "Jute, Not Plastic" means environmental and energy conservation

It takes four times as much non-renewable energy to make a plastic sack as it does a jute sack. This means that the production of one plastic sack uses almost as much energy as a human being needs for one day: 2.8 kilowatts for the human being, as against 2.3 kilowatts per day for the plastic sack.

Jute can be composted, rotted and burned. But there are no satisfactory ways of eliminating plastics as yet. They cannot return to nature by rotting or similar processes. Some synthetic materials, when being destroyed, are extremely pollutant.... The burning of four plastic sacks consumes as much oxygen as a human being needs in one day.

3. "Jute, Not Plastic" means a shift towards new mental attitudes and a simpler life-style.

... The consumption economy has reached a threshold, beyond which higher consumption risks giving us a poorer, not a better, quality of life. The "Jute, Not Plastic" action gives people the opportunity of taking stock of our present situation, a tool for bringing about a change of attitude, a symbol of the refusal to continue participating in an economy based on consumption and waste . . . .

The "Jute, Not Plastic" campaign can help promote the discussion of themes such as: "Living in greater solidarity"; "What kind of growth?"; and "A new way of thought for a new way of life". Such questions can be approached from very different angles: from that of the ecologist, the development policy-maker and the progressive trade unionist. What is usually lacking is the overall perspective and inter-relationships between the various aspects of the problem.

Conducting the operations

The jute bags are only meant to serve as a stimulus to a learning process. Of course, this learning process is not triggered off when someone buys a jute bag. It is more complex than that. Those who are selling the jute bags are encouraged first to attend a local group training course, which may last for several evenings. For this purpose, a "sales training kit" is available, as well as other information material (transparencies, films, etc.). These group discussions are one of the most important parts of the operation. The participants get to know each other, organize themselves, exchange experiences and in general go through a common learning process.

Only when the training has been completed are the preparations made for the sale of jute bags, which is then done on streets, in stands, and in front of churches and stores. People who buy the jute bags are also supplied with information material. The price of the jute bags can be kept extremely low even though the jute cooperative in Bangladesh earns a fair profit. The cost of the imported and stamped jute bag is about one Swiss franc (40¢ in the U.S.). They will be sold for double this in order to pay for the accompanying information materials and the media and distribution costs. The entire operation is self-financing.

Ten Swiss development organizations are participating in the "Jute, Not Plastic" campaign which is being coordinated by the Berne Declaration Movement. Further inquiries may be addressed to: Declaration de Berne (French-speaking Switzerland), Case postale 97, CH1000 Lausanne 9, Switzerland.

Current U.S. Campaigns Needing Our Support

Such support can take the form of appropriate letter-writing, public education efforts in our own community, organizing a support group, or seeing if an existing local group (especially one with which we are active) would be willing to integrate this new concern with its existing priorities. Relating to existing efforts increases our awareness and effectiveness. It also helps us realize that we are part of a larger group of people struggling for justice. By inserting ourselves in networks that can put us in contact with increasing numbers of people, we are generally strengthened in our commitment and see many more possibilities for action and even some career choices.

The following campaigns and groups are focused on the issue of land use and export cropping. Some of them concentrate on this issue in Third World countries. Others have a U.S. focus. One is presented in some detail: Del Monte, because it has been used as an example throughout Part II.

1. *The Del Monte Campaign*

For several years, a number of people, particularly on the West Coast where Del Monte has its international headquarters (San Francisco), have been challenging Del Monte's land use policies in the Third World. At one point, the group was involved in a boycott of Del Monte products. Earthwork, as the group is called, is now encouraging schools, churches and individuals to do a number of things.

(a) *Fasting and sharing.* School cafeterias might organize a day of fasting as an act of solidarity with the small Filipino farmers displaced by Del Monte actions. Participants would eat only a small serving of rice (equivalent to what many poor Filipinos eat daily). Donations of the food money saved could be sent to either Earthwork (3410 19th Street, San Francisco, CA 94110) or to Fr. Ed Gerlock (c/o Maryknoll Fathers, Maryknoll, N.Y. 10545) for distribution in ways that will best promote both social change and satisfaction of immediate needs of Filipino workers. It would be good to tell them of your concern and urge them to continue their efforts on behalf of the Filipino people.

(b) *Food Store Displays.* We might call a local supermarket and ask if we can have permission to set up an information table on world hunger. Fact sheets on world hunger can be obtained from a variety of sources, such as the American Friends Service Committee (15 Rutherford Place, New York, N.Y. 10003). Combine such information with short handouts on the involvement of corporations like Del Monte and Nestlé. In addition to *Food First,* Al Krebs at the Agribusiness Accountability Project and Jim Hightower (*Eat Your Hearts Out: How Food Profiteers Victimize the Consumer,* New York: Random House, 1975) are excellent sources for this information.

Such handouts and fact sheets on hunger might be best constructed by the participants themselves as a way of orienting our research to action. Translating information in ways that both attract and make sense to ordinary people is not easy, but it is crucial for effective communications and action. "Del Monte Supports *Apartheid,*" a poster encouraging a boycott of Del Monte products, is available from the San Francisco Poster Brigade, P.O. Box 31428, San Francisco, CA 94131.

(c) *Stockholder Resolutions.* If you happen to own some Del Monte stock, you can support the stockholder resolutions filed each year with the corporation. In 1978, as the "Land Acquisition Resolution" printed below indicates, stockholders were asked to support an effort to get the corporation to reveal the current and future impact of its control over land in the Philippines. The resolution was filed by the Northern California Interfaith Commission of Corporate Responsibility (NC-ICCR) on behalf of a number of very small stockholders. Chap. 6, pp. 105-6) provides some of the background behind the resolution. Write NC-ICCR (870 Market Street, San Francisco, CA 94101) for information on stockholder resolutions with Del Monte after 1978.

DEL MONTE CORPORATION
Land Acquisition Resolution
1978

WHEREAS, the Philippine government, since martial law was declared in September 1972, has been accused by Amnesty International and the U.S. House Committee on International Relations of violations against human rights, and Filipino workers have been denied the right to assemble, strike and collectively bargain; and

WHEREAS, Del Monte defines Philpak, its Philippine subsidiary, as "one of the strongest arms in Del Monte's international operations": and

WHEREAS, Philpak has extended its planting acreage in the Province of Bukidnon with apparent disregard for small landholders and farmers; and

WHEREAS, there is increasing protest by small Filipino farmers whose lands have been taken away from them by Philpak, directly and indirectly, and in many cases by forcible means; and

WHEREAS, Del Monte has continued to deny Philpak's involvement in such unfair land acquisition practices in the Philippines;

BE IT RESOLVED that the shareholders urgently request the Board of Directors to disclose information to shareholders in a written report within four months of the Annual Meeting. The report shall contain the following information, provided that information directly affecting the competitive position of the Company may be omitted, and provided that the cost of preparing this report shall be limited to an amount deemed reasonable by the Board of Directors:

1. The status of land owned and or cultivated by small farmers in the Province of Bukidnon, Philippines, whose lands have been acquired by Philpak through lease, contract, or purchase as a result of the Company's expansion policies within the past ten years.

2. Plans for future expansion of Company operations where they involve further land acquisition through purchase, lease, or in any other mode of acquisition, direct or indirect.

Statement of Security Holders

New information has come to light over the past year which has strengthened the contention of shareholders that Del Monte's operations in the Philippines, through its subsidiary, Philpak, have been in direct contravention to the basic regard for human rights. Concern over conditions in the Philippines where human rights, political freedom and economic stability are severely threatened, has increased. Del Monte has a duty to its stockholders that it not be part of the process that continues to deny Filipino farmers and peasants basic human rights to own and work land which they have cultivated in past years.

We have continued to receive legally documented papers attesting to the take-over of farm lands in Bukidnon Province by Philpak. The take-overs are questionable legally, as well as on the basis of the Company's professed policy of assisting the host country's economic and social development. Any action that deprives farmers of their basic rights to till their land can only reflect badly on the Company that is doing business in an area that involves these farmers.

The report requested by this resolution will be of great service to shareholders of Del Monte in assessing the Company's land use and ownership policies and practices in light of current conditions and the continued violation of human rights under the state of martial law in the Philippines declared and maintained by President Ferdinand Marcos.

2. Bread for the World—a Legislative Campaign

Each year this Christian citizens' lobby on behalf of hungry people has focused on a particular legislative aspect of world hunger. Having succeeded in mobilizing people around the U.S. to persuade the U.S. Congress to pass the "Right to Food" Resolution and then the U.S. component of a World Food Reserve, Bread for the World decided in 1978 to make aid for self-reliance and export cropping major concerns. In 1978 and 1979, BFW has been encouraging citizens to urge their Congressional representatives to request a "nutritional impact study." This means asking Congress to ask the General

Accounting Office to study the impact of U.S. corporations involved in Third World export cropping on Third World peoples. If the GAO comes to the same conclusions that others have (see Chapter 6) about the negative impact of export cropping, then Congressional action is more likely.

Specifically, the questions to which BFW wants answers from the GAO include—

(a.) What is the effect on the nutrition of Third World peoples from U.S. corporations moving into Third World export cropping?

(b.) What percentage of U.S. corporate investment is involved in food production and what percentage is in export cropping in the Third World?

(c.) What is the effect on employment and wages in the Third World from U.S. corporations moving into Third World export cropping?

(d.) What is the effect on land ownership and land reform from U.S. corporations involved in Third World export cropping?

It seems clear that Bread for the World has made a long-term commitment to this issue of export cropping. Write them for additional legislative suggestions in this regard. The April 1978 issue of the BFW newsletter contains an excellent four-page description of the export cropping issue and a two-page supplement on the GAO study.

3. National Land for People—Agribusiness in the U.S.

National Land for People (NLP) is a movement of small farmers, former farm workers, and others in California and around the country. Its main purpose is to gain access to federally subsidized irrigated lands in the San Joaquin Valley of California. This struggle against agribusiness in the U.S. is specifically aimed at the U.S. Government and its obligation to enforce the 1902 Land Reclamation Act that is being violated by corporations and other large landowners. There are acreage limits, land residency requirements, and sales limitations that are being violated flagrantly. The result is lack of opportunity for small farmers to have access to this highly desirable land. Visually, three of NLP's major concerns are as follows:[6]

HIGHLIGHTS OF NLP PROPOSALS

LOTTERY MOST IMPORTANT
All reclamation lands not transferred to family members must be sold through public lottery.

Land Sales and Leases by Lottery

#10

LOTTERY

LAND ACCESS

NEW FARMER OPPORTUNITY
To encourage new farmers, the government would buy a certain amount of reclamation lands for leasing through public lotteries to new farmers who will have the option of purchasing said land anytime within five years.

#10

NO MORE THAN 640 ACRES, NO WAY
No person or legal entity, directly or indirectly, may hold an interest in more than 640 acres receiving federal water.

Except in High Plains

200 acre average 640 acre maximum

640   160   320
320   320   80 80
640   160
160   320

15 MILE RESIDENCY
All buyers of reclamation lands including family members must be or agree to become resident (within 15 miles) operating farmers.

Small Town

15 Miles

House On Land

There are several things we can do to assist NLP.

(a.) Write NLP (2348 N. Millbrook, Fresno, CA 93711) for details on the legislation it is promoting in the U.S. Congress to ensure that the Land Reclamation Act will finally be enforced. Then write your Congresspersons and the Secretary of the Interior on behalf of this legislation.

(b.) Write NLP about taking out a certificate of deposit in NLP's Agricultural Development Bank. NLP plans to establish this Bank by 1980 as a way of enabling small farmers or non-farmers to make their beginning in farming, specifically in the Westlands area (where the controversy is centered).

(c.) Use NLP's excellent slide show—"Discover America"—as a way of doing public education on the issue and of raising money to support NLP's court challenges over violations of the Land Reclamation Act. The slide show documents the issue, illustrates the greater efficiency of smaller farmers, and identifies a number of actions we can do to support NLP's efforts.

(d.) To see this struggle firsthand, take NLP's one-day tour of the Westlands area. It brings people into contact with NLP farmers, with the land, with the specifics of the legal and legislative challenges, and with the possibilities of personal action. Contact NLP for specific dates (generally once a month).

4. Clergy and Laity Concerned (CALC)[7]

CALC's Politics of Food Taskforce has been working on export cropping and agribusiness for several years. A campaign that CALC embarked on in the fall of 1978 is described below.

"Regional Food Self-Reliance". As noted above (p. 119) many parts of this country are becoming highly dependent on agribusiness and foreign sources for basic foods. With National Land for People, CALC is working with local chapters and communities to investigate the extent of their dependency and to organize a campaign to reduce this dependency. Write CALC's national office (198 Broadway, New York, NY 10038) for details and for local chapter closest to your area.

CALC's land use/food self-reliance focus affirms the need to link local and regional hunger concerns with global hunger issues. Unless people recognize their own vulnerability within the system of global farms and supermarkets, it is unlikely that they will be able to identify with poor people in other countries. Thus, CALC members and local communities are seeking answers to the following questions related to trends in land use and land ownership over the past thirty years:

(1) Has the number of farms declined?

(2) Has the amount of acres farmed decreased dramatically?

(3) Has the average size of farms increased? Is there evidence of increased corporate farming? Is there evidence of foreign ownership of land?

(4) Identify shifts in what is being produced. Is there a move away from diversified production? Is food once produced locally now being imported? Where is it coming from? California? Mexico?

(5) What is the impact of imported food on local producers?

(6) Do retailers in your area buy from local producers?

(7) Does the work of your local land grant college and/or extension agent foster or hinder regional food self-reliance? Whose interests do they serve—agribusiness, large farmers, or small farmers?

(8) How many people in your state are employed in agriculture—in production? in processing? in transport? in marketing? What are the trends in these sectors over the past 30 years?

What Should I Do?

Deciding on what each of us can do and should do is not always easy. This chapter has suggested many different possibilities. Hopefully, one or more of these suggestions are appropriate for each of us as we try to decide what to do. For some, maybe none of these suggestions are appropriate but maybe they help stimulate other possibilities. Since none of us can do everything, try to choose *one* action. The following two sets of questions are designed to help evaluate all the possibilities suggested in this chapter—

1. Which action(s) have the best chance of succeeding?
2. Which actions are important enough to do, whether or not they have a chance of succeeding?
3. Which actions mobilize (or have the potential to mobilize) the largest number of people?

4. Which actions put us (or come closest to putting us) in direct contact with the victims of the injustice(s)?
5. Which actions do the victims say they want other people to do?
6. Which actions involve the victims themselves in leadership positions?
7. Which actions have the greatest potential for long-term change in the practices and policies of the institution(s) involved?
8. Which actions have actual groups working on them?
9. Which actions have the best potential for surfacing links between local problems and global problems?

Having sorted through these possible actions, try to answer the following questions to help you decide which one of the actions makes the most sense for you at this point in your life—

1. Which action seems to fit best with your own concerns, knowledge, skills, and time?
2. Which action is most likely to deepen and sustain your commitment to bread and justice?
3. Which action would have the best potential for generating the support of others that you feel you would need to carry it off?

Resources

In addition to the groups and materials mentioned in the text and footnotes, there are a number of other groups working on export cropping and agribusiness. Among them are

—The Institute for Food and Development Policy (Joseph Collins, Frances Moore Lappe, and others) is exploring action possibilities around their excellent research on land use and export cropping in the Third World. Write them about their "Rural Realities Project."

—NACLA's Agribusiness Project (contact Roger Burbach, 464 19th Street, Oakland, CA 94612) is doing the same thing. Their bi-monthly publication, *NACLA Report on the Americas*, contains a wealth of information on these issues.

—*Food Monitor* is the monthly magazine published by the Institute for Food and Development Policy and World Hunger Year (P.O. Box 1975, Garden City, NY 11530), analyzing these issues and suggesting action possibilities.

—The Agribusiness Accountability Project (Sue Sechlar and Al Krebs, 1095 Market Street, San Francisco, CA 94103) is working on corporate ownership of land in the U.S. and publishes a fine journal entitled the *Ag Biz Tiller.*

—*Travels of a Green Banana* (from the Canadian Council for International Cooperation, 75 Spark Street, Ottawa, Ontario, Canada) is a 28-minute slide-tape presentation on the history of the banana trade; on how bananas are grown, transported and marketed; and on the issues of the NIEO, especially corporate concentration in the food industry. An excellent resource for the third action suggestion on p. 120 above.

—The National Catholic Rural Life Conference (3801 Grand Ave., Des Moines, Iowa 50312) is also working on U.S. national land policy and publishes a monthly magazine for non-experts entitled *Rural Life.*

—The Interreligious Task Force on U.S. Food Policy (110 Maryland Ave. NE, Washington, DC 20002) works with Bread for the World and others in legislative action on global hunger issues, including trade and export cropping. Its monthly newsletter and short studies are good sources of information.

—The National Coalition for Development Action (NCDA) brings many of these and other similar groups together around food and global economic issues, with land use and export cropping a major concern. NCDA is part of an International Coalition for Development (ICDA) and shares ICDA's concern about moving First World governments to a more cooperative approach to Third World needs in the New International Economic Order negotiations. Write NCDA (c/o Steve Hayes, YMCA International Division, 291 Broadway, New York, NY 10007) for information on the Coalition and its members.

—For resources on several of the multinational corporations involved in export cropping, see Chapter 11, Resources.

Part III

HUNGER, MULTINATIONAL
CORPORATIONS AND THE NIEO

Introduction

As Part II clearly indicated, "bread" and "justice" necessitate changes both in the international economic order and within Third World countries themselves. Part III on "multinational corporations" combines with Part IV on "new internal economic orders" to make the same point. While a number of multinational corporations are coming to be seen as major contributors to world hunger, they do not operate alone. Rather, in many Third World countries, especially in Latin America, they work side by side with local elites. Thus, multinationals often reinforce the power and wealth of the few over the vast majority of the populations. Both factors need to be addressed.

Part III addresses the first of these two factors. Chapter 8 provides data about the organization, size, and operation of multinational corporations. Chapter 9 offers a point-counterpoint consideration of ways in which these corporations are a force for and a force against the realization of bread and justice. Chapter 10 examines NIEO proposals to regulate the multinationals and evaluates the adequacy of these proposals. Chapter 11 offers a variety of action suggestions for challenging the corporations to be more socially responsible. Finally, Chapter 12 presents a case study of one multinational corporation involved in world hunger.

Chapter Eight

WHAT ARE MULTINATIONAL CORPORATIONS?

This chapter presents a variety of facts about multinational corporations and reasons for their growth—as background for evaluating their impact on Third World countries and peoples.

1. Historical Development

The past half century has witnessed a profound change in the international economic order. One of the most far-reaching aspects of this change has been the development of the multinational corporation, sometimes called transnational corporations or enterprises. Up to World War I, corporations were generally national, since their production and other activities were located in *one* of the industrialized countries. Their overseas investments were not large and were generally

confined to buying stock in other companies ("portfolio investments"). Finally, the overseas sales of these national corporations were in the form of exports, mainly to developing countries.

This picture has changed dramatically in the past sixty
years, especially since 1945. The overseas investments of multinational corporations have increased considerably. Direct
investments—that is, establishing branches or subsidiaries
overseas to provide themselves directly with the raw materials they need—grew many times larger than portfolio investments. Rather than concentrating on exporting their goods to
foreign countries, multinational corporations have penetrated
foreign markets by establishing subsidiaries to produce and
sell goods right within foreign countries. Thus, already by
1971, the total value of this overseas production of multinational subsidiaries had surpassed the value of all goods traded
around the world—$310 billion to $300 billion.[1]

Most people agree that it is primarily two realities that
make a corporation "multinational." First, it must have
branches, affiliates or subsidiaries in a number of foreign
countries. Secondly, its management would thus have the
ability and resources to make fundamental decisions on marketing, research, production, and supplies in terms of alternatives available to it in various parts of the world. The world
has come to be seen by the multinational corporations, in the
words of IBM President Jacques Maisonrouge, as "one economic unit."[2]

Manufacturers Hanover Bank, for instance, can boast in
full-page ads that "through our growing network of overseas
facilities—branches, representative offices, subsidiaries and
correspondents—Manufacturers Hanover offers international
customers direct access to virtually any marketplace in the
world." A corporation like General Motors, with assembly
plants worldwide, can ship cars to markets in several continents in a matter of hours. As "one economic unit," multinational corporations also have choices in how they do their

accounting. One option for corporate accountants is called "transfer pricing" and is described below.

2. Why Corporations Become "Multinational"

Four major reasons are generally cited for the expansion of corporations overseas: tax breaks, expanded markets, cheaper labor, and environmental regulations.

a. Tax Breaks

Some countries or zones within countries—like Panama, the Philippines, Ireland, several Caribbean islands, and others—offer tax-free havens on income earned within their borders. Further, through the mechanism of "transfer pricing", multinational corporations are able to take additional advantage of these tax breaks. It works like this:

A large portion of the imports and exports of a multinational corporation are really intra-company transactions. That is, several branches of the same corporation buy and sell to one another. This allows the corporations to overvalue their exports and undervalue their imports (or vice versa) across a number of countries. The reason is to have their books show higher profits in countries with lower tax rates and lower profits in countries with higher tax rates. For example, consider the following hypothetical operation of a multinational automobile company.

Multinational Automobile Company Operation

1. Its aluminum plant in Jamaica buys equipment from the international headquarters in New York
2. Its assembly plant in Colombia buys aluminum parts from its aluminum plant in Jamaica
3. Its shipping company in Panama buys cars from the assembly plant in Colombia
4. Its company dealerships in Florida buy cars from the shipping company in Panama
5. Customers buy cars from the Florida dealerships

Stages #1–4 in this operation are intra-company transfers since each plant is owned by the parent company. The prices that one plant charges another are determined at the international headquarters in New York. In this case, since Panama is a "tax-free zone", it would be best from a profit perspective to have the company's profits be made by the shipping company in Panama. Thus, on the multinational corporation's books, its aluminum plant, its Colombian assembly plant, and its Florida dealerships would all pay high prices for their purchases. Its shipping company in Panama, on the other hand, would be charged a very low price for the assembled cars. In this way, a large part of the corporation's total profit would appear on the books as being made in Panama. Thus, since very little tax would be paid on the entire operation, total profits would be higher than otherwise possible. Because the multinational corporation is "one economic unit", its figures (transfer pricing) as well as its products can be moved all over the world. Since there are not as yet any internationally agreed upon rules for accounting, the multinational corporation is able to operate virtually unchecked.

b. *Expanded Markets*

Secondly, corporations move abroad to penetrate what are called "protectionist markets", like the European Common Market, where high tariff barriers keep out foreign goods. Thus, for instance, when a U.S. razor blade company like Gillette was not allowed by the French government to export its razor blades to France, Gillette bought a French razor blade company. In this way, the Gillette subsidiary was then able to sell razor blades to the French people. This explains why 87% of French razors and razor blades are owned by U.S.-based multinational corporations, like Gillette.

c. *Cheap Labor*

Thirdly, cheap labor overseas accounts for corporations becoming multinational, especially for their subsidiaries in the Third World. Many corporations prefer not having to pay union wages. So, for example, Dole and Del Monte have been shifting their pineapple production from Hawaii, where workers are unionized, to the Philippines, where labor is cheap and independent unions are prohibited. In 1975 Philpak, Del Monte's Philippine subsidiary, employed about 5,600 workers (almost 10,000 by 1977) in its pineapple and banana operations. But more than half of these workers are "casual" or seasonal rather than "regular". Seasonal workers are not paid the same wages as the regulars. According to the *Far Eastern Economic Review*, in 1974 these "casual" workers were paid 4.8 pesos a day, below the then minimum wage for agricultural workers in the Philippines of 6.25 pesos a day (about $1.00). The "regular" workers received 9.6 pesos a day (about $1.50).[3] This situation continues today.

"Runaway shops" and "export platforms" are multiplying elsewhere too, especially in Mexico, Taiwan, South Korea, and Hong Kong. Electronics corporations, for instance, like Zenith, close down their plants in the U.S. and move their operations a few miles into Mexico. With much cheaper Mexican labor, they produce TV sets and other items at less cost. Then they export these items back across the border for sale at higher profits. That is why such operations are referred to as *runaway* shops and *export platforms*.

d. Environmental Regulations

Finally, some corporations become multinational to escape stricter environmental regulations in their home country. Also, they are concerned about public outcry at contaminating factories. It is much easier to move their pollution overseas, far away from the more politically effective resistance of First World citizens.

Primarily because of these four reasons, many multinational corporations generally realize higher profits on their overseas operations than on their domestic ones. This is especially true in certain industries, as the following chart points out:[4]

Type of Industry	Overseas Profit Rate	Domestic Profit Rate
Office Equipment (1971)	25.6%	9.2%
Pharmaceuticals (1971)	22.4%	15.5%
Food (1971)	16.7%	11.5%

The distribution of this overseas investment of the multinational corporations presents an interesting picture. Most direct investments are in the industrialized world.[5]

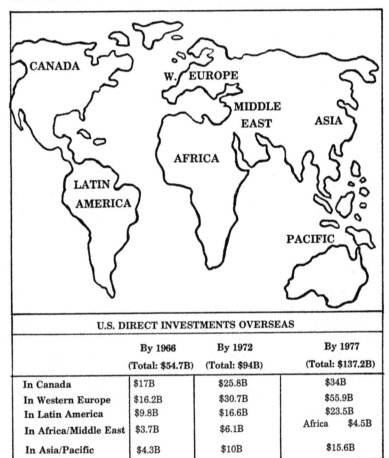

U.S. DIRECT INVESTMENTS OVERSEAS			
	By 1966 (Total: $54.7B)	By 1972 (Total: $94B)	By 1977 (Total: $137.2B)
In Canada	$17B	$25.8B	$34B
In Western Europe	$16.2B	$30.7B	$55.9B
In Latin America	$9.8B	$16.6B	$23.5B
In Africa/Middle East	$3.7B	$6.1B	Africa $4.5B
In Asia/Pacific	$4.3B	$10B	$15.6B

3. Magnitude of the Multinationals

For the four main reasons we have just seen, it is no wonder that many multinational corporations have moved many of their activities overseas. According to the European Commission survey just mentioned, there are about 10,000 multinational corporations around the world. 4,534 of them are based in Western Europe and 2,570 are based in the U.S. These multinational corporations have roughly 50,000 foreign affiliates. Of the largest 650 of these multinational corporations, 638 have their corporate headquarters in the U.S., Western Europe or Japan.[6]

Direct investments in the Third World by these multinationals based in the First World jumped from about $4.4 billion in 1972 to $6.7 billion in 1973. The top 298 U.S.-based multinationals studied by the U.S. Department of Commerce earned 40% of their entire net profits outside the U.S. by 1973, almost double the 1966 percentage.[7]

With banks, it is the same story. According to Howard Wachtel in *The New Gnomes*, by 1975, 63% of the total income of the twelve largest multinational banks headquartered in the U.S. originated in their thousands of foreign branches. Only two years earlier, the total had been 43%. In 1971, the total was only 23% of their total income generated overseas. In other words, in just four years, the total almost tripled. To cite but one example, Chase Manhattan Bank obtained 78% of its 1976 profits from foreign lending activities.[8]

The size and the extent of control of these multinational corporations are staggering. Of the largest one hundred economic entities in the world, only fifty-nine are countries. Forty-one are multinational corporations. Comparing gross annual sales of the multinational corporations with the gross national products (GNP) of the countries, we get the following chart:[9]

Gross National Products and Net Sales of Nations and Corporations

Figures are given in billions of dollars. GNPs are for fiscal year 1975 unless otherwise indicated. Net sales are for 1976.

1. U.S.A. 1,516	51. Unilever 15.7 B, F
2. U.S.S.R. 865.3	52. General Electric 15.69 A
3. Japan 488	53. Chrysler 15.5 A
4. Fed. Rep. of Germany, West 423	54. Portugal 14.8 (est. 1975)
5. France 336 (est. 1975)	55. Taiwan 14.7
6. People's Rep. of China 299	56. Colombia 14.51
7. U.K. 226	57. Thailand 14.5
8. Italy 172	58. Kuwait 13.9
9. Canada 152 (est. 1975)	59. Iraq 13 (est. 1975)
10. Spain 102.7 (est. 1976)	60. Peru 12.7
11. Brazil 90	61. Algeria 12.5
12. Poland 89.9	62. Pakistan 12.2 (fy 1976)
13. India 85 (fy 1976)	63. Libya 11.9
14. Australia 83	64. ITT 11.76 A
15. Netherlands 80.4	65. New Zealand 11.7
16. Mexico 78.6	66. Standard Oil Indiana 11.53 A
17. German Dem. Rep., East 70.2	67. Philips' 11.5 F
18. Sweden 68.8	68. Israel 11.4
19. Belgium 59.1	69. Egypt 11.2
20. Czechoslavakia 56.6	70. ENI 9.98 D
21. Switzerland 56.03	71. Francaise des Petroles 9.92 C
22. Romania 51.4	72. Renault 9.35 C
23. Iran 50	73. Hoechst 9.33 I
24. Exxon 48.63 A	74. Shell Oil 9.22 A
25. General Motors 47.18 A	75. BASF 9.2 I
26. Yugoslavia 39.19 (est. 1975)	76. Petroleos de Venezuela 9
27. Argentina 37.8 (1974)	77. Daimler-Benz 8.9 I
28. Turkey 36.5	78. U.S. Steel 8.6 A
29. Royal Dutch/Shell Group 36 B, F	79. Volkswagenwerk 8.5 I
30. Denmark 32.8	80. Atlantic Richfield 8.4 A
31. Saudi Arabia 31 (est. 1975)	81. Du Pont 8.36 A
32. South Africa 29.6	82. Chile 8.3
33. Indonesia 29	83. Bayer 8.29 I
34. Ford Motor 28.8 A	84. Malaysia 8.1
35. Hungary 27.8	85. Nippon Steel 8 H
36. Venezuela 27.3	86. Siemens 8 I
37. Texaco 26.45 A	87. Continental Oil 7.95 A
38. Nigeria 26	88. Thyssen 7.94 I
39. Finland 26	89. Ireland 7.9
40. Mobil 26 A	90. Toyota Motor 7.69 H
41. Norway 24.6	91. Nestle 7.6 G
42. Bulgaria 23.1	92. ELF-Aquitaine 7.53 C
43. Greece 21.1	93. North Korea 7.5 (est. 1975)
44. National Iranian Oil 19.67	94. Cuba 7.5
45. Standard Oil of California 19.4 A	95. Imperial Chem. Industries 7.46 B
46. British Petroleum 19 B	96. Peugeot-Citroen 7.3 C
47. South Korea 18	97. Petrobras 7.2 E
48. Gulf Oil 16.4 A	98. Western Electric 6.93 A
49. IBM 16.3 A	99. Morocco 6.9
50. Philippines 15.8	100. Hong Kong 6.8

Code for Countries where Headquartered

A. U.S.	D. Italy	G. Switzerland
B. U.K.	E. Brazil	H. Japan
C. France	F. Netherlands	I. West Germany

Examining this chart, we find that Exxon and General Motors rank 24th and 25th, ahead of Yugoslavia, Argentina, South Africa and most countries of the world. Mobil, Ford, and Royal Dutch Shell are all in the top forty. One interesting comparison is ITT in 64th place and Chile in 82nd place. It is reported that the corporate power of ITT contributed greatly to the attempt to keep Chile's President, Salvador Allende, from taking office in 1970.

With the growth rates of these multinational corporations at an average of about 10% a year,[10] their size relative to that of countries should continue to increase. By 1972, the gross annual sales of the twelve largest multinational corporations was $144 billion—more than the total annual national income of the world's poorest thirty-five countries with approximately one billion inhabitants!

4. "Diversification" and "Vertical Integration"

Some multinational corporations are giants because of their diversification. That is, they are involved in a wide variety of products and/or industries. As we saw in Chapters 4 and 5, single export economies are quite vulnerable. Corporations that produce only one product can also be vulnerable. If something happens to that product—like a change in consumer taste or increased costs of one of the product's key components—then the corporation is in jeopardy. So, most corporations protect themselves by diversifying into a number of products.

Tenneco, for instance, boasts that it is "the most roundly diversified and solidly successful multimarket company in all industry," because it is involved in synthetics, mining, packaging, food, gas, tractors, shipbuilding, toys, furniture, auto parts, and a host of other products. In another of its corporate ads, Tenneco says it is "like a supermarket for the necessities of life." Almost every multinational corporation is diversified to some extent. Among the 187 U.S.-based multinational corporations selected for the Harvard Multinational Enterprises study, the average corporation produced twenty-two products and operated in over eleven countries.[11]

Other multinational corporations are giants because of "vertical integration." That is, they control all or at least most phases of a single operation or industry. Like diversification, vertical integration provides protection at the same time as it increases the corporation's options. Controlling all phases of the production and distribution of a particular product prevents unexpected costs in any one of the phases. It also makes possible such benefits as transfer pricing, as we saw earlier.

Among corporations known for their vertical integration are Del Monte and Exxon. Similar to Safeway's motto "from seedling to supermarket," Del Monte is a classic example of vertical integration in the food industry. In the following chart, Jim Hightower points out the extent to which Del Monte was involved in each phase of the food industry by 1974: from the farm to the cannery and other processing facilities, to transporting that food and storing and distributing it, to marketing a variety of well-known brands and finally to an extensive food service operation.

"From the ground to the tank," Exxon's vertical integration in the oil industry is even more extensive than Del Monte's in the food industry. In 1976, Exxon had worldwide sales of $48.63 billion from its oil operations.

(1) Rigs working for Exxon or companies it partially owns bring up oil from the Arctic tundra, the Arabian deserts, the Gulf of Mexico, and Venezuela.

(2) Giant tankers owned by Exxon ship that oil.

(3) Exxon refineries in California, Rotterdam, Saudi Arabia, and Singapore refine the oil.

(4) Gas station pumps bearing Exxon labels dispense gasoline in Canadian fishing villages, African jungle outposts, as well as in the U.S.

(5) Finally, Exxon petrochemical operations produce materials that go into fertilizers, records, panty hose and many other products.

VERTICAL INTEGRATION IN THE DEL MONTE CORPORATION

Del Monte Corporation
(1974 sales of $1,042,608,000)

FOOD AND AGRICULTURAL RESEARCH

$7,500,000 annual budget
500 full-time employees
6 research and new-product
development laboratories

SEED FARMS

AGRICULTURAL PRODUCTION
55 farms, ranches, plantations and
orchards 132,700 acres of Del-
Monte-farmed land in the U.S.,
Canada, Kenya, Latin America
and the Philippines
Unknown number of beef feedlots in
the U.S., the Philippines and
South America, and fishing fleets
in the Pacific and Atlantic Oceans

FARMERS
10,000 U.S. farmers
under contract

INPUTS
15 can-manufacturing plants
2 label-printing plants

PROCESSING
(In 15 states and 9 foreign countries)
59 canneries
3 dried-fruit plants
15 snack-food, specialty and frozen-food plants

TRANSPORTATION
21 air-freight forwarding stations
5 banana-transport ships
9 tuna seiners and transport ships
Salmon boats
1 ocean terminal
7 trucking operations

STORAGE & DISTRIBUTION
15 distribution warehouses
1 tune freezer-storage plant

BRANDS
Argo canned seafood
Award frozen foods
Del Monte
Dew Drop asparagus

Grand Tour frozen foods
Granny Goose snacks
Perky meat and fruit
pies

MARKETING
1,220 salespeople in 58 sales offices
throughout the U.S. and abroad
250 independent brokers
Market research staff

ADVERTISING
$16+ million an-
nual budget for
national net-
work TV, radio,
magazines, etc.

FOOD SERVICE
712 food-service accounts (United
Airlines, nursing homes, hotels,
school lunch programs, industrial
plants, etc.)
409 food-vending accounts (3,000
Del-Monte-owned vending machines)
28 public restaurants catered by Del
Monte.

SOURCE: Hightower, Jim: *Eat Your Heart Out* (1975), Crown Publishers, pp. 26–27.
Reprinted with permission from the publisher.

5. Conclusion

The big question is whether multinational corporations, with all this wealth and power, are or can be a positive force in the development of the Third World. As General Motors put it a few years ago, in one of their ads: "World peace and human progress are necessary to our business. That's the single most important point about a corporation, like General Motors, being multinational in its operations." Can this be true? We will examine this question in the next chapter.

Discussion Questions

1. What makes a multinational corporation "multinational"?
2. Explain some ways in which the multinational corporations have made the world "one economic unit."
3. Why are some multinational subsidiaries called "runaway shops" and "export platforms"?
4. Explain the four reasons for corporations becoming multinational. Can you think of other advantages?
5. How big are the multinational corporations? What are some of the possible consequences of this bigness?
6. What is the difference between diversification and vertical integration and what advantages do they give multinational corporations?

Resources

On Multinational Corporations in General
   —Of the dozens of bibliographies on the subject, the best may be *The Transnational Corporations and the Third World* (produced and distributed by CoDoC—Cooperation in Documentation and Communication, 1500 Farragut St., NW, Washington, DC 20011). Done in 1975, it lists hundreds of resources produced between 1970 and 1974 on the general theory and

description of multinational corporations and on their impact in the Third World.

—The United Nations Center on Transnational Corporations publishes a newsletter on its work and on the operations of the corporations (see Chapter 10).

—"Multinational Corporations—The Quiet Revolution?" is the title of *Intercom* magazine #74 (Center for Global Perspectives, 218 E. 18th, New York, NY 10003). It presents summaries of various perspectives on the multinationals (from labor, government, the corporations themselves, and the Third World) and offers a variety of classroom suggestions.

Chapter Nine

THE IMPACT OF THE
MULTINATIONAL CORPORATIONS

Introduction
Tenneco accurately sees itself as a "global supermarket." The unique ability of Tenneco and other multinational corporations to centralize global economic resources and integrate production on a worldwide scale is the reason for their fantastic growth in the past few years. More specifically, the growth and profits of the multinationals derive from three basic sources—their influence over finance capital (money for investment), technology, and marketing and communications.

Each of these areas has a significant impact on the Third World. Returning to the question asked at the conclusion of Chapter 8, is this impact a positive or a negative one for the Third World? Mr. Lee Iacocca's essay from *Newsweek* magazine is the multinational corporation's answer to its critics. The impact of a multinational corporation like Ford, in the view of its then President, is both significant and positive for the Third World. The bulk of this chapter disputes Iacocca's claim. Specifically in terms of world hunger, the overall impact of the multinational corporations generally seems to be both significant and negative for the Third World.

Myth of the Big, Bad Multinational

Industrial productivity, according to the myth of exploitation, is still a controversial term in many places the world over. After more than 100 years of highly visible material gains, this dramatic multiplier of human effort is still often regarded as a mean, immoral way of wringing more work out of people for minimal wages. In fact, rather than diminishing in power and appeal as evidence of productivity's benefits mounts, the myth has taken on a new and more damaging dimension by featuring the multinational corporation as the global villain.

The myth says the multinational corporation, if not rigidly controlled, would take all and give nothing to host countries. And the myth too often finds expression in unrealistic government policies that prevent resident multinationals from doing the job they could be doing for these countries, or that drive off foreign investment altogether.

The fact is the modern corporation, national or multinational, is the most effective, most accessible source of productivity any country has, and productivity is absolutely essential—there is no alternative—to the material hopes and aspirations of all nations, rich or poor.

Elements of Productivity

Productivity is *the* fundamental reality of economic life, and no matter where you are, it consists of five basic elements:

First, capital, which must be brought to bear on human needs through machines and facilities.

Second, talented people, who are needed to work on those same problems, people with brains and the technological ability to invent and constantly improve new designs and processes.

Third, a well-motivated and trained labor force, essential in carrying out production with maximum efficiency.

Fourth, an organization, one designed to manage the people, the capital, the machines and the know-how so that everyone involved can extend his labor and skills a hundredfold.

And fifth, governmental cooperation, which is necessary to create a climate of investment that attracts the people and the capital to do the job. Needless to say, if the organization of human effort is not made economically viable through sensible, realistic regulatory and tax policies, no work will get done, whether it's by a ten-man machine shop or by a multibillion-dollar multinational.

Without all five of these elements, you can't get productivity. Obviously, where there is great and widespread material need, as in many emerging nations, increasing productivity is the problem, not exploitation. Getting the horse in front of the cart is the first order of business in closing the gap in living standards between the Northern and Southern hemispheres. And the multinational corporation can pull that cart better and faster than anyone else.

The Spanish Example

It has been called the most creative economic invention of the twentieth century, an "engine of growth" that can accelerate development the world over. Moreover, the multinational offers less-developed nations the best available linkage with the markets, technology and know-how of the industrialized world. In addition, through direct foreign investment in plants and equipment, it provides a ready source of scarce capital without adding to the considerable debt burdens of these countries.

Ford Motor Co.'s recent investment in Spain is an example of what a multinational company can do. It took us just three years to the day to build an industrial complex 2½ miles long and half a mile wide, with 55 acres under roof. To get from farmland to an annual capacity of 250,000 cars and 400,000 engines, we drew on the experience of 75 years in the automotive business, utilizing personnel and technological resources from all over the world.

You just can't go out and buy that kind of know-how on the open market, no matter what you're willing to pay.

In the course of those three years, we invested close to $800 million—$500 million in Spain and $300 million more for the expansion of related facilities in Europe. In addition, we contracted with and coordinated the efforts of more than 200 Spanish suppliers, who provide 65 per cent of the content of production, under very specific quality controls that we continuously monitor. The plant itself now employs 9,000 workers. They are all local people and all well paid by local standards.

We couldn't have done this—and we wouldn't have done it—if the Spanish Government hadn't provided a favorable investment climate. It made provisions in its law that allow us to compete for a fair share of the Spanish domestic market, and it permitted us to have 100 per cent ownership of the facility. Spain, in turn, now has a valuable link with the Common Market, and exports of our cars and engines should add about $170 million to its foreign-exchange earnings this year, rising to over half a billion dollars in 1978 and 1979.

You might assume all nations would welcome investments like this. But the malevolent multinational of the exploitation myth dies hard, and many governments actually discourage such massive infusions of capital and know-how, unwittingly or otherwise. Bureaucrats dictate how much a company can export, what local materials and parts it must use, what prices it can charge and how much money it can take out of the country to finance operations elsewhere in the world. Worse yet, the uncertain investment climate is being further clouded by the proliferation of codes and guidelines now under study by various bodies in the United Nations, primarily at the urging of the developing nations.

Tragic 'Protection'

Spokesmen for the developing world often assert they want the benefits multinationals have to offer. But their restrictive terms rarely take accurate account of global economic realities. No one benefits if multinationals are welcomed with one hand and cut to pieces by the other.

It is a tragic irony to try to "protect" the people of the developing world by denying them the help of multinational corporations. According to an extensive United Nations study, the world is fully capable of reducing by 50 per cent the income gap between "have" and "have not" nations by the year 2000.

The know-how and the technology are available. The resources and manpower are there. The capital can be generated. The challenge—for developed and developing nations alike—is to put them all together in the right combination: to make them productive.

It's what the multinational corporation does best.

Lee A. Iacocca

Iacocca was president of Ford Motor Co.

Three Sources of Multinational Control

1. *Control over Finance Capital*

The most persistent claim of the multinational corporations, in their defense of themselves as agents or "engines" of development, is that they provide badly needed capital without which economic growth would be impossible. Actually, the situation is often quite different, in a number of ways. Let's look at four of these ways.

(a.) *A Net Flow of Capital Back to the U.S.* As we saw in Chapter 8, multinational corporations have indeed invested billions of dollars in foreign countries. However, with regard to multinationals based in the U.S., for example, the actual flow of capital has been in this direction, back to the U.S. Capital from direct foreign investment (subsidiaries overseas) returns to the corporate headquarters of the multinational corporations in at least four ways: from profits on past investments, from interest payments on loans to the subsidiaries, from royalties on the use of patented technology, and from fees for the technical expertise of the home office. The total of this capital return to the U.S. exceeds the amount being currently invested abroad, and by greater margins each year. In 1961, the net flow to the U.S. was $1.2 billion. By 1967, it was up to $1.4 billion. By 1973, the total had reached $6.2 billion.[1]

With regard to Latin America specifically, the data is even more devastating. Sol Linowitz, one of the two key U.S. negotiators on the Panama Canal Treaty, estimates that the average direct new investment each year by U.S.-based multinational corporations is $235 million (not counting reinvested earnings). In contrast, the average annual repatriation (return) of profits is about $1 billion. That's four times as much coming back to the U.S. as is going out. [2]

(b.) *A Large Percentage of Local Capital Is Tied Up.* Contrary to Iacocca's claim that multinational corporations provide "massive infusions of capital," more and more of the capital invested, especially in Third World countries, is not from corporate headquarters. Rather, it is local capital drawn generally from the branch banks of the multinational banks. These branches control more and more of the private deposits of the country (50% in the case of Bolivia). Because of credit ratings and business and friendship ties, these branch banks would much prefer to lend to the subsidiaries of U.S.-based multinational corporations than to local business. [3] Raymond Vernon's important study of the multinational corporations, *Sovereignty at Bay*, estimates that in the 1960s, less than 25% of the investments of multinational corporations came from the home office of the parent company. [4]

This is particularly true for multinational investments in Latin America. According to the research of Barnet and Muller, for instance, in mining, oil, and smelting industries, 83% of the capital for multinational enterprises came from local sources. In contrast, these enterprises repatriated 79% of their profits to corporate headquarters. [5] This does not reflect any "massive infusion of capital". Neither does it support the claim that multinational corporations are doing things *for* host countries. In monopolizing local capital, the multinational corporations severely limit the possibilities of local businesses developing.

(c.) *The Character of the Investments.* The character or type of investment is equally important. The multinationals claim to supply new capital through which their superior management skills can be channeled into new productive facilities. In this way, new Ford plants, such as Iacocca's example in Spain, are created. However, according to the Harvard Multinational Enterprises study mentioned in Chapter 8, the 187 largest U.S.-based multinationals between 1958 and 1967 used "a substantial part of their investment" in Latin America to buy up local firms rather than create new ones. 46% of all manufacturing operations established by multinational corporations during that decade were these take-overs (331 of 717).[6] Certainly new plants are created, but not nearly as many as the corporations would like us to believe.

(d.) *Foreign Exchange.* Finally, the claim of multinational corporations to provide increased foreign exchange earnings (income from exports) to host countries seems to be something of a myth itself. Who is the actual recipient of these earnings? In Iacocca's example, he says Spain. Spain may benefit from the taxes it levies on the export of Ford cars and from taxes on both Ford's profits and on the incomes of Ford workers. However, the bulk of the foreign exchange earnings is not Spain's. It is income for Ford, which is distributed in a variety of ways. One of the main concerns of many Third World countries is that a large part of such earnings is channeled into management salaries. In this way, foreign exchange earnings are often wasted on luxury consumer imports for the higher salaried members of the multinational's management staff. Imported air-conditioners make the homes of corporate managers comfortable, but are in no way beneficial to the host government or to the people of that country. The precise extent to which this is true in Spain is unknown, but it remains a major concern to host governments the world over.

To conclude this examination of capital, many Third World countries may be currently low on capital. However, this is the result of a series of decisions made by those who control the capital and/or the sources of capital in those countries. As Barnet and Muller point out, historically—

The finance capital generated by the natural wealth of many countries of the underdeveloped world was not used to develop local factories, schools, and other structures for generating more wealth but was siphoned off to the developed world—first as plunder, then in the more respectable form of dividends, royalties, and technical fees—where it was used to finance the amenities of London and Paris and more important, the industrial expansion of affluent societies. Most of the capital left in the poor countries was in the control of a small local elite closely tied to foreign capitalists who knew how to consume it in lavish living and where to invest it abroad for a good return.

Thus, because the power over the national wealth was largely in the hands of foreigners, the finance capital generated by past wealth-producing activities was not used to maintain, much less to expand, the local economy. The result was a process of wealth depletion which has resulted inevitably in lower consumption for the local population. The net outflow of finance capital from the underdeveloped societies weakened their capacity to develop the knowledge to produce wealth, and this further decreased their bargaining power.[7]

This is exactly what the example of Potosi, Bolivia, revealed in Chapter 2. The silver wealth of Potosi and the creativity of its residents were extracted in brutal fashion to finance the development of Spain. Chapter 4 showed how Third World wealth continues to be extracted, but more subtly, through a whole series of trade policies. It is important to remember that the current need for capital is a created need. That is, it is only once a country's resources have been drained that it can be said to need foreign capital. Actually, Third World countries need foreign capital much less than they need to change the rules and institutions governing the international order, so that they can keep their own capital and human resources.

2. Control over Technology

The second source of multinational corporate power is its control over technology. The multinational corporations operate on the very frontiers of technology. Compared with other companies, they spend more on research and development, receive the bulk of government money for technological development, use a more skilled and specialized workforce, and introduce the vast majority of new products and processes into the mainstream of economic life.[8] This control over technology creates a series of problems for Third World countries. Let's examine three of these problems.

(a.) *Dependence.* A good illustration of the problems facing Third World countries in their efforts to get modern technology is the international patent system. Patents confer on their owners a monopoly on production and distribution of products in each country granting the patent and for a specific period of time (usually 10, 15, or 20 years). So when a multinational corporation like Monsanto develops a product—for instance, an agricultural chemical like Lasso—it obtains a patent in the U.S. to be its exclusive producer and distributor. If Monsanto wants this same exclusive opportunity in other countries, it applies for a patent in the desired countries. Thus, with patents in over 60 countries, mostly in the Third World, Monsanto's subsidiaries are protected in their production and distribution of Lasso. No other company—foreign or local— can manufacture or even import and sell the same product. This is the monopoly that patents confer.

According to a 1976 United Nations study, 3.5 million patents had been granted by the mid-1970s. Yet, only 200,000 (6%) had been granted by Third World countries. And of these 200,000, only one out of six was held by Third World citizens. The bulk were and are held by foreigners, mostly multinational corporations headquartered in the U.S., England, West Germany, France, and Switzerland.

Thus, because most manufactured goods and manufacturing processes are controlled by foreign corporations, it is difficult for Third World countries to develop their own manufacturing industries. One option for Third World countries is to pay the foreign owners of patented technology—again, generally multinational corporations—for the use of their technology. But the cost is quite high and the products and processes are often restricted in their uses. According to the United Nations Conference on Trade and Development (UNCTAD), Third World payments for the use of patented technology reached about $1.5 billion by 1970 and could reach $9 billion by 1980![9]

Iacocca claims that the multinational corporations provide this technology to Third World countries to increase their productivity. But the reality seems to be a little different. The control that multinational corporations exercise over technology seems rather to translate into restricted competition and thus to higher profits for the multinationals.

(b.) *Corporate Goals vs. Third World Needs.* The transfer of the technology of multinational corporations is often not helpful for Third World countries. This is not only because of the high cost, but also because the multinational corporations and many Third World countries often have different goals and interests. Multinational control over technology means that research and development funds will generally go to the corporation for its own profits. If this goal happens also to promote the development needs of Third World countries, fine. If not, then the corporation comes first.

Because of corporate control, the transfer of technology contracts will often restrict the uses that the Third World recipients can put the technology to. Often these contracts have required Third World countries to buy raw materials, plant and equipment, and spare parts from the corporation as well. Further, Third World users of foreign technology are often prohibited from exporting the products generated by the technology.[10]

For instance, before the Andean Pact (5 countries negotiating as a group with the multinationals) was created in 1971, 80% of the technology transferred to the Andean countries of Peru, Chile, Bolivia, Ecuador, and Colombia could not be used for exports.[11] Iacocca's essay stresses what the multinational corporations could be doing *for* foreign countries. A more accurate word, in light of the evidence, might be *in*. This does not mean that multinational corporations have not done or can not do things for Third World countries. It does mean, though, that they have not done nearly as much as they claim to have done and that much of what they have done has not been beneficial to Third World countries.

(c.) *Inappropriate Technology and Loss of Jobs.* Because the technology transferred to the Third World by the multinational corporations is geared more to corporate goals than it is to Third World needs, it is often inappropriate for the human and natural resources and the values of Third World countries. Usually the technology is heavily capital-intensive, rather than labor-intensive. That is, it requires machine and money power, rather than labor power. Allis-Chalmers is a good example:

Allis-Chalmers, International Harvester, John Deere & Co., and the other large multinational agricultural equipment corporations have all kinds of machines to sell. Mammoth combines and expensive irrigation systems may be appropriate to the needs of corporate farmers in the U.S. and to a few very large farmers in the Third World. But it does not seem that the Third World "needs more of what Allis-Chalmers makes."

Corporations want machines that can do the work of many workers and do it more efficiently and reliably. Third World countries, however, have an abundance of labor power and generally little money for such machines. Appropriate technology for most Third World countries, then, would be designed to put the maximum number of people to work.

A special aspect of the inappropriateness of much of the technology transferred to the Third World is the development of technology appropriate for Third World women. While women do the majority of the farming in much of Africa and a little less than 20% of the farming in Asia and Latin America, development workers teach new techniques and supply farm machinery and other inputs only to the men. Why? Because men are involved in cash cropping and women in subsistence farming. It is the men who bring in cash.

Thus, the transfer of technology often means increased unemployment for women. For instance, women haulers in Asia and Africa have been replaced by trucks, whose drivers are always men. Home-based weaving done by women is disappearing in the face of manufactured textiles.[12] And the infant formula corporations (see Chap. 3, pp. 43-44, and Chapter 12 on Nestlé) continue to market their technology to Third World women who are (1) often too poor to afford the formula and (2) generally capable of breast-feeding their infants.

Inappropriate technology, then, often means less jobs. Returning to Iacocca's essay, we find some interesting figures. He speaks of Ford's investment as $800 million, $500 million of it in Spain. That $500 million, he says, produced 9,000 jobs.

That translates into about $55,000 per job. That is precisely the problem with capital-intensive technology. It generates far fewer jobs per amount of investment than labor-intensive technology. But the multinational view of development is measured in higher levels of technology, bigness, quantity of goods produced and consumed—not in terms of increased jobs for people.

3. Control over Ideology and Marketing

Spain's acceptance of a Ford plant on its farmland reveals the third source of the power of multinational corporations. As Barnet and Muller note, "no aspect of the technological superiority of the developed world is more important than its mastery of the techniques of ideological marketing."[13] This technological know-how, combined with the multinationals' growing control over the communications media of Third World countries, means that the tastes, goals, and values of people are being shaped increasingly by the consumption goals and values of corporations. Commercials sell a way of thinking and living as well as specific products. Their underlying message is generally "more is better" and "consumption is the key to happiness." Certainly, the automobile industry has been among the leaders in sending this message around the world.

Illustrations of multinational corporate control over communications in the Third World reveal a frightening picture. Advertising firms have become multinational corporations. In 1954, the top thirty U.S. advertising agencies received only 5% of their total billings from overseas campaigns. That 5% figure, however, jumped to 33% by 1972. 33% of $7 billion worth of advertising in 1972 is a lot of selling of consumption to the Third World.[14]

TV and radio are the most effective channels for advertising, especially in countries with high illiteracy rates. And, characteristically, it is U.S. networks that have played the dominant role in Third World countries, especially in Latin

America. By 1974, CBS was distributing its programs in 100 countries. In 1970 and 1971, CBS and NBC combined sold more than $500 million worth of programming to foreign countries. Today in Peru, for instance, the U.S. way of living is conveyed via TV through such favorites as "Hawaii Five-0" and "The Streets of San Francisco." By 1968, ABC had controlling interest in 16 foreign companies that operated 67 TV stations in 27 countries.[15]

Further, it is the multinational corporations that are the most frequent advertisers on these stations. Barnet and Muller cite the example of Channel 5 in Peru, which received 63% of all TV advertising revenues in that country for 1969. 11% of those revenues came from only two firms—Procter & Gamble and Colgate Palmolive.[16] Today, TV commercials are urging Peruvians to drive Toyotas and Datsuns (from the Japan-based multinationals Toyota and Nissan), as well as chew Chiclets gum (from the Warner-Lambert Company) and drink the ever-present Coca-Cola.

The effects of this control over the media are generally negative. Distinctions between rich and poor are sharpened. Traditional values and cultures are shoved aside for more "modern" ways of thinking and living. A sense of urgency about the need for serious social change can be dulled. And the lives of the poor are devastated, as we will see in Chapter 12.

It is here, in the economic growth models of the multinational corporations and their consumption-oriented way of living and thinking, that the fundamental difference between their worldview and the vision of life and development presented in Part I of this book is most clearly evident. Let's go back to Iacocca's essay.

He writes, "Increasing productivity is the problem . . . ." To the question—"Productivity for what?"—his answer would be, according to his essay, "To get from farmland to an annual capacity of 250,000 cars and 400,000 engines . . . ." Ford may be proud of using farmland for its auto plant and Ford may need more cars, but does the world? In view of Chapter 6 on export cropping, it seems that Spain and even more so the countries of the Third World need to convert their agricultural resources to food for local consumption first, not to cars.

Cars benefit only a tiny fraction of the human family— primarily those whose view of development is more in terms of modern buildings, luxury consumer goods, mobility, technological gadgets, large-scale machines, etc. Most people, on the other hand, are more concerned about adequate sources for food and other basic necessities and for a greater opportunity to control their own lives a little more. It would be interesting to know how many Spanish farmers, displaced by the Ford plant, now buy their food at much higher cost. It would also be interesting to know how many of them are driving Fords.

Multinational Corporations and World Hunger

Precisely because of their control over technology, capital, and ideology and marketing, some multinational corporations—far from being the "engines of development" they claim to be—actually contribute to hunger in the Third World. There are three main ways in which this happens, paralleling the three sources of multinational corporate power.

1. Control over Technology: Increasing the Gap Between Rich and Poor and Eliminating Jobs

Chapter 6 on export cropping pointed out how the transfer of corporate technology has enriched the wealthier farmers of several Third World countries at the expense of poorer farmers. First of all, poorer farmers cannot afford such farm machinery and fertilizers and pesticides. Secondly, wealthier farmers want even larger tracts of land to take greater advantage of this large-scale machinery. Such additional lands come, obviously, from the holdings of the poorer farmers who are gradually moved off their land.

Further, the agricultural technology exported by such giant corporations as International Harvester, John Deere, and others has often been capital-intensive and thus job-reducing. The mechanization and concentration of agriculture in fewer and larger units means less and less work. For instance, in Sonora, Mexico, farm workers today average 100 days of work a year. Prior to extensive mechanization, they averaged 194 days a year.[17]

But even in labor-intensive operations, there is less work. Former small farmers, who owned their own land and grew year-round rotating crops, have frequently been reduced to seasonal farm laborers harnessed to a single crop. Farm workers who are paid less in wages than they once made on the land themselves face the serious problem of purchasing enough to eat, especially when they must pay higher prices for food staples no longer grown in that area. Let's look at Del Monte's operation in the Philippines.

According to Del Monte in 1975, its Philippine subsidiary Philpak employed 5,600 people in jobs that did not exist before Del Monte came to the Philippines in 1926. Most of these jobs, it claims, are full-time, because tropical fruits grow year round. Finally, they cite the fact that their cannery and "regular" plantation workers are paid above the Philippine minimum wage.[18]

From the point of view of the workers and a number of missionaries who have worked with them for many years, the picture is quite different. At least half of Del Monte's workers are classified as "casuals" and are thus paid half of what the "regulars" get (see Chap. 8, p. 143). Many of the agricultural workers are now paid employees on land they once considered their own. A recent estimate suggests that 80% of the rural labor force, once landholders, are now landless laborers.[19]

Fr. Ed Gerlock, who worked in the Philippines with many of these dispossessed farmers and who knows the psychological costs of this arrangement, calculated its cost in dollars. He estimated in 1977 that a farmer on one hectare (about 2.5 acres), employing the crudest means of agriculture, and growing two crops per year, could earn about $600/annually. When

this same farmer leases this hectare to the company at between $30 and $70 and works as a laborer for $1.00 a day (the
wage for "casuals"), he can only earn about $420 a year, even
if he works 350 days a year. Not only do these farmers make
less, but now they have to buy food staples which they used to
grow themselves.[20] Hunger, thus, becomes a much more serious situation.

2. Control over Capital: Control over Land and the Production and Distribution of Food

As we saw in Chapter 6 on export cropping, the multinational corporations exercise greater and greater control over
the agricultural resources of Third World countries. Some of
this is done with the blessing of Third World governments.
Sometimes it is imposed as one of the conditions for a crucial
loan from the International Monetary Fund (see Chapter 4, p.
70).

In the Philippines, for instance, Del Monte's Philpak
worked around the legal limit of about 2,500 acres of land
under corporate ownership by leasing most of the land it uses.
In fact, Philpak has a leasing agreement with an agency of the
Philippine Government for 17,000 acres until 1988. In addition to these leases, the United Nations Conference on Trade
and Development estimates that Del Monte controls at least
another 9,000 acres, where it has begun to expand banana
production.[21]

What does this kind of control over land mean with regard to world hunger? First, as we have just seen, the farmers
who once controlled this land face a serious hunger situation.
Secondly, as Chapter 6 pointed out, lands controlled by multinational corporations are often producing export crops and
non-food items like flowers and marijuana. Such items do not
reach the stomachs of the hungry majority of Third World
peoples. Thirdly, some lands controlled by the corporations
are not used at all. The aluminum companies and Jamaica
provide a good example.

As indicated in the map below, six aluminum companies control and sit on vast areas of land. They do not want their competitors to have access to the bauxite below. But idle land produces no food. Thus, with hunger a real problem, Jamaica is renegotiating ownership of these lands.[22] Meanwhile, however, a valuable source of food has been taken.

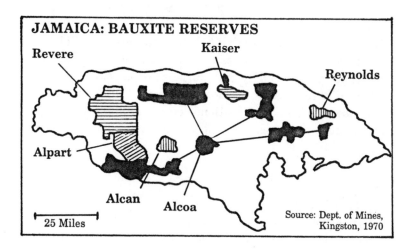

JAMAICA: BAUXITE RESERVES
Revere
Kaiser
Reynolds
Alpart
Alcan
Alcoa
25 Miles
Source: Dept. of Mines, Kingston, 1970

3. Control over Attitudes and Values through Advertising: Harmful Changes in the Dietary Habits of the Poor

If the food produced and distributed by the multinational corporations were limited to export crops of fruits and vegetables, the overall picture would not be as bleak as it currently seems to be. There are two additional problems that relate directly to hunger. First, multinational advertising is selling the poor food they cannot generally afford. Secondly, much of this food is of little nutritional value. The result is less money available for nourishing food and thus a malnourished population.

As Barnet and Muller put it, "the most important impact of this shift in eating habits in poor villages is that it takes a much greater share of the virtually nonexistent family food budget."[23] According to one executive of a British-based multinational corporation, "It is a sad fact that most nutritional food products marketed by commercial firms are aimed at the segment of society least in need of them."[24]

The poor spend their meagre resources in response to the high-powered advertising campaigns of the soft-drink corporations more than on any other single item. Coke, its co-product Fanta, and Pepsi are the big three. But soft drinks are not the only villain. ITT packages its Hostess Twinkies singly; Nabisco does so with individual Ritz crackers; and Del Monte has its single slices of pineapple—all to reach into the pocketbooks of an increasingly malnourished population.[25]

Collins and Lappe provide two devastating illustrations of this power of the multinational corporations. The first is a letter from a Mexican priest, Father Florencio, written in June 1974:

> It seems that soft drinks are a very important factor in the development of villages. I have heard some people say they can't live one day without drinking a soft drink. Other people, in order to display social status, must have soft drinks with every meal, especially if there are guests . . . .
>
> Near the larger towns where daily salaries are a little higher, soft drinks are cheaper. But in the very remote villages where people earn much less, and where soft drinks have to be transported in by animals, soft drinks cost in many places up to twice as much. The typical family in Metlatonoc can't earn more than 1,200 to 2,000 pesos a year. But even the little they receive each year they spend drinking soft drinks. In the richest village in this area, Olinala, where the majority of people are artisans and earn from 25 to 70 pesos a day ($2.00 to $5.60), about 4,000 bottles of soft drinks are consumed each day. Olinala has 6,000 inhabitants.
>
> The great majority of people are convinced that soft drinks must be consumed every day. This is mainly due to extensive advertising, especially on the radio which is so widespread in the mountains . . . . In the meantime, in these same villages, natural products such as fruit are consumed less—in some families just once a week. Other

families sell their own natural products in order to buy
soft drinks . . . .[26]

The second statement offers a sharp contrast. In the
words of Mr. H. Walter, Chairman of the Board of International Flavors and Fragrances (IFF)—

> How often we see in developing countries that the poorer
> the economic outlook, the more important the small lux-
> ury of a flavored soft drink or smoke . . . . To the dismay of
> many would-be benefactors, the poorer the malnourished
> are, the more likely they are to spend a disproportionate
> amount of whatever they have on some luxury rather
> than on what they need . . . . Observe, study, learn (how to
> sell in rapidly changing rural societies). We try to do it at
> IFF. It seems to pay off for us. Perhaps it will for you
> too.[27]

Conclusion

According to Iacocca, multinational corporations are "engines of growth that can accelerate development the world
over." We have just seen that they are, in fact, engines of
growth. More Fords, more Hostess Twinkies, more Cokes,
more pineapples and bananas, more Ritz crackers, more of
many things are being produced and consumed. But is this
"development"?

The development track that Iacocca's multinational engine travels is very different than the one being travelled in
this book and in many parts of the world by many different
people. The evidence presented in this chapter seems to indicate that it is time to trade in Iacocca's multinational engine.
The question, however, is whether we should trade it in for a
different model of multinational engine or for an entirely
different form of transportation. In other words, can multinational corporations *become* a positive force for "development"
as it is understood in this book or do they have to be scrapped
before development can take place in the Third World? The
next chapter tries to answer this question.

Discussion Questions

1. What are Iacocca's main arguments in defense of multinational corporations?
2. In what ways is or can control over capital by the multinational corporations be helpful and harmful to Third World countries?
3. In what ways is or can control over technology by multinational corporations be helpful or harmful to Third World countries?
4. In what ways is or can control over ideology and marketing by the multinational corporations be helpful and harmful to Third World countries?
5. In what ways does multinational control over technology affect world hunger?
6. In what ways does multinational control over capital affect world hunger?
7. In what ways does multinational control over advertising affect world hunger?
8. What are the differences in worldviews or in understandings of development between Iacocca and the rest of this chapter?
9. In general, do you think that the interests and goals of multinational corporations and Third World countries are more in harmony or in conflict with each other? And why?

Resources

On the Impact of Multinational Corporations in General
   —In addition to the audio-visual resources listed in Chapter 10, there is a 1978 16mm color film (40 minutes) entitled "Controlling Interest: The World of the Multinational Corporations" (from California Newsreel and available through Resolution, 630 Natoma St., San Francisco, CA 94103, for $60 rental). It examines multinational involvement in Chile, the meaning of the "Brazilian miracle", an electronics factory

leaving Massachusetts, and especially how corporate officials view these matters.

—*The Corporate Examiner*, the monthly 8-page publication of the Interfaith Center for Corporate Responsibility, is excellent on stockholder resolutions and other actions being directed at the corporations. The 4-page insert each month focuses on a specific aspect of the whole question of corporate social responsibility.

—*Catholic Church Investments for Corporate Social Responsibility* is a similar 8-page publication, produced by one part of ICCR—the National Catholic Coalition for Responsible Investment (c/o Justice and Peace Office, 3900 N. Third, Milwaukee, WI, 53212).

—Robert J. Ledogar, *Hungry for Profits: U.S. Food and Drug Multinationals in Latin America* (IDOC/North America; available for $4.95 from ICCR)—a study of the impact of corporations on consumers in Latin America, including Nestlé's marketing of infant formula, Gulf & Western in the Dominican Republic, and Coca-Cola in Brazil.

—Many of the resources listed in Chapter 6 are quite appropriate here, especially the whole issue of "Agribusiness Targets Latin America" (*NACLA Report on the Americas*).

—*Development—Dependency: The Role of the Multinational Corporations* (Dept. of Social Development and World Peace, U.S. Catholic Conference, August 1974). This 11-page booklet summarizes Papal reflection on capitalism and socialism as the background for some observation on the impact of multinationals in Latin America and in the U.S. and on the role of the Church.

—"Caribbean Conflict: Jamaica and the U.S." is the theme of the May–June 1978 issue of NACLA's *Report on the Americas*. It presents historical background on the bauxite issue as well as a detailed examination of the issue of multinational aluminum corporations and Jamaican efforts to pursue something of a socialist model of development.

—Raymond Vernon, *Sovereignty at Bay: The Multinational Spread of U.S. Enterprises* (New York: Basic Books, Inc., 1973), and *Storm Over the Multinationals* (Cambridge, Ma.: Harvard University Press, 1977). The author is a highly respected analyst of multinational corporations. Both books are worth reading for greater depth on multinational corporations in general.

On Del Monte Corporation in Particular (see also Chapters 6 and 7)

—*Del Monte Working Papers* is a packet of resource materials compiled by the Del Monte Working Group. Available through Earthwork, 3410 19th St., San Francisco, CA 94110, this is probably the best collection of shorter items on Del Monte, including the NACLA issue entitled "Bitter Fruits", cited here and in Chapter 6.

—See the references cited in the footnotes in this chapter and in Chapter 6.

—"Collision Course," 45 minutes, color, 1978, BBC production distributed by Maryknoll, is a 16mm film describing the struggle between Church and state in the Philippines over human rights. One part of the film presents an interview with Fr. Vincent Cullen on the struggle of the peasants in the Bukidnon Plain area.

On Gulf & Western in Particular

Besides the slide presentation "Guess Who's Coming to Breakfast?" (Chapter 10), the Dominican Republic Task Force (P.O. Box 641, Cathedral Station, New York, N.Y. 10025) publishes a fine newsletter on Gulf & Western. Write for their "Resource List on the Dominican Republic."

—Of the many good short articles on Gulf & Western, you might start with the two "CIC Briefs" in *The Corporate Examiner* (from ICCR). Each is 4 pages and they were written in late 1975 and late 1976. Joe Mulligan, S.J. updates them in an article in *The Christian Century*, January 1977.

On Multinational Corporations and Technology
   —Denis Goulet, "Exporting Technology to the Third World," in the Perspectives on Development and Social Change series (Center for the Study of Development and Social Change, 1430 Massachusetts Ave., Cambridge, MA 02138), is a good concise pamphlet (25¢) on the meaning and kinds of technology. It outlines the various questions facing the Third World as it pursues economic development and is especially careful to respect the values/cultures of Third World peoples.
   —"Agribusiness and World Hunger: Can Corporations Produce Appropriate Technology?", CIC Brief (The Corporate Examiner, ICCR, March 1976), is an excellent 4-page summary of the issue, with specific examples, pictures, charts.
   —"Dancing South to South: A New Partnership in Technology—Of, By and For the Third World" is the May 1978 issue of the *New Internationalist.* Its essays examine "technical cooperation among developing countries", appropriate technology, patent problems. A page of charts and graphs is especially helpful.

Chapter Ten

WHAT NEEDS TO BE DONE?

This chapter examines various ways of regulating the activities of the multinational corporations and is designed to lead us to a decision about what needs to be done regarding multinational corporations.

Introduction

There is a growing realization among Third World countries that political independence did not bring them economic independence. Instead, it seems to have brought a new and more subtle form of foreign control over their resources and destinies. In light of the evidence presented in the last chapter especially, this should not surprise us. Consequently, many Third World countries denounced the multinational corporations at the third United Nations Conference on Trade and Development (UNCTAD III) in 1972. That Conference increased the momentum toward a series of provisions for regulating the multinational corporations.

The corporations are clearly aware of this struggle. As the President of IBM put it, "the critical issue of our time is the conceptual conflict between the search for global optimization of resources and the independence of nation-states."[1] In his view, the resolution of the conflict between Third World countries and the multinational corporations is the most important global economic issue today. Further, he feels that the economic future of the world will be threatened unless the world's resources are organized by those most capable of doing so—the multinational corporations. This seems to be what "global optimization of resources" means. As we have seen, many disagree with this corporate view.

Several factors have helped to surface this basic conflict to the point where it may be dealt with seriously.

(1) There is the economic leverage of the raw materials located in the Third World. These resources are so vital to the interests of the First World and its multinational corporations that they do not want to push the Third World to the point of restricting these resources. OPEC did it with oil in 1974 and it hurt.

(2) There is the increasing political leverage of the Third World within the United Nations. First World governments often find themselves in the minority now in voting in the UN's General Assembly.

(3) There is additional leverage for Third World countries because of increasing competition among First World countries for Third World markets and raw materials. For instance, Japan and Western European countries have taken positions on the Arab-Israeli conflict different from the U.S., partially because of their almost total dependence on Arab oil. Competition among First World (and Second World) countries in arms sales to the Third World has increased in the last few years.

(4) Finally, alliances among Third World countries ("collective self-reliance") have reduced somewhat the tremendous gap in bargaining power between the multinational corporations and Third World countries. Jamaica, for example, took the lead in organizing the International Bauxite Association (a group of eleven bauxite-producing nations). This OPEC-type

producer association has begun to negotiate with the multinational aluminum corporations for a redistribution of control over bauxite and over the revenues from it.

Four Major Conflict Areas

Chapter 9 pointed out a number of areas where Third World countries and the multinational corporations are in conflict. These included multinational take-overs of local Third World firms, multinational advertising, government anti-union activity as a way of attracting the multinationals, and others. But four issue areas continue to be the most pressing.

1. Economic Sovereignty

As Chapters 3 and 9 have shown, foreign ownership of land and other resources and control over decision-making in major sectors of the local economy are a serious matter for Third World countries. It is a concern shared by a number of First World countries as well. Canada is an excellent example. According to a *Time* magazine report,[2] direct investment by multinational corporations based in the U.S. has penetrated deep into Canadian industry. The following graph reveals how much Canada resembles a Third World country in this regard.

Canadian industries (1972)	% owned by U.S. corporations	Chilean industries[3] (1970)	% owned by First World (U.S.) MNCs
Oil refineries	99%	Automotive assembly	100%
Rubber factories	84%	Copper industry	80%
Chemical industry	78%	Chemical industry	60%
Transportation equipment'	73%	Iron, Steel & metal products	60%
90% of all Canadian plants that employ 5,000 or more workers are owned by U.S.-based multinational corporations		100% or nearly 100% of tobacco, copper fabricating, office equipment, pharmaceuticals, television and radio.	

2. Host Country's Share of the Wealth Created

This is the question of whether there is a net flow of capital into Third World countries. We saw in Chapter 9 how often the flow is actually in the opposite direction, that is, toward the corporate headquarters in the First World. This negative flow results from a combination of ingredients, primarily tax rates, dividends and royalties, the extent of corporations repatriating their profits, the cost of technology, and the mechanism of transfer-pricing. Remember how that hypothetical multinational automobile corporation was able to increase its profits by adjusting its costs around the world, so that the largest profits would show up in countries with the lowest tax rates. Third World countries would like to get a handle on all these channels through which money leaves their countries.

3. Extent of Local Processing

Third World countries are quite concerned that their raw materials are often not processed in their countries but are exported to First World corporations for processing. Chapter 4 showed how profits are usually much greater for manufactured or processed goods than for raw materials. Why should Ghana have to have its cocoa beans processed by Nestlé and Hershey? Why should Bolivia not be allowed to process its own tin? Why should its tin be exported to First World firms for conversion into manufactured goods like tin plate for roofing, tin foil, tin cans, many other tin goods, all of which Bolivia must then import back at much higher costs?

Similarly, we saw in Chapter 4 how Honduras gets only 1.8¢ for every 20¢ worth of bananas sold in the First World. It is the multinational corporations—United Brands (Chiquita), Castle & Cooke (Dole), and Del Monte who package and ship the bananas and Safeway and others who distribute them— that get the bulk of the 20¢. Honduras and other members of the Union of Banana Exporting Countries tried to change this situation by taxing every box of bananas exported, just as

Jamaica had done on its bauxite. But with alleged bribes for Honduran officials, according to the United Nations Development Program, United Brands was able to divide the Union and bring the tax down considerably.[4] Thus, the conflict remains.

4. The Existence of a Foreign Enclave

The multinational business community is frequently isolated from the Third World societies where they are located—physically, economically and socially isolated. In New Delhi, India, for instance, the US embassy compound (beautiful embassy headquarters, large swimming pool, snack bar and fine restaurant) and a US residential area effectively create an American ghetto. US government and business people work together, live together, socialize together, go to church together. While this is in many ways quite natural, it is also quite isolating. Living at the Gandhi Peace Foundation in New Delhi, I was amazed to discover that, even after just a few weeks in the country, I was being asked about what was going on in the country by people from the U.S. who had been in India for a couple of years.

If multinational corporations and banks want to become more sensitive to the needs of the Third World countries in which they are operating, their people have to break out of this ghetto and put themselves in touch with a variety of individuals and groups within those countries. When they are isolated from Third World societies, multinational corporations can easily engage in discrimination toward Third World individuals and businesses. Many multinationals make real efforts to hire Third World nationals for management as well as laboring positions. Others, however, do not. Some multinationals also tend to go to other First World firms for their supplies, for needed services, as well as for their banking. This is a sore point for many Third World countries.

These conflicts become even clearer in the following example. Although Energy Enterprises, Inc. is a hypothetical corporation trying to enter a hypothetical African nation, the scenario is not far from reality and the issues are quite real.

"Energy Enterprises, Inc.—Multinationals and the Third World"

Energy Enterprises, Inc. (EEI) has just made an offer to a central African country to mine and process that country's recently discovered uranium deposits. Only a month earlier, EEI had been stopped in its effort to develop the uranium on Native American reservation lands in the U.S. and is thus anxious to move into Africa. Aware that its competitors have similar agreements with other uranium-rich countries, EEI made the following offer to the government:

"To explore, mine, and process all uranium deposits for 25 years, under an agreement that would:

(1) allow EEI to have majority ownership of the operation (51% of the stock);

(2) allow EEI profits to be taxed at a 10% rate for the first 10 years once mining and processing had begun, with a willingness to renegotiate the tax rate after the 10-year period;

(3) establish no restrictions on how much of EEI profits could be repatriated or on what they can be reinvested in locally;

(4) permit EEI to limit the percentage of Black Africans in its managerial staff to 10%, with EEI willing to hire up to 75% of the remainder of its workforce from among Black Africans;

(5) establish a no-union clause, with government assurances that concrete steps will be taken to curb the growing union movement in the country;

(6) allow EEI to borrow up to $^2/_3$ of its investment capital from local sources."

This offer has been formally presented to the national legislature, with a request from EEI for a prompt response, to be followed immediately by a meeting to negotiate the agreement.

The situation in the Central African country is as follows: a high degree of dependence on its exports of coffee and tin. It imports much of its food, most of its manufactured goods, and all of its weapons. It has few highly qualified technicians and is considered by industrialized countries to be technologically "backward." Its national debt is rising alarmingly—because of rising costs for food, manufactured goods, and oil. Also, its tin prices have fallen. It has a history of comparative political stability, with three major political groupings represented in the national legislature: the Development Party (moderate) presently controls 50% of the seats; the Land Reform Party (left-wing) controls 25% of the seats; and the Security and Freedom Party (right-wing) controls the other 25%.

The negotiating positions of each group is as follows:

Energy Enterprises, Inc.

Anxious to gain a foothold in the vital uranium business, EEI is nevertheless aware that its offer asks no more than existing contracts in other countries. Each of the six items is important to it.

Item #1 allows EEI to dominate decision-making;

Item #2 increases its profits, as the corporate tax rate in the U.S. is 48%;

Item #3 protects EEI in case of nationalization and increases profitable investment possibilities; as with its bauxite lands in Jamaica, EEI wants to reinvest in land so it can limit any future competition;

Item #4 responds to EEI's skepticism about the managerial ability of Black Africans and its concern that its customers would probably be more comfortable dealing with white rather than Black EEI representatives;

Item #5 minimizes potential labor problems;

Item #6 allows EEI to minimize the use of its own capital in this venture, so as to free it for other ventures.

The Development Party

This party represents mostly urbanites, a small but growing business community, the moderate majority of the military, and others. It is anxious for the country to industrialize, to increase and diversify its exports, to shed its "backward" image, and play a prominent role within the Third World and the United Nations. It wants EEI to come in, but has difficulty with items #2, #3, #4, and #6 in EEI's offer. It wants more of the profit generated by the project to be available to the country. It is somewhat incensed by EEI's position on Black managers. And it is afraid that capital for local business operations will dry up if EEI gets item #6.

The Land Reform Party

This party represents the small farmers, farm workers, the tin miners, and many of the intellectuals. It is strongly opposed to the terms of the EEI offer. It sees EEI dominating the land resources which desperately need to be redistributed already. It is afraid of increasing industrialization, which would mean less national investment in rural development and a growing urban class wanting cheap food. It rejects item #5 completely and is skeptical about any agreement being possible.

The Security and Freedom Party

This party represents some of the military officers, all the large landowners, and some of the business community. It sees real possibilities in EEI's offer. It is particularly interested in the uranium as a source of weapons development and thus has trouble with item #1. It wants majority ownership to ensure that the uranium can be used for both weapons development and world military prestige. It is also hesitant about item #3, because its members own most of the land in the country and are not interested in EEI taking over any of it. Like the Development Party, it would like to keep more of the profits in the country, but it is generally attracted by the EEI offer.

Consider yourself a citizen of this central African country and answer the following questions:

(1) Which of the three political parties do you tend to identify with?

(2) What do you see as the advantages and the disadvantages of the project with EEI?

(3) What do you think your government's response to EEI should be?

(4) If "yes, but under certain conditions," then what would these specific conditions be and why?

Multinational Corporations and the NIEO

The EEI scenario and Chapter 9 both raise the same question. Can multinational corporations become a positive force for the development of the Third World, in cooperation with both the governments and the people of the Third World? Recent history shows that this question has been answered in several ways. "No" is the answer Third World countries give when they nationalize the corporations. They have come to the conclusion that the multinational corporation will not act in the interests of the country and so it must be taken over. A "code of conduct" for multinational corporations represents the "yes, if" answer. Multinational corporations need to be carefully regulated. If an effective set of conditions for the operations of multinationals can be designed with enforceable sanctions in case these conditions are not met, then, say many others, the multinational corporation may be a constructive institution. Both of these answers are found in the New International Economic Order.

1. The NIEO and the Right of Nationalization

As Chapter 3 pointed out, the NIEO—both in its *Charter of the Economic Rights and Duties of States* and in *The Principles for a NIEO*—makes a strong claim for the right of countries to nationalize foreign corporations in their countries. The NIEO calls for:

Full permanent sovereignty of every State over its natural resources and all economic activities. In order to safeguard these resources, each State is entitled to exercise effective control over them and their exploitation with means suitable to its own situation, including the right to nationalization or transfer of ownership to its nationals.[5]

Nationalization represents the most drastic exercise of this "full permanent sovereignty" in relationship to the multinational corporations. Between 1960 and mid-1974, the United Nations has identified 875 cases of nationalization in 62 Third World countries. According to the same UN report, 50% of these nationalizations involved multinational corporations based in England. While US-based multinationals account for about 50% of all direct foreign investment, 25% of nationalizations have involved these US-based corporations.[6]

Nationalization is an extremely emotional and volatile issue. Perhaps the best, as well as the most well-known, example in recent history was Chile's nationalization of its copper industry in 1971.[7] The economic situation in Chile in 1970 when Salvador Allende was elected its president was reflected in the graph on page 178. Much of Chile's economy was under foreign—mostly U.S.—control. Kennecott, Anaconda, and ITT had the largest direct investments in the country. Kennecott and Anaconda had controlled Chile's all important copper industry for about fifty years and accounted for 80% of Chile's foreign exchange earnings in 1970. No wonder Allende had committed himself to nationalizing the copper industry. No wonder Isabel Letelier, one of Chile's most courageous citizens, now in exile in the US, could exclaim:

In Chile, copper is life—because it is our main resource. We let the foreign companies come to our country and invest in our country, but they left very little tax money. In many ways foreign corporations were able to take out enormous wealth from Chile ...
The vote in Chile's Congress to nationalize the industry was unanimous. For the first time all the opposition

political parties agreed: "Copper for the Chileans." I
would love to share with you the exhilarating feeling that
people in my country had when Allende won the election . . . . It meant everything for us.[8]

Anaconda's 1972 Annual Report showed that while Chile
represented only 17% of Anaconda's worldwide investments,
it accounted for 80% of the company's worldwide net profits in
1969. According to a Jamaican economist, between 1915 and
1968, Anaconda's and Kennecott's combined net profits and
depreciation allowances from Chile totaled $2.011 billion.[9] No
wonder these multinational corporations fought Allende before the nationalization decision and wanted to get rid of him
after the decision. No wonder they went to court again and
again to get all the compensation they could. As Anaconda's
1972 Annual Report states:

> The expropriation [nationalization] of the company's in-
> vestments in Chile, which in the past constituted a major
> source of its funds and profits, required management to
> take extraordinary measures so as to minimize the effects
> of the expropriation on the company's future profitabil-
> ity.[10]

Pressed by the multinational corporations involved, concerned about further nationalizations of US-based multinationals and about similar actions by other governments, and
determined to discourage any further socialist governments
from coming to power, the U.S. Government seemed to want
to make an example of Allende and Chile. U.S. Senate staff
reports entitled *Covert Action in Chile: 1963–1973* and *Alleged
Assassination Plots Involving Foreign Leaders* reveal the incredible lengths the U.S. Government went to in trying to
undermine Allende and to discourage any further nationalizations. No wonder the U.S. Ambassador to Chile could write to
former Chilean president Eduardo Frei in September 1970:

> Not a nut or bolt will be allowed to reach Chile under
> Allende. Once Allende comes to power we shall do all

within our power to condemn Chile and the Chileans to
the utmost deprivation and poverty, a policy designed for
a long time to come to accelerate the hard features of a
communist society in Chile.[11]

Obviously, not all 875 nationalizations between 1960 and
1974 produced as intense a situation as the nationalizations in
Chile, but some did. To conclude this section, it is important to
consider whether nationalization is the best answer to those
multinational corporations perceived to be acting against the
interests of Third World countries. To answer this question in
any specific situation, it would be good to try to answer a
series of additional questions—

(1) How vital is the operation to the economy of the Third
World country involved?

(2) How intense and widespread among the people of the
country is support for the nationalization? They will have to
live with the repercussions.

(3) How quickly will the country be able to operate the
enterprise on its own or in cooperation with other Third
World countries?

(4) What other sources of capital and technology and
parts are available?

(5) What kind of retaliation can be expected from the
multinational corporation(s) and the First World?

2. A Code of Conduct for Multinational Corporations

Nationalization represents the drastic attempt of an individual country to get a hold on massive economic institutions
that span many countries and are really accountable to none.
The traditional institutional checks and balances on national
corporations—government, labor, and competition from other
corporations—are generally ineffective in face of the global
nature of the multinational corporations.

(a.) *Governments:* multinational corporations play one
government off against another. If you raise your corporate
income tax, we'll go somewhere else, they say. Unfortunately,

some Third World governments, anxious to pursue the style of development and way of living represented by the giant corporations, are quite willing to give the multinationals much of what they want. Breaking the united front among the banana countries, as we saw earlier, was a relatively simple matter.

(b.) *Labor:* although the term "international" appears in the title of a number of labor unions (e.g., the International Brotherhood of Teamsters), labor is *much* less unified internationally than the multinational corporations are. The corporations pit the unions in this country against Third World workers. They threaten to move their plants overseas ("runaway shops") if the union's wage demands escalate. The corporations have many choices; workers have few.

(c.) *Competition from other corporations:* we saw in Chapter 9 how multinational control over capital, technology, and communications has driven many local Third World enterprises into selling out to the multinational corporations. Some competition among the multinationals themselves exists, but more often these corporations form what is called an "oligopoly." That is, in contrast to a monopoly where a *single* corporation controls an industry, an oligopoly is several corporations controlling an industry. Examples are numerous: the seven giant multinational oil firms, the "big three" auto makers, the four breakfast cereal corporations that control 90% of the industry.

This is what many analysts call an "institutional lag." That is, there are no effective institutions to regulate the global activities of the multinational corporations. But two possibilities have begun to take shape, both of which involve a code of conduct for multinational corporations.

The first possibility has already been mentioned—collective self-reliance. We saw in Chapter 9 (p. 161) that the Andean countries of Latin America formed a united front called the "Andean Pact" to negotiate a better arrangement with the multinational corporations in their countries. Other Third World countries formed OPEC and the International

Bauxite Association for the same purpose. Joint regulations or a code of conduct (on tax rates, on % of foreign ownership, on repatriation and reinvestment limitations, etc.) prevent the corporations from playing one country against another.

In the hypothetical case of Energy Enterprises, Inc., the corporation had an advantage in that other Third World countries had already agreed to contracts similar to the one EEI was offering. If the central African nation had been part of a unified Organization of Uranium Exporting Countries, for instance, it might have had the leverage it needed to negotiate terms more favorable to its national interests.

The second possibility for regulating the multinational corporations is an expansion of the first—an international code of conduct. Third World countries have turned to the United Nations as the possible source of effective international restraints on the activities of the multinationals. In turn, with 875 nationalizations in a 15-year period, the First World countries where the corporations are based have been willing at least to look at something short of nationalization.

The alternative that has emerged from UN deliberations contains a threefold approach—

(1) a broad, internationally agreed upon code of conduct relating to the rights and duties of host countries, home countries (where the multinationals are based), and the corporations themselves. Such a code would have to be backed by appropriate arbitration machinery for resolving conflicts among the three groups.

(2) a firm and specific set of terms and conditions of entry and operation laid down by each host government regulating the activities of the multinational corporations. Both the country involved and the corporation need a degree of certainty for rational economic planning.

(3) adequate publicity, both of government regulations and of corporate performance. Regular evaluation of the relationship between the host country and the multinational cor-

poration enables the code of conduct to be kept up to date and in the best interests of all parties involved.[12]

More specifically, the code of conduct mandated by the *Programme of Action for the Establishment of a NIEO* is supposed to achieve five goals:

(1) "To prevent interference in the internal affairs of the countries where they operate and their collaboration with racist regimes and colonial administrations;

(2) "To regulate their activities in host countries, to eliminate restrictive business practices and to conform to the national development plans and objectives of developing countries, and in this context facilitate, as necessary, the review and revision of previously concluded arrangements;

(3) "To bring about assistance, transfer of technology and management skills to developing countries on equitable and favorable terms;

(4) "To regulate the repatriation of the profits accruing from their operations, taking into account the legitimate interests of all parties concerned;

(5) "To promote reinvestment of their profits in developing countries."[13]

The one item in this statement of goals that has not been discussed yet is #2—specifically, the notion of a national development plan. Without such a plan, the Third World country really has no basis for negotiating with a multinational corporation or any way of evaluating whether the activities of the corporation are consistent with national interests.

Progress to Date. As a result of this United Nations mandate, an intergovernmental Commission on Transnational Corporations was set up to advise the UN Economic and Social Council (ECOSOC) and a Center of Transnational Corporations was created to formulate the code of conduct. ECOSCO, the UN Development Program (UNDP), and other UN agencies have held a number of workshops around the world to assist Third World countries in the formulation of national rules governing foreign investment.

But little other progress is being made. In May 1977, the meetings to formulate the code of conduct were suspended. Representatives of First World and Third World countries were unable to agree on the specifics of the agenda. As of the spring of 1978, the stalemate continued.

Meanwhile, individual multinational corporations or groups of corporations have begun to formulate their own codes of conduct. Often under pressure from corporate responsibility groups (see Nestlé, Chapter 12), the corporations in these self-imposed codes generally address the bare minimum. For instance, with regard to multinational corporations in South Africa, at least 61 of them have agreed to a set of six principles calling for things like non-segregated facilities, equal pay for equal work for non-white workers, training programs and supervisory opportunities for non-white workers.[14] But these principles avoid the real justice issues in South Africa—denial of majority rule, severe repression, and the corporations' and banks' financial support of the government responsible for both.

Conclusion

Thus, there is a double problem with a code of conduct approach to regulate multinational corporations. First, the prescribed UN code of conduct is a statement of principles, not a treaty with legally binding sanctions. So long as First World governments obstruct an agreement even on principles, there will not be even a draft of a treaty or law to regulate the multinationals.

The second problem holds for the nationalization strategy as well as for the code of conduct. Unless the Third World governments formulating the code (or nationalizing the corporations) are committed to bread and justice, that is, to the vision of development summarized in Girvan's last statement, then the additional benefits reach only a fraction of the population of the Third World. So we come to the same conclusion as we did in Part II on trade. A New International Economic Order without fundamental changes within many Third World countries (a "new internal economic order") may actually impede the realization of bread and justice.

Discussion Questions

1. Why are each of the four areas of conflict between Third World countries and multinational corporations important to the Third World?
2. See the questions about Energy Enterprises, Inc., on page 184.
3. Do you think nationalization of multinational corporations is ever necessary? If not, why not? If so, under what circumstances?
4. Why is *international* regulation of multinational corporations necessary?
5. How adequate do you think the UN's code of conduct is?
6. What would be the most effective strategy or combination of strategies to ensure that Energy Enterprises, Inc. operates in the best interests of the central African country—a clear code of conduct from the beginning, the formation of an Organization of Uranium Exporting Countries to deal collectively with companies like EEI, or nationalization of EEI?

Resources

On the Conflict between Multinational Corporations and the Third World
    —*The Impact of the Multinational Corporation on Development and on International Relations* (Report of the Group of Eminent Persons to the Secretary-General of the UN; New

York: United Nations Publications, 1974) is one official resource to go with the many works cited in Chapters 8–11.

On the Code of Conduct, the UN, and Multinational
Corporations
        —The UN Center on Transnational Corporations puts out
a newsletter that updates its efforts at establishing the code of
conduct as well as provides information of the multinational
corporations. Write the Center at United Nations Plaza, New
York, NY 10017.
        —For a critique of the multinational corporations' own
codes of conduct, write the Interfaith Center for Corporate
Responsibility.

On the Chapter as a Whole
        —Two outstanding AV resources on multinational corpo-
rations and the Third World are
        "Sharing   Global   Resources"   (NARMIC/American
Friends Service Committee), a 45-minute filmstrip (or slide)
presentation featuring the multinational corporations in
Chile, Jamaica, and Appalachia (a little more than half of the
total presentation); and
        "Guess Who's Coming to Breakfast?" (Packard-Manse,
Box 450, Stoughton, MA 02072), a 20-minute filmstrip on the
impact of Gulf and Western on the Dominican Republic where
the corporation controls a large part of the sugar industry.
Like "Sharing Global Resources," it also shows how the corporation relates to us. Both AVs were well-done technically as
well as in terms of their content.
        —Rev. Michael Crosby, *Catholic Church Investments for*
Corporate Social Responsibility (Justice and Peace Office, 3900
N. Third, Milwaukee, WI 53212; 1975), presents a theological
rationale, plus ethical guidelines, for calling corporations to
social responsibility.

Chapter Eleven

WHAT CAN I DO?

Chapters eight, nine, and ten have shown us that multinational corporations need to be radically changed if bread and justice are to become realities for people in the Third World. This Chapter is designed to help us see ways in which we might participate in bringing about such change. Before considering these action possibilities, let's see how closely linked with the multinational corporations our lives are.

How Multinational Corporations Relate to Us

Some of us have close ties with the multinationals. We may own stock in one or more of them. We may have relatives who work for one of them. We may put our money in banks that loan to South Africa. Those of us who do not have these direct connections are nevertheless linked to the multinationals in many other ways.

As the title of the excellent filmstrip asks, "guess who's coming to breakfast?", if we examine what we eat for breakfast, we will probably find that a number of multinational corporations have joined us at table.

—Perhaps Coca-Cola, source of all those soft drinks that undermine the diets of people in almost every village of the world (Chap. 9, pp. 169-171). Coke owns the Minute Maid orange juice we may be drinking.

—Perhaps General Foods, formerly the world's largest purchaser of Ugandan coffee so necessary for Idi Amin's economic survival (Chapter 7, p. 118). General Foods is also one of the four members of the breakfast cereal oligopoly, providing us with a variety of Post cereals for our breakfast.

—Perhaps our bowl of Post Grape Nuts Flakes has a slice of Del Monte pineapple or a United Brands (Chiquita) banana on it. We have seen the impact of Del Monte and United Brands on the Third World, especially on small farmers (Chapters 6 and 9).

—Perhaps we sweeten our cereal or our cup of coffee or tea with some Domino sugar. Who controls Domino sugar? The same multinational corporation that controls a large part of the sugar industry in the Dominican Republic and that has relentlessly fought the unionization of its workers there—Gulf and Western.

—Perhaps we top off our breakfast with a big cup of Nescafe or Tasters' Choice coffee. Sure enough, another multinational at our table—this time it is Nestlé. Chapter 12 describes their impact on the Third World.

—Where did we buy all these breakfast foods? On the West Coast, perhaps it was from Safeway, another of the agribusiness giants that have caused great concern to many people, especially small farmers.

But we have only been up for one hour and have not even left the house and yet half a dozen multinational corporations have entered our life. It is hard to avoid meeting them, for they are part of our lives in myriads of ways. And when we buy their products, we lend—unintentionally—a tiny bit of support to their activities.

The point here, though, is not to overwhelm us with guilt (guilt comes only when we are aware of an evil and choose to continue to support it). Nor is it to call for one great act of boycott—no more Safeway or any other multinational corporation in my stomach ever again! There are too many of them to get rid of them all at once. Chapter 7 (pp. 126-7) examined this question of boycotts more carefully. Here the point is rather one of awareness—how much we participate in a multinational corporate world.

But we are much more than passive, unwitting supporters of the corporations. We are also their victims. It is not just Third World people who have to worry about the impact of the multinationals on their lives. We do too. After examining six areas of our lives as individuals and as a community that are negatively affected by the multinationals, maybe we will be even more ready to act.

1. Food

How costly and nutritious is the food we get from the multinational corporations? Coke, Del Monte's Granny Goose potato chips, Nestlé chocolate bars, General Foods' Cocoa Pebbles and Fruity Pebbles cereals are all low-nutrition foods on which more and more of us are getting hooked each year. There is a growing problem of malnourishment in the U.S. as well as in the Third World.

2. Needs and Values

Corporate advertising tells us that having things is what will make us happy. To be liked and valued by others, we should dress, smoke, drive, eat, drink, brush our teeth, and use deodorants in certain ways. Women are treated as sex objects and told that it is how they "wrap their package" that will determine their happiness. "We are what we have" is the message drummed into us by commercial after commercial.

THIS IS WHAT YOU PAY ...

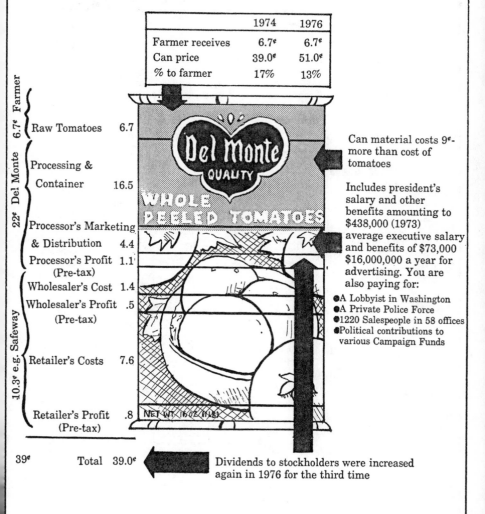

	1974	1976
Farmer receives	6.7¢	6.7¢
Can price	39.0¢	51.0¢
% to farmer	17%	13%

Farmer 6.7¢

Raw Tomatoes 6.7

Del Monte 22¢

Processing & Container 16.5

Processor's Marketing & Distribution 4.4

Processor's Profit 1.1
(Pre-tax)

Safeway 10.3¢ e.g.

Wholesaler's Cost 1.4

Wholesaler's Profit .5
(Pre-tax)

Retailer's Costs 7.6

Retailer's Profit .8
(Pre-tax)

39¢ Total 39.0¢

Can material costs 9¢ more than cost of tomatoes

Includes president's salary and other benefits amounting to $438,000 (1973) average executive salary and benefits of $73,000 $16,000,000 a year for advertising. You are also paying for:
- A Lobbyist in Washington
- A Private Police Force
- 1220 Salespeople in 58 offices
- Political contributions to various Campaign Funds

Dividends to stockholders were increased again in 1976 for the third time

CAN YOU AFFORD ALL THESE COSTS?

It is estimated in Jim Hightower's *Eat Your Heart Out* that in 1972 consumers were overcharged $193,000,000 on canned fruits and vegetables.

THIS IS WHAT YOU PAY FOR ...

The food in this can was inspected by a government inspector—but Del Monte pays half the cost of the inspector, including half the salary of the inspector.

The brand name you pay for: Delmonte products sell at a premium, from a few pennies to 15¢-20¢ more than other lesser known brands, massive advertising ($16 MILLION - 1974 -), and a sales force of over 1200 convinces many people and stores to buy Delmonte products.

Del Monte QUALITY
WHOLE PEELED TOMATOES

Major food companies have consistently lobbied against more accurate labelling, such as listing ingredients by percentage & contents by drained weight.

Not only does processing destroy large percentages of important nutrients, it has been recently suggested that the quantity of certain minerals in such vegetables as tomatoes has been diminishing because of decreasing soil quality, unbalanced use of fertilizer, and development of mechanically harvestable tomatoes.

NET WT.. 16 oz (1LB) or 454 grams CUPS. APPROX 2

INGREDIENT: TOMATOES, TOMATO JUICE, SALT, WITH TRACE OF CALCIUM SALT ADDED.

CALORIES...50   CARBOHYDRATE 10 gm
PROTEIN..2 gm   FAT.......0 gm

PERCENTAGE OF US. RECOMMENDED DAILY: ALLOWANCE (U.S. RDA) PER ONE CUP SERVING
VITAMINS   MINERALS

VITAMIN A   NIACIN   6
VITAMIN C   CALCIAM   4
THIAMIN B,   IRON   4
RIBOFLAVIN B2   PHOSPHORUS   4
                   MAGNESIUM   6

24000 01326

Net weight tells you how much the contents weigh minus can weight. It does *not* tell you how much of that is tomatoes, water, sugar, or added starch. For example:

1969 USDA figures showed that:

Townhouse
whole leaf spinach 15 oz.
= About 8% more spinach than ...
    Del Monte 15 oz.
    Whole leaf spinach
Hanover house
Cut green beans 16 oz.
= 3-4% more beans and less liquid than ...
    Del Monte 16 oz.
    cut green beans
Townhouse
Fruit cocktail
= 4-5% more fruit cocktail, less liquid than
    Del Monte fruit cocktail

An informal survey by Earthwork showed that ...
Contadina
whole peeled tomatoes 14½ oz.
= about 8% more tomatoes than ...
    Del Monte 16 oz.
    whole peeled tomatoes

This computerized code, chosen in a secret meeting in March 1973, was worked out by representatives from Delmonte, Gen. Foods, Greenbelt Co-Op Stores, H.J. Heinz, Proctor & Gamble, Red Owl Stores, Safeway, and Winn Dixie Stores, and an attorney. The public interest was not represented. This system will cost $5 Bill. to install (about 150,000/store), will eliminate more jobs and individual item pricing and result in little if any saving to consumers.

"For the good life" we are told we need Lancers wine, a beautiful escort, and a moonlit lake resort. Novelty and "more" are king. The corporations try to shape our feelings, wants, and even values to expand their sales. We are victims, though all too willing victims at times.

3. Jobs

As we saw in Chapters 6 and 9, "runaway shops" and "export platforms" mean fewer jobs for us. A 1973 U.S. Senate Finance Committee study put the figure at 1.3 million jobs. According to Barnet and Muller,[1] between 1966 and 1972, more than 50,000 jobs were created along the Mexican border, paying one-sixth of the U.S. wage scale. The pattern of employment in the U.S. is changing. Production jobs are moved away and service jobs like computer programming and packaged-food sales are created. The result is a redistribution of income and wealth from the working class to middle and upper middle class management people. It seems to get harder for many of us to find jobs each year.

4. "Participation"

Growing multinational corporate control over U.S. food production, corporate power to further shape us into a nation of consumers through advertising, and control over the kinds and number of jobs available all mean a reduction in our control over our own lives. This is true of us as individuals and as a society. The planning power of the multinationals is enormous. The multinational energy giants, for instance, have the power to decide how much and what kinds of oil, gas, and other forms of energy will be available and at what price and in what parts of the country. Every cold winter we struggle through, every enormous heating bill, and continuing high prices at gas station pumps should remind us of our victimization.

5. Public Services

Working class and middle class people are increasingly angry and frustrated as their taxes go up and their purchasing power goes down. They are the "have-lesses" who have been convinced for the most part that their enemies are the communists and the "have-nots" (the poor and their welfare programs). As a result, multinational corporations involved in military-related production, with very few exceptions, continue to prosper and military priorities continue to eat up our tax dollars. Badly needed public services like mass transportation, education, health care, housing, food programs, job training, and others continue to suffer underfunding. The victims? *Both* the "have-nots" and the "have-lesses."

6. Our Environment

As the law of supply and demand makes food, energy, and other precious aspects of our existence more and more profitable, primarily for the corporations with the power to cash in, we are victimized in yet another way. The eco-system in which and on which human existence is based is threatened today as never before. Fish, and thus people, are the victims of industrial pollution. Farm lands have been destroyed by mining companies. Radio-active wastes from nuclear weapons and nuclear power plants—both multinational operations in most cases—threaten life and the environment on an unprecedented scale.

What Others Are Doing

1. Action-oriented Research

Researching multinational corporations and banks is listed under action suggestions because it is crucial that research be geared to action. Chapter 1 pointed out how overwhelmed and paralyzed we can feel when we become aware of problems but do not have opportunities for action to address these problems. Students need, we all need, and the world needs ways of using research for building the human community—for promoting justice and human development.

(a.) *How to do a case study of a multinational corporation.* Write to the Interfaith Center for Corporate Responsibility (ICCR) for a list of corporations about which it is most concerned, for a list of action coalitions dealing with specific corporations that you might be interested in researching, and for some specific research leads on the particular corporation(s) you chose to research.

Write the appropriate action coalition(s) and other action-oriented groups dealing with the corporation(s) selected, asking for information they have on it, where further information is available, some action possibilities, and whether there are aspects of the corporation(s) that need to be researched and whether you would be able to help them in this.

Write the appropriate multinational corporations themselves, asking for their annual reports, for any specific reports or publications they have available on specific aspects of your study (the more specific you can be the better the information you will generally receive), for answers to pertinent questions you have already identified and for which you want the corporation's perspective.

Obtain a copy of *Open the Books: How to Research a Corporation* (written by The Community Press Features and available from Urban Planning Aid, Inc., 639 Massachusetts Ave., Cambridge, MA 02139) and of the *NACLA Research Methodology Guide* (NACLA, Box 57, Cathedral Station, New York, NY 10025). NACLA's 72-page *Guide* has a 5-page section on how to research a corporation that is excellent. *Open the Books* is a 100-page volume that expands NACLA's *Guide*, adding such things as how to read bank and corporate financial statements. It focuses on banks as well as corporations. NACLA's *Guide* does shorter pieces on elites, political parties, the media, labor organizations, universities and the military-industrial complex, the police, the churches and the health industry, and imperialism in the Third World.

The standard library volumes to consult for information on the history of a particular corporation, its domestic and foreign affiliates, its plant locations, the type of products it generates, etc., are *Moody's Manuals* (separate volumes are published annually on four areas—industrial corporations, utilities, transportation, and banking and finance) and *Standard & Poor's Corporation Records* (6 volumes are published annually, with up-dated daily news items).

Write the Corporate Data Exchange (198 Broadway, New York, NY 10038) for information on who owns stock and how much in each corporation. Their focus in 1977–1978 was on corporations involved in food and agriculture.

(b.) *How to research multinational banks.* The first four steps on doing a case study on a multinational corporation are appropriate here too, especially the use of *Open the Books.* Another valuable research guide here is William Batko, *How to Research Your Local Bank (Or Savings & Loan Association)* (Institute for Local Self-Reliance, 1976, 34 pages).

Howard M. Wachtel, *The New Gnomes: Multinational Banks in the Third World* (Washington, DC: The Transnational Institute, 1977, 60 pages) is an excellent overview of the growth of multinational banks and their activities in the Third World.

Find local groups involved in local banking issues like the "red-lining" (refusing to give mortgage and home improvement loans) of neighborhoods. They are valuable allies, sources of information and strategies, and provide the opportunity to make some of the local-global linkages so important in research and action. The Association of Community Organizations for Reform Now (ACORN, 628 Baronne, New Orleans, LA 70113) has offices in the states of AR, LA, TN, TX, FLA, MO, CO, NV, PA, SD, IA, OK, MI.

Write the Committee to Oppose Bank Loans to South Africa (305 E. 46th St., New York, NY 10017) for copies of their excellent 3-page guide on "Suggestions on How to Research Your Bank's Possible Involvement in Making Loans to South Africa." It offers suggested questions for raising with your bank itself, ways of finding out information that the bank will not release to you, and some background reading.

2. Action Based on This Research

The Nestlé case study in the next chapter provides a variety of action suggestions, as Chapter 7 does on Del Monte. In relationship to multinational banks as well as to multinational corporations, the following action possibilities have been generated by groups working to end the support of *apartheid* in South Africa. ICCR, the Committee to Oppose Bank

Loans to South Africa (COBLSA), the American Friends Service Committee, and the American Committee on Africa (305 E. 46th St., New York, NY 10017) are the best sources of information on the suggestions and on what groups are available in your local area to consult and work with. These action possibilities are based on an ICCR list and are included here to open up our imaginations as to what is possible.

(a.) Support stockholder resolutions filed by ICCR groups, if you own stock in Citibank, Continental Illinois, First National Bank of Chicago, Manufacturers Hanover Trust, Morgan Guaranty, Bank of America, Crocker National Bank, First Boston Corporation. ICCR knows where and when to write.

(b.) Withdraw your bank account from these and other banks making loans directly or indirectly to South Africa and deposit them in banks that do not make such loans (write COBLSA for lists of both), or write to the Corporate Data Exchange, 198 Broadway, N.Y., N.Y. 10038, for the most up-to-date list of banks involved in South Africa. There are other important criteria for where to bank, so ask around.

(c.) Show the slide presentation "Banking on South Africa" (see Resources) to church, school, and civic groups.

(d.) Encourage your Congresspersons, the President, and our UN ambassador to press the issue of South Africa at the United Nations and in direct U.S.-South Africa dealings.

(e.) Become a resource center for information on this issue, using ICCR's "Bank Packet", the World Council of Churches' booklet "The WCC and Bank Loans to Apartheid" (from ICCR), and COBLSA's materials including "The ABCs of U.S. Bank Loans to South Africa: A Primer."

(f.) Write (letters to editors and articles in school papers, neighborhood newspapers, and other local newsletters and journals) an article on this issue and on what people can do.

(g.) Help organize and release an open letter from prominent Black persons and others in your area condemning the banks for their loans and calling for their cessation.

(h.) Help organize an effort to get your school, church, union, or other group to examine whether it has stock or does business with banks that are involved in South Africa. If so, visit with these groups and ask that the issue of continued participation in such a bank (or corporation) be considered and what other actions might be taken. Church boards, parish councils, or church finance committees ought to consider such moral questions. Write the National Council of Churches (475 Riverside Drive, New York, N.Y. 10027) for a description of their actions and statements in withdrawing their funds from such banks in November 1977.

(i.) Oppose the sale of the Kruggerrand (the South African gold piece highly advertised in major U.S. cities) by any bank anywhere, as another tangible link with *apartheid*.

(j.) Participate in personally and/or help organize local participation in national days of bank withdrawals—as on March 21, the day commemorating the massacre at Sharpsville in 1961, and June 16, the anniversary of the 1976 Soweto uprising. Activities can include
  —lines of people making withdrawals inside banks;
  —demonstration picket line outside the bank;
  —distribution of anti-loan materials inside the bank;
  —guerrilla theatre activity, where the issue is dramatized;
  —special letter to bank employees explaining the campaign.

(k.) If you or some friends belong to a union, raise the question of where the union pension fund is invested (contact COBLSA and ICCR for details on the Furriers Joint Council of New York withdrawals of more than $10 million from Manufacturers Hanover Trust on July 21, 1977).

3. Community Organization to Oppose the Multinational Corporations

One of the most important actions that Barnet and Muller describe in *Global Reach* challenging the inequities of present multinational involvement in First and Third World communities is for the communities to organize themselves, formulate economic development plans, and to negotiate with the corporations on the basis of these plans.[2]

One impressive example of how a community successfully resisted a multinational corporation is provided by Community Action on Latin America (CALA). Residents of Rusk County, Wisconsin, with some help from this small Wisconsin-based group of researchers and organizers, challenged the re-entry of Kennecott in their county. Rusk County was one of the areas of northern Wisconsin which Kennecott and others had deserted a couple of decades earlier, to concentrate on operations in Chile, Puerto Rico, and elsewhere. With the nationalization of the copper mines in Chile in 1971 (see Chapter 10, pp. 185-7), Kennecott began returning to the U.S.

Kennecott found, however, that the memories of severe economic depression that resulted from the earlier abandonment had not been erased in the minds of workers and their families. Food and the environment were also crucial issues. As Roscoe Churchill, educator and part-time farmer, testified before the Rusk County Board of Supervisors, November 10, 1976:

Kennecott tells us that the mine will be a boost for the local economy. But we have seen that eleven farms have already been bought up which could have supported generations of farmers on them. We're trading good farmland for eleven years of mining employment and irreversible damage to the environment. I want to be able to pass on to my daughters this good farmland. I want them to be able to draw sustenance from the earth, drink the water and breathe clean air. Kennecott will take this away from all of us forever if we allow them to mine here.[3]

The Rusk County Citizens Action Group was formed in March 1976. It used the public hearings on Kennecott's environmental impact statement as a focus for public education. In less than a year, Kennecott's copper mining plans for Rusk County had come to a halt. Other groups in the region— the Chippewa Indians in their dealings with Exxon and the Phelps Dodge Corporation—have been encouraged by the Rusk County Citizens Action Group.

With this and other models and with the realization that multinational corporations can be successfully resisted, despite their tremendous power, local groups can begin to assess their situations and develop strategies. ACORN and other groups challenging the private utilities around the country, National Land for People and the other groups described in Chapter 7 on trade would be valuable sources of information and strategies, as well as good subjects for research projects. If a multinational corporation is considering moving its plant out of your community, especially if it is moving it to the Third World, you have a clear issue around which to mobilize people.

4. Other Action Possibilities

(a.) *Peace Conversion Campaigns.* One special case of communities challenging corporations to be more responsive to human needs concerns the corporations involved in military production. The Mid-Peninsula Conversion Project (c/o American Friends Service Committee, 2160 Lake St., San

Francisco, CA 94114) is one group working to convert some of the defense industry in the San Francisco Bay Area (Lockheed and a number of electronics firms) to production for human needs. Clergy and Laity Concerned and the American Friends Service Committee (see Appendix) have organized national campaigns on this issue, including the successful effort to terminate the B-1 Bomber. Currently these groups are focusing on multinational corporations like General Electric, General Dynamics (makers of the Trident submarine), and others. Local chapters of CALC and AFSC can use our help. Write the national offices for local addresses, if necessary.

(1) Creative public demonstrations have included a "tug-of-war" between people dressed as corporations and weapons and people representing unmet human needs like clinics, houses, schools. Others have organized festivals or marches celebrating life in the face of weapons of death.

(2) Especially effective as a community event have been the "peace conversion fairs" organized in different communities around the country. Groups representing many of the alternative uses for the billions of dollars of waste in the military budget set up booths describing or offering their alternatives. These fairs are celebrations of life at the same time that they challenge corporate involvement in weapons production.

(3) Civil disobedience has also been part of the nonviolent resistance to corporations producing nuclear weapons. On the two Coasts, the Pacific Life Communities (Seattle; San Francisco; Westminster, B.C.; and elsewhere—write 335 8th St., New Westminster, British Columbia V3M 3R3) and Atlantic Life Communities (c/o Jonah House, 1933 Park Ave., Baltimore, MD 21217) have been challenging Lockheed, General Dynamics, and the military over the Trident submarine.

(b.) *Agribusiness Campaigns.* In addition to the actions suggested in Chapter 7, the Agribusiness Accountability Project (1095 Market Street, San Francisco, CA 94103) recommends two actions to support the small farmers in their struggle against the corporations taking over farming in this country. First, they urge us to buy our fruits, vegetables, and other items directly from the small farmers. Farmers' markets in urban areas are excellent places to buy from area farmers. Secondly, they suggest that we write to our State agricultural college(s) and urge them to research and develop agricultural technology that is appropriate for smaller farmers. At present, most of the technology developed addresses the needs of corporate farmers.

(c.) *Television Campaigns.* Groups working to reduce television violence; to change the images and roles assigned to women, the elderly and handicapped, and racial minorities; and to challenge the corporations on their advertising, especially to children, have come up with a variety of strategies and some successes. Action for Children's Television (ACT—46 Austin Street, Newtonville, MA 02160) has been especially resourceful and successful in their efforts to eliminate commercialism from children's TV. Subscribe to their newsletter and write them for action suggestions. In general, letter-writing campaigns to the local TV stations, to the national networks, and to the corporations sponsoring the shows or responsible for the ads have proven successful on occasion.

What Do I Do?

As we did in Part II, let's examine a series of questions that will help us evaluate all the possibilities suggested in this chapter—

(1) Which action(s) have the best chance of succeeding?

(2) Which actions are important enough to do whether or not they have a chance of succeeding?

(3) Which actions mobilize (or have the potential to mobilize) the largest number of people?

(4) Which actions put us (or come closest to putting us) in direct contact with the victims?

(5) Which actions do the victims say they want other people to do?

(6) Which actions involve the victims themselves in leadership positions?

(7) Which actions have the greatest potential for long-term change in the practices and policies of the institution(s) involved?

(8) Which actions have actual groups working on them?

(9) Which actions have the best potential for surfacing links between local problems and global problems?

Having sorted through these possible actions, try to answer the following questions to help you decide which one of the actions makes the most sense for you at this point in your life—

(1) Which action seems to fit best with your own concerns, knowledge, skills, and time?

(2) Which action is most likely to deepen and sustain your commitment to bread and justice?

(3) Which action would have the best potential for generating the support of others that you feel you would need to carry it off?

Resources

On How Multinational Corporations Relate to Us
   —Regarding food, three resources would be helpful: the Agribusiness Accountability Project and its *AgBiz Tiller* (see Chap. 7, p. 135); *Food for People, Not for Profit: A Source Book on the Food Crisis* (New York: Ballantine Books, 1975); and James Hightower, *Eat Your Heart Out.*
   —"Hamburger USA: A Closer Look" is a slide presentation produced by the American Friends Service Committee (2160 Lake St., San Francisco, CA 94114). It examines the ingredients of the hamburger (bun, lettuce, tomato, cheese, meat) pointing out numerous problems with the food industry in this country as it becomes more and more controlled by multinational corporations.

—Regarding advertising, John Kavanaugh, SJ, has prepared a graphic slideshow on ads depicting persons as objects, objects as personal, and the extent of manipulation in advertising. Invite him to share his presentation (c/o St. Louis University, St. Louis, MO 63103). The Economic Justice Program of the Justice and Peace Center (3900 N. Third, Milwaukee, WI 53212) has prepared a booklet entitled "Children and Ads." It is an excellent guide for working with young people, parents, and teachers on commercialism and young people.

—Regarding public services, Clergy and Laity Concerned (CALC) and the Coalition for a New Foreign and Military Policy (120 Maryland Ave SE, Washington, DC 20002) are two of the groups working on what is called the "Transfer Amendment", a piece of legislation designed to transfer several billions of dollars from the military budget to areas of human needs.

—Regarding the environment, National Land for People's "Discover America" slideshow (see Chapter 7, p. 132); NARMIC's "Sharing Global Resources" slideshow, especially the section on Appalachia (see Chapter 10 "Resources"); and the pastoral letter of the Appalachian Catholic bishops, *This Land Is Home to Me* (see Chapter 13 "Resources").

On What Others Are Doing
—See "Resources" in Chapters 7, 9 and 10.
—On the Kennecott example, Al Gedicks, *Kennecott Copper Corporation and Mining Development in Wisconsin* (Community Action on Latin America, 731 State Street, Madison, WI 53703) provides an excellent outline of a research-action project and relates the Rusk County issue with corporate involvement in Chile and Puerto Rico. $1.00. Gedicks has also produced a 25-minute, 16mm film entitled "The Shaping of an Era". This gives an oral history by retired miners who worked for the multinational corporations in northern Wisconsin. It has been used as an effective organizing tool in mobilizing

Rusk County residents in their efforts to stop the return of Kennecott. Available for rental from CALA.

—Susan Kinsella, *Food on Campus: A Recipe for Action* (Emmaus, PA: Rodale Press, 1978) is a step-by-step guide to improving a college food service operation, with a consideration of junk foods, nutritional education, and good vending.

—The Food Action Center and the Center for Science in the Public Interest (1755 "S" Street NW, Washington, DC 20009) also publish a teaching and action guide entitled *Food: Where Nutrition, Politics and Culture Meet.* It examines nutrition, advertising and marketing of foods, food and the environment, and the relationship between U.S. policy and world hunger. The Center's *Nutrition Action* is a monthly magazine on these same issues.

Chapter Twelve

NESTLÉ: A CASE STUDY OF A MULTINATIONAL CORPORATION

Nestlé has been chosen for special consideration not because it has the worst record of corporations operating in the Third World. Rather, because of what the corporation has revealed about itself and because of the extensive research on Nestlé by many different groups around the world, we know more about Nestlé than many other corporations. Because of this wealth of information both from Nestlé and from its critics, this chapter is presented in "point-counterpoint" fashion. It concludes with an invitation to action and a number of suggestions about what to do.

Introduction[1]

N-E-S-T-L-E-S is a familiar household jingle in this country. But not many people know that Nestlé of White Plains, New York, is actually a subsidiary of the largest multinational food corporation in the world. Nestlé Alimentana S.A. (the corporation's full name) is headquartered in Vevey, Switzerland, and is the 19th largest multinational corporation outside the U.S. With over $10 billion of sales in 1977, Nestlé is larger than the Gross National Product of 108 countries! By 1978, Nestlé had 140,000 employees and 294 plants in some 52 countries, 70 plants in Latin America alone. It does about 47% of its business in Europe, 20% in the Third World, and most of the rest in Japan and the U.S. By 1977, Nestlé's U.S. sales had reached $2 billion (about 20% of the total) and the corporation is committed to doubling that total to $4 billion by 1982.

Although today, *Fortune* magazine can call Nestlé the most "multi" of the multinational corporations, it was not always so. Begun in 1866 as a baby food business, Nestlé first expanded in 1905 when it merged with another small condensed milk business. The 1947 takeover of Alimentana, an important Swiss food company, brought Nestlé into the food business in a bigger way. In 1974, Nestlé took over a French cosmetics company and began its diversification efforts in earnest. The purchase of Alcon Laboratories shortly after that made Nestlé a large pharmaceutical company as well. But as a Swiss-based corporation with tight control over its limited and very expensive shares of stock (about $1500 per share), Nestlé stock is not available on either the New York or the American Stock Exchanges.

In this country, we know Nestlé through a variety of products. Nestlé's Quik, Nestlé's Crunch, Nescafe, Nestea, and Tasters' Choice are the most familiar. But there are also Libby's packaged foods, Stouffer's Restaurants and Frozen Foods, Souptime instant soups, Sunrise instant coffee with chicory, Choco-Chill cold chocolate drink, and Lunchtime 3-minute casseroles.

In the Third World, Nestlé is also known for its infant formula—Lactogen and Nan—and its weaning food—Cerelac. Nestlé's involvement in the Third World really began in 1921 when it opened its first plant—a factory in Brazil. Now it employs about 42,000 workers in the Third World. As the largest buyer of cocoa in the world and as Europe's largest buyer of coffee, Nestlé has a profound effect on single export economies, as we saw in Chapter 4 (pages 63-65). Nestlé considers itself an important engine of development for the Third World and points to the fact that it was almost the only foreign company not nationalized by Allende in Chile. As the cover of its own publication, *Nestlé in the Developing Countries*, states—

> While Nestlé is not a philanthropic society, facts and figures clearly prove that the nature of its activities in developing countries is self-evident as a factor that contributes to economic development. The company's constant need for local raw materials, processing and staff, and the particular contribution it brings to local industry, support the fact that Nestlé's presence in the Third World is based on common interests in which the progress of one is always to the benefit of the other.[2]

But many people and countries have come to a different conclusion. Nestlé has been challenged in recent years by church groups, the health profession, some Third World governments, and many others because of one item—its infant formula. The concern is not so much the formula itself. It is as good as any other infant formula. Rather, the concern stems from the aggressive marketing of this artificial formula to poor women in the Third World. The results of these marketing practices are summarized in the chart on the next page and are the focus of this case study.

But Nestlé is not the only "villain." The other major infant formula multinationals have similar marketing practices with similar consequences. Abbot Laboratories, American Home Products, and Bristol-Myers, are engaged in similar efforts to offset declining birth rates and the rate of growth of formula sales in the First World by rapid expansion of sales in the Third World. Such expansion means selling formula to the many poor women as well as the few rich women.

Nevertheless, Nestlé is the focus of a national boycott campaign for three main reasons. First, it sells more infant formula in the Third World than any of its competitors. The most frequently used conservative figure is 33% of the Third World market—more than $300 million.[3] Nestlé's standard response to this figure is to ask for its source, but it has never provided any figure of its own. Secondly, because Nestlé stock is not available to U.S. citizens, it cannot be challenged through stockholder resolutions as all the U.S.-based infant formula corporations have been for several years. Finally, Nestlé has been the least cooperative and responsive of all the infant formula corporations. Several years of dialogue with the corporation has produced no substantial changes. Thus, a boycott is the only means left to challenge Nestlé's destructive marketing practices in the Third World.

The three categories for presenting the case study in Chapter 9 will also be used here—control over capital, technology, and marketing. Although this will mean putting an item in one category when it could fit two categories, it does provide continuity and a little extra clarity.

Three Ways Nestlé Affects Hunger

1. Control over Capital

Infant formula means spending scarce capital on an expensive, generally unnecessary "modern convenience." Among affluent women, the choice between breast feeding and bottle feeding may be based on personal choice, but this choice is a critical one for poor women. As the following graph from the United Nations' Protein Advisory Group[5] indicates, the cost of infant formula in many Third World countries is more than half of the total income of families receiving the minimum wage! As the document from Fatima Patel—a nurse who has worked with Third World women for more than 15 years—indicates (see pages 220-22), few of these poorer fam-

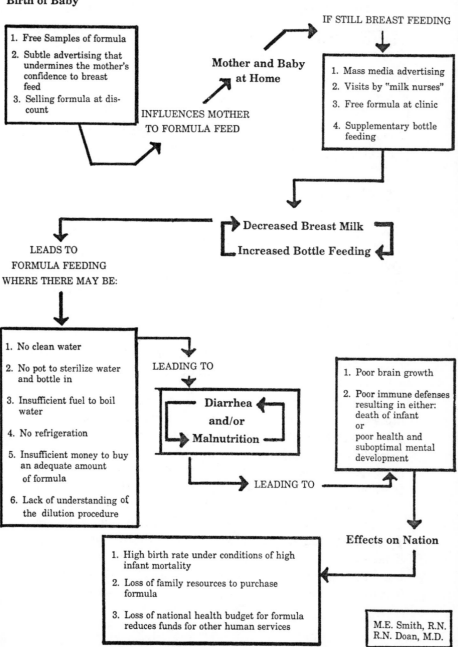

EFFECTS OF BOTTLE FEEDING
under conditions common in third world countries [4]

Birth of Baby

IF STILL BREAST FEEDING

1. Free Samples of formula
2. Subtle advertising that undermines the mother's confidence to breast feed
3. Selling formula at discount

Mother and Baby at Home

INFLUENCES MOTHER TO FORMULA FEED

1. Mass media advertising
2. Visits by "milk nurses"
3. Free formula at clinic
4. Supplementary bottle feeding

Decreased Breast Milk

Increased Bottle Feeding

LEADS TO
FORMULA FEEDING
WHERE THERE MAY BE:

1. No clean water
2. No pot to sterilize water and bottle in
3. Insufficient fuel to boil water
4. No refrigeration
5. Insufficient money to buy an adequate amount of formula
6. Lack of understanding of the dilution procedure

LEADING TO

Diarrhea and/or Malnutrition

1. Poor brain growth
2. Poor immune defenses resulting in either:
   death of infant
   or
   poor health and suboptimal mental development

LEADING TO

Effects on Nation

1. High birth rate under conditions of high infant mortality
2. Loss of family resources to purchase formula
3. Loss of national health budget for formula reduces funds for other human services

M.E. Smith, R.N.
R.N. Doan, M.D.

ilies actually receive the minimum wage. So the infant formula takes an even greater percentage of their income.

COST OF ARTIFICIAL FEEDING IN SOME COUNTRIES AND % OF MINIMUM WAGES					
Country	Minimum wage per week US $	Cost at 3 months per day US $	% of wage	Cost at 6 months per day US $	% of wage
United Kingdom	39.20	0.84	2.1	1.30	3.3
Burma	5.01	0.53	10.6	0.81	16.2
Peru	5.60	0.84	15.0	1.30	23.2
Philippines	9.69	1.67	17.2	2.59	26.7
Indonesia	5.60	1.05	18.8	1.62	28.9
Tanzania	7.62	1.57	20.6	2.44	32.0
India	4.62	1.05	22.7	1.62	35.1
Nigeria	5.18	1.57	30.3	2.44	47.1
Afganistan	2.80	1.05	37.5	1.62	57.9
Pakistan	5.18	2.09	40.3	3.23	62.4
Egypt	4.09	1.67	40.8	2.59	63.3

Accurate information on wages and costs of food is difficult to find. Here they are expressed at US $ for comparative purposes. It is assumed that the artificial food, a full-cream modified milk, supplies the infant's total daily need for food.

The information in this table comes from a joint seminar held on March 24, 1970 at the London School of Hygiene and Tropical Medicine (UNICEF/WHO course for senior teachers of child health and students taking their postgraduate diploma in nutrition). Reprinted from the Protein Advisory Group Manual on Feeding Infants and Young Children, PAG Document 1.14/26, December 1971.

Because of these extraordinary costs, mothers stretch formula intended for four days to last three weeks and longer. In
a 1969 survey in Barbados, only 18% of the families using
formula were emptying the tin of milk in the prescribed four
days. 82% were watering it down considerably. Others turned
to water, chocolate or tea as substitutes when the formula ran
out. The result in both cases has been the same: malnutrition,
disease, and a mortality rate among bottle-fed babies in the
Third World double that of breast-fed babies. Even if the baby
lives, early malnutrition can cause brain damage. And if that
brain damage occurs in the first six months of the baby's life,
it is irreversible.[6]

To Nestlé, the redirection of Third World capital from breast feeding to the bottle is an economic necessity. To cite one of its annual reports:

> Generally sales developed satisfactorily; although the continued decline in birth rate, particularly in countries with a high standard of living, retarded growth of the market. This resulted in considerably increased competition and a far greater choice of products available to the consumer. In the developing countries our own products continue to sell well, thanks to the growth of population and improved living standards.[7]

The Interfaith Center for Corporate Responsibility discovered in a 1977 supermarket sales print-out from Brazil that the profit rate for infant formulas were 72%, while all other supermarket products ranged between 15% and 25% in their rate of profit.[8] No wonder Nestlé and the others want to cultivate this growing market.

But to many Third World governments and people, this redirection of capital has disastrous economic consequences. Mothers' milk is a natural resource and ought to be regarded as one of the country's assets. By transferring consumption patterns from the country's natural resource to an artificial formula, this resource is wasted. Alan Berg, a nutritionist for the World Bank, estimates that the loss from non-use of breast milk had reached $780 million by 1973. In Kenya, for instance, the estimated $11.5 million annual loss in breast milk is equivalent to 2/3 of the national health budget and 1/5 of the annual foreign economic aid Kenya receives.[9] This wasting of a country's natural resources also means less self-reliance.

National governments in the Third World have begun to recognize this problem. However, they often find themselves with few resources to challenge these multinational corporate marketing practices. Since colonial times, the Third World's source of capital and the markets for its agricultural products have been the industrialized West. As we saw in Chapters 4, 8 and 9, the terms of economic development have been and continue to be dictated by those with economic resources. To illustrate where these resources lie, Nestlé's gross annual sales exceed the GNP of 108 countries.

Nevertheless, following a World Health Organization resolution in 1974 condemning the marketing practices of the infant formula corporations (see pages 226-27), Kenya and other Third World countries began to act. Their actions have ranged from public education campaigns on the value of breast feeding to requiring a doctor's prescription for infant formula. Zambia even nationalized the infant formula industry and tightly controls its activities.[10]

2. Control over Technology

Is infant formula an appropriate technology to introduce to Third World countries? Although the bottle is never as good as mothers' milk, infant formula is a high quality product that has been successful in Western society. Here, with refrigeration, pure water, and sterile bottles, infant formula has been a workable substitute for mothers' milk. Yet, even in the First World, concern is growing about the extent to which we are becoming dependent on artificial and processed foods.

In the Third World, hygienic conditions are generally quite different. These conditions for the majority of Third World families are graphically described by Fatima Patel, speaking from her 15 years of field experience working among the lower income peoples of South Africa, Jamaica and South America:

I will give just a few of the disadvantages and difficulties one encounters when formula feeding:

(1) When you have to buy that vital liquid—water—from a guy on a bicycle or horse back, or you have to queue up at 4:00 AM at the communal village tap to carry home a bucket or two, or you have to go down to the river to get a pail or two and carry it on your head all the way

home; you're definitely not going to do what sweet, little nursie who just turns on the tap and has all the water she needs, told you about boiling the baby's bottle and nipple at least six times a day.

(2) Besides, nursie doesn't have fuel problems. She just touches the electric switch or puts a match to the gas and she has all the fuel she can use. I, the mother, have to queue up before dawn to get a gallon of kerosene (paraffin) and that takes one-sixth from the daily income, or I have to go into the bush and chop a log with a hand machete, all morning. Does nursie realize what great problems I have getting fuel?

(3) Living in the slums is just like living on a garbage dump—no water, no toilets, no sewage disposal and no garbage collection. So the area is infested with flies. As we all know, flies carry disease and these just love a taste of baby's formula. They settle on the rubber nipple and the baby ingests all these germs when it's thirsty.

(4) Mother goes to work, leaving baby, bottle and formula with either an elder sibling or granny. Elder sibling mixes the formula with much more [formula] than her mother instructed, so that the baby can fill up and go to sleep, so that she can go out to play. Granny isn't going to be wasteful and use all that amount of formula as instructed by the mother. So she uses half the amount or less. The results—elder sibling's concentrated bottle means an upset stomach, diarrhea, vomiting; Granny's diluted bottle means an unhappy, crying, irritable baby, leading to malnutrition and low resistance to infections. The baby has to be seen by the doctor, which means bus fares, maybe even a taxi if the weather is bad and the baby's very ill, doctor's fees, medicines, etc. This can cost up to a week's wages, not to mention the sufferings of the poor little one.

(5) The minimum legal wage per day is $1.88 [in Peru]. But nobody pays that. If you ask for the minimum, you can enjoy unemployment with its hundred and one worries—the same as the unhygienic artificial formula feeding, which burns holes in the family budget.

222 · BREAD AND JUSTICE

Her conclusion is as graphic as her description above:

> Bottle-feeding is *poison* for the majority of the infant population of the Third World; in fact, not only the developing countries, but also the lower income group of the so-called developed countries. I won't say that bottle feeding is the only cause filling up the cemetery, but it is a major cause in the deaths of babies. For example, we don't find monkey babies dying from all those diseases, related to human babies. Why? Because Mama monkey just feeds her dear one on the nutritious formula God provided . . .[11]

While mothers' milk does not have the highest amounts of proteins and minerals as advertised on infant formula cans, it does have the proper amounts, plus the protective antibodies that formulas lack. In the past, breast feeding has postponed the mortality rate of infants in the Third World beyond the critical first year. But with the advent of the bottle, the death rate among newborn infants is increasing.[12]

Nestlé recognizes the problem of improper use of its product. Together with the other infant formula companies, Nestlé formulated a code of conduct in which they agreed to promote the concept that mothers' milk is best. Thus, a Nestlé pamphlet now reads: "It may happen that you do not have enough milk to feed your baby. In this case, the meal must be supplemented by bottle feeding."[13] See pages 228-229 for the code of conduct.

This ad does give credit to an appropriate technology—the use of the natural resource of mothers' milk. It also suggests that mothers might not have enough milk and thus must rely on another technology—the artificial formula. Doctors generally agree that about 5% of the population is unable to nurse their babies for physiological reasons. But they also agree that frequent nursing is the best way to produce more milk. Anxiety is often the cause of stopping the milk flow in mothers.

Certainly the Nestlé suggestion that mothers may not be giving enough to their babies could trigger such anxiety. If a mother is relying totally on breast feeding, she produces milk according to her baby's need. With mixed feeding (breast milk and bottle milk), as promoted by Nestlé, the mother's production decreases as soon as the baby is introduced to formula. The sweeter taste of the formula, plus easier sucking with the bottle increases the baby's desire for formula and thus decreases the amount of milk being produced by the mother.[14]

Nestlé's control over technology, then, affects the Third World in several ways. First, Nestlé and the other infant formula corporations encourage Third World peoples and countries to give up a technique which is under their own control—breast feeding—and to substitute a technique which is under the corporations' control. This increased dependency, as Chapters 1 and 4 pointed out, has negative psychological as well as health and economic consequences. Personal and national self-reliance are further undermined.

Secondly, as Chapter 9 pointed out, inappropriate technology generally means a loss of jobs. Is this the case with Nestlé? Nestlé employs 42,000 people in the Third World. How many of them are employed in its infant formula operations is unknown. However, since the Lactogen and Nan are produced in the First World, it would seem that all of Nestlé infant formula employees in the Third World are involved in selling the product in some way. Doug Johnson, director of the boycott campaign against Nestlé, estimates that 40 to 50 of Nestlé's sales persons are what are called "milk nurses" or "mother craft advisors". Many of these women are trained nurses who advise mothers in child care while promoting the Nestlé products at the same time. The higher pay offered by Nestlé unfortunately attracts nurses who were trained at public expense into the Nestlé sales force. Thus, these women are no longer involved in full-time health care work for their country.[15] The result is a loss of urgently needed jobs, even though the total number of employed persons has probably been increased.

3. *Control over Marketing and Marketplace Attitudes*

Nestlé's control over consumers' use of capital and their choice of technology is due to its control over marketing and its advertising. Although Nestlé and the others claim that women are abandoning breast feeding for reasons that have nothing to do with company promotional activities—mothers working, the bottle as a status symbol, the idea of the breast as a sexual object rather than a source of food—marketing is clearly a major factor. In the Third World at least, most working mothers are able to continue breast feeding their babies. To return to the experience of Fatima Patel—

> I personally don't think that breast feeding can be a handicap to any working mother, since most of the places of employment now have a nursery where babies can be left and taken care of while the mother works and she can slip down to the nursery when it's feeding time. For the mother who works as a domestic or other home help, I very much doubt that the Governess, who needs the help desperately, will object to the maid having the baby with her and feeding it when necessary.[16]

The second reason offered by Nestlé is also clearly related to advertising. Where does the image of the "modern" mother and woman and of the bottle as a status symbol come from, if not from the corporations' marketing practices? Mothers put empty Nestlé's Lactogen cans and feeding bottles on their dead babies' graves because they believe that formula and the bottle are the most valuable possessions their babies once had.[17] The corporations use five main channels to help foster this belief among Third World women.

(a.) *Mass Media Advertising.* As a food-based corporation without the kind of inroads to the medical profession that the pharmaceutical-based infant formula corporations have, Nestlé relies most heavily on the mass media. Newspaper, billboards, radio and television have all been used to promote Lactogen and Nan. Pictures showing healthy babies and their bottles are prominently displayed for both the rich and poor.

Radio is the most effective means for reaching of masses of illiterate peoples. According to *Food First*, during one day in Sierra Leone, there were fifteen 30-second advertisements for Nestlé. A 1973 study showed that ads for Lactogen accounted for 11.26% of all Swahili radio advertising in Kenya.[18]

Nestlé claims that it does not promote its products to those who cannot afford to use them properly. Yet the Sierra Leone ad is in the common dialect of the poor: "Now Lactogen a better food cos it don get more protein and iron, all de important things dat go make pikin strong and will ... Lactogen and Love."[19] Nestlé claims now that such advertising has stopped, but reports from Third World countries continue to dispute this claim. Write to Nestlé and to INFACT (see Resources) for the most recent developments.

(b.) *Hospital Advertising.* In hospitals and clinics, Nestlé provides posters and pamphlets with baby care instructions. These educational services are a cost-saving factor for the hospital, but they endorse the use of Lactogen in baby care. The unaware mother thinks that she is receiving information from the medical profession, not Nestlé.

(c.) *Free Samples.* Nestlé gives free samples to hospitals, clinics, and new mothers to get the infants started on the formula. It pays off, as often hospitals will start the baby on formula even if the mother intends to nurse her child.[20] Once the baby is started on the formula, however, it is more difficult for the mother to lactate. Further, the parents are not aware of the cost when given free samples. It is only after the free samples run out that they often discover that Lactogen is more than they can afford. By that time, it may be too late for the mother to be able to breast feed her baby.

(d.) *Mother-craft Advisors.* A company sales person, often a qualified nurse, visits the new mother in the maternity ward or home to promote the formula. Until recently, they dressed in white uniforms and gave child care tips, while actually promoting the formula. This clearly implied an endorsement by the medical profession. As noted on page 229, pressure on

Nestlé resulted in a change of the *color* of the uniform, but not the practice. Mother-craft advisors now wear a small patch bearing the name of Nestlé and only wear the nurse's uniform if they are a nurse. Otherwise, they wear a blue uniform. Several countries, including Jamaica, have banned mother-craft personnel from public hospitals. But the practice often continues, because of the expense of enforcement.

(e.) *Promotion to the Medical Profession.* Although the pharmaceutical-based infant formula corporations concentrate a greater percentage of their promotional efforts on the medical profession, Nestlé has not left this channel unattended. Nestlé sponsors conferences and courses on nutrition for pediatricians. Doctors tend to rely on the milk companies for their updated information on infant feeding, as they do on pharmaceutical companies for drug information. Nestlé prints professional journals and provides other courtesy services to pediatric associations. They also issue prescription blanks with the hospital name and Nestlé products already printed for the doctor's use.[21]

It is not just a few radical groups in the U.S. and Western Europe who are concerned about these marketing practices. It has been the judgment of the World Health Organization and the International Pediatric Association as well. On May 23, 1974, the World Health Organization passed the following resolution in Geneva:

> Reaffirming that breast-feeding has proved to be the most appropriate and successful nutritional solution for the harmonious development of the child; Noting the general decline in breast-feeding, related to socio-cultural and environmental factors, *including the mistaken idea caused by misleading sales promotion that breast-feeding is inferior to feeding with manufactured breast-milk substitutes;*
>
> Observing that this decline is one of the factors contributing to infant mortality and malnutrition, in particular in the developing world; and

Realizing that mothers who feed their babies with manufactured foods are often unable to afford an adequate supply of such foods and that even if they can afford such foods the tendency to malnutrition is frequently aggravated because of lack of understanding of the amount and correct and hygienic preparation of the food which should be given to the child.

A. Recommends strongly the encouragement of breast feeding as the ideal feeding in order to promote harmonious physical and mental development of children;

B. Calls the attention of countries to the necessity of taking adequate social measures for mothers working away from their homes during the lactation period, such as arranging special work timetables so that they can breast-feed their children;

C. Urges member countries to review sales promotion activities on baby foods and to introduce appropriate remedial measures including advertisement codes and legislation where necessary . . .[22] (italics mine)

A year later, the International Pediatric Association issued a series of recommendations to encourage breast feeding. The section entitled "Curtailing Promotion of Artificial Feeding" reads:

1. Sales promotion activities of organizations marketing baby milks and feeding bottles, that run counter to the general intent expressed in this document, must be curtailed by every means available to the profession, including, where necessary and feasible, legislation to control unethical practice.

2. Dissemination of propaganda about artificial feeding and distribution of samples of artificial baby foods in maternity units should be banned immediately.[23]

Nestlé's Response to Its Critics

Nestlé's response to its critics has been basically threefold. It argues that it does not force anyone to buy its products, but merely makes an alternative available. It has formulated and imposed a code of conduct on itself. And it has repeatedly denied the charges of its critics and has published a number of papers and books defending itself.

1. Freedom of Choice

Three statements of the corporation make this point clearly:

> "Breast-milk substitutes are intended to supplement breast-milk and for use when mothers cannot or elect not to breast feed for medical or other reasons."

> "We have a milk on the market; naturally that milk is going to be available to the people . . . . If the mother comes to a decision not to breast feed because she has to use an alternative for some reason, then this is not our promotion against breast feeding. We make a product available on the market, but the onus cannot be on us to stop mothers from taking such a product into consideration."

> "No one has yet hit on the idea of demanding that wine be sold through doctors or pharmacies because hundreds of people get drunk on it and sometimes cause fatal accidents."[24]

2. A Code of Conduct

The "Code of Ethics and Professional Standards for Advertising, Product Information and Advisory Services for Breast-Milk Substitutes" adopted in 1975, six days before Nestlé went to a Swiss court to sue a Western European group for libel by the International Council of Infant Food Industries (ICIFI) contains 13 provisions. The most important ones are as follows:

> (2) "Product information for the public will always recognize the milk of healthy, well-nourished mothers as the feeding of choice with the recommendation to seek professional advice when a supplement or alternative may be required."
> (3) "Product labeling will affirm breast feeding as the first choice for the nutrition of normal infants."

(4) "Product claims will reflect scientific integrity without implication that any product is superior to the breast milk of healthy mothers."

(5) "To insure optimal nutritional intake, explicitly worded instructions and demonstrations for product use will be provided for the hygienic and correctly measured preparation of breast-milk substitutes."

(6) "In cooperation with health authorities, professional communications and educational materials will be provided to caution against misuse and to inform mothers on the importance of and methods for obtaining safe water for the preparation of breast-milk substitutes."

(7) "Members' personnel will observe professional ethics and established rules of conduct in medical/nursing centres, maternities, and physicians' offices and in all contacts."

(8) "Members will employ nurses, nutritionists and mid-wives whenever possible to perform mothercraft services...."

(11) "Nurses' uniforms will be worn only by persons who are professionally entitled to their use. The attire worn by mothercraft personnel will bear the identification of the respective ICIFI member. It is recommended that an ICIFI emblem be worn."[25]

3. Denial of Critics Charges

First of all, Nestlé has published several expensive public relations portrayals of its operations in the Third World, including *Nestlé in the Developing Countries* and *An Illustration of Nestlé's Role in Developing Countries: Example of the State of Chiapas, Mexico.* Thanks to the research of Susan George, we have a way of reading such documents. Her article entitled "Nestlé Alimentana S.A.: The Limits to Public Relations" (available from INFACT) analyzes the information provided by Nestlé in the first source cited above.

Secondly, Nestlé has prepared responses to specific charges. Write them for their 4-page refutation of an INFACT ad printed in "Mother Jones" and write INFACT for their counter-response.

Critics' Counter-Responses to Nestlé

Although much more is available from INFACT, this section will be restricted to the UN's Protein Advisory Group's response to the ICIFI Code of Ethics.

Code of Conduct

In a four-page document, the Protein Advisory Group of the United Nations critiques the ICIFI Code of Ethics point by point. Its major concerns center on three areas:

(1) The language in Code items #2, #3 and #4— "healthy and well-nourished mothers", "normal infants", and "healthy mothers"—suggests that other mothers ought not to breast feed their children, which is not true. Generally, even malnourished mothers can adequately feed their infants.[26]

(2) Agreeing with the observations of Fatima Patel, above, the Group writes:

"Clearly worded instructions and demonstrations [Code items #5 and #6] and educational material will be useful *only* for families who have some minimum education and facilities to adopt. In the poverty groups, who form the majority, it is impossible to follow instructions, understand demonstrations, or read educational material; besides, they cannot put these things into practice. One may tell them methods to obtain safe water; but sterilizing containers, bottles, storing foods, etc., are too complex in their situation. Hence, it is unwise for industry to expose these poverty groups to the availability of the formula products. The health authorities should take the responsibility to determine if and when substitute products are required and how to provide the same in a hygienic way."

(3) Referring to Code item #7, the Group states:

"The statement that a members' ' personnel' should be visible in medical wards and maternity institutions is not acceptable. Visits to a physician's office outside of his/her consulting hours seem reasonable. A clear decision on this is essential if ICIFI has to draw a line between ethical and unethical promotion."[27]

As a way of summarizing the concern of the World Health Organization, the UN's Protein Advisory Group, and many others in the health care profession, and as a way of summarizing this case study, let us look at Fatima Patel's letter contrasting the bottle and the mother:

Nursing Bottle	Mother's Milk
1. It is artificial.	1. Baby likes it more because it is natural.
2. Sometimes there is no milk powder.	2. It is always on hand.
3. It needs 180 big tins of milk for the first six months.	3. It is very economical.
4. If the proportion of milk is inadequate, the baby can die of hunger.	4. It is a whole food and it is always ready.
5. It causes a lot of digestive problems.	5. It is easy to digest.
6. You have to boil the nursing bottle six times a day and the milk or water for more than 10 minutes.	6. It does not need preparation and has no microbes that can make the baby ill.
7. If you don't boil the nursing bottle or the milk well, your baby can sicken & die.	7. The mother's milk is always clean and guarantees the baby's life.
8. It soon becomes sour.	8. It never becomes sour.
9. It contaminates with flies or dust which bring illness.	9. It does not get contaminated.

What Can I Do?
As discussed above (pp. 215-216), many people have decided that a national boycott of Nestlé's products is the only effective strategy at this time. There are a number of ways in which to participate in this boycott.

1. Check your own home for Nestlé products and personally join the boycott. Be sure to write a letter to Nestlé (100 Bloomingdale Rd., White Plains, NY 10605) to explain your reasons for participating in the boycott. Send copies of your

letter to your Congresspersons and to INFACT. If a number of students in the same class write Nestlé, be sure to compare the responses that Nestlé makes. Perhaps a whole class could make a joint response back to Nestlé.

2. Write your Congresspersons to tell them why you are supporting the boycott and urge them to initiate and/or support legislation to control corporate marketing practices in the infant formula business. Ask them for a copy of the Congressional hearings held in May 1978 on this whole issue.

3. Write to Clergy and Laity Concerned (198 Broadway, New York, NY 10038) to ask if there is a CALC chapter in your community that is working on the infant formula issue. Write INFACT (The Infant Formula Action Coalition, 1701 University Avenue SE, Minneapolis, MN 55414) for names of people working on this issue in your community. Also ask them for any buttons, leaflets, posters, articles you might need for any of the suggestions that follow. Also ask them for strategy ideas, once you have mapped out your goals.

4. Organize a teach-in or guest speaker at your school or church group. A showing of the film *Bottle Babies* (see "Resources") would be good. A follow-up to the presentation would

be to work to get your school's food service or cafeteria to stop buying Nestlé products. Be sure to consider candy and coffee machines as well. INFACT materials would be invaluable for the educational process that should precede any school-wide decision.

5. Urge some interested individuals or existing social action groups in your community to organize a local coalition to promote this issue locally. If a coalition is not possible, then ask existing groups—like your church's social action committee—to endorse the boycott and participate in it. Be sure to contact your local La Leche League group (promoting breast feeding) about the boycott.

6. Contact local grocers, inform them about the boycott, and ask their support by not re-ordering Nestlé products. Ask them if you can put up a poster on the boycott and/or set up a table to display materials and to talk with shoppers. They will probably say "no", but even so, it is important that they be asked to consider their participation in this whole issue.

7. Write a letter to the editor of your local paper(s), explaining why the boycott should be supported.

8. Urge your school or church group not to use Nestlé candy for fund-raising efforts. You might also think about substitutes that are far more nutritious, like raisins and peanuts. Holy Name Academy in Seattle cancelled its candy sales contract with Nestlé in 1978.

9. Urge conference planners to consider locations for their conferences other than Stouffer's Inns. If you are a member of the National Catholic Education Association or any other professional education group or attend teachers' conventions, check the display booths for Nestlé. If Nestlé is present (as it was at the 1978 NCEA Convention), raise the issue with those in charge and ask them to reconsider the corporation's presence the next year. Ask if there are any criteria for determining who can have a booth. Be sure to ask for "equal time" at a minimum. That is, ask to have the film *Bottle Babies* shown during the convention and ask permission to leaflet about Nestlé's activities in the Third World.

If you want to do something but are not sure which of these suggestions to follow, you might go back to the questions in Chapter 11 (pp. 209-210) to help you decide. If you come up with something different than these nine suggestions, be sure to send it to INFACT so that they can suggest it to others.

Resources

Bottle Babies is a 28-minute color 16mm documentary produced by German filmmaker Peter Kreig and filmed in Nairobi and rural Kenya (write INFACT for a list of places where it is available). It starkly details the conflict of interest between the needs of growing children for good nutrition and the needs of the infant formula corporations.

In addition to the "point-counterpoints" presented in this chapter, two others are good:

(1) an INFACT ad that appeared in "Mother Jones", Nestlé's critique, and INFACT's response (available from INFACT)—addressing 11 points.

(2) Nestlé's "Infant Feeding in the Developing Countries" (available from Nestlé) and INFACT's response, along with Susan George, "Nestlé Alimentana S.A.: The Limits to Public Relations" (available from INFACT).

Formula for Malnutrition: A filmstrip on the infant formula problem.

In cooperation with the Interfaith Center on Corporate Responsibility, the United Methodist Church A-V Dept. has produced an excellent filmstrip with soundtrack cassette. The filmstrip provides a basic introduction to the infant formula problem and to the more general issue of the role of multinational corporations in the Third World.

The 30 minute filmstrip will cost $10.00 and can be ordered from:

> Service Center
> United Methodist B.G.M.
> 7820 Reading Rd.
> Cincinnati, OH 45237

Part IV

HUNGER AND A NEW INTERNAL ECONOMIC ORDER

Introduction

If the New International Economic Order is to bring both bread and justice, as has been repeatedly stated in this book, there must also be a new internal economic order within Third World countries. Otherwise, it would be just the elites, and not the majorities, of Third World peoples who would be the beneficiaries (and agents) of the changes brought about by the NIEO. And justice is concerned with all, not the few. To summarize what has been said so far:

(1) The components of justice in Part I clearly implied the need for an internal redistribution of wealth and especially power (Ch. 1, pp. 14-15; Ch. 2, pp. 32-35; Ch. 3, pp. 48-49). They called for development models and strategies to focus first on meeting the basic human needs of the poor (Ch. 1, p. 10; Ch. 3, pp. 41-43) and be built on the resources, values, and cultural traditions of Third World societies (Ch. 1, pp. 12-13; Ch. 3, p. 43).

(2) In Part II on trade, Ch. 5 pointed out that the justice claim behind all the proposed changes in trade is on behalf of the poor in Third World countries, not the elites (pp. 92-95). Ch. 6 concluded that, without a series of basic structural changes within Third World countries, the eight key NIEO trade measures and a continuation of export cropping would impede the achievement of bread and justice for the majority of Third World peoples (pp. 110-113).

(3) Part III on multinational corporations came to a similar conclusion. The changes envisioned in the NIEO and other codes of conduct for multinational corporations could well result in a new alliance between the multinational corporations and the elites of Third World countries, an alliance that would continue to frustrate the achievement of bread and justice. Ch. 10 thus concluded that what needs to be done is for communities, rather than a few wealthy individuals, to gain some real control over the operations of the multinationals (pp. 191-192).

(4) In each Part, the phrases "self-reliance", "self-reliant development", "collective self-reliance", and "food self-reliance" were used to indicate a model of development that was probably unfamiliar to most readers. This model emphasizes meeting the basic human needs of the masses of people in a country through strategies geared to the particular human and natural resources, the values, and the traditions of the country or region, and through strategies maximizing the collective efforts of people within each country and among Third World countries.

For most Third World countries, such a model would clearly require a new internal economic (and social, political, and even cultural) order. As we have already seen (Ch. 5, pp. 92-95), progressive Third World spokespersons like Julius Nyerere, Michael Manley (President of Jamaica) and Mahbub ul Haq recognize the need for both a New International Economic Order and a new internal economic order. As ul Haq puts it, "fundamental reforms in the international order will be meaningless, and almost impossible to achieve, without corresponding reforms in the national orders."[1] The NIEO is necessary to transfer some First World wealth to the Third World and thereby provide the material conditions (financial possibility) for such reforms. Otherwise, as Nyerere noted, "we are merely redistributing poverty." But the NIEO cannot guarantee these reforms and might actually hinder a redistribution of power and wealth within Third World countries.

Since there are different visions and models of "development" and of what constitutes this new internal economic order, Chapter 13 will compare the three most prevalent models of development. The excellent work of Sheldon Gellar will be used to make these models graphic. Chapter 14 will outline the basic components of a new internal economic order based on a self-reliance model of development. A case-study of the village of Patti Kalyana in northern India will illustrate such a model. Chapter 15 will focus on how we are related to these issues and what people are doing about promoting self-reliance models of development and what we might do.

Chapter Thirteen

THREE MODELS OF
DEVELOPMENT

This chapter compares three models of development and uses the story of One Flew over the Cuckoo's Nest *to demonstrate the need for a new* internal *economic order to ensure that a new* international *economic order benefits the majority.*

For many people, the terms "developed", "underdeveloped", and "developing" refer to how modern or wealthy a society is. Most U.S. citizens would view the U.S. as a "developed" society, pointing to things like its technological achievements and the high standard of living of most of its people. Third World countries would be measured against this standard and be considered as either "underdeveloped" or "developing." Thus, most of us in the U.S. would feel that we have the development that others need.

It is very difficult to avoid measuring others against one's own society and way of life. But if we are to be able to identify what kind of development is really needed in Third World countries (and maybe in our own as well), we have to try to step back and consider alternative models of development. The standard for evaluating these models will not be our own model of development but the principles of bread and justice on which this book is based.

In trying to answer the question "what kind of a new internal economic order should we be working for in the Third World?", we will examine three models of development.[1] The first two come readily to our minds—capitalism and socialism or communism. The third is more difficult to identify. Since the best illustration of it lies in the model of development Mahatma Gandhi struggled to create in India and which his followers continue to try to implement today, it could be called the Gandhian model. Gellar prefers the terms "Mainstream" (capitalist), "Marxist", and "Moralist-Idealist" (Gandhian) for these three models. Since this chapter relies in part on his analysis of these models,[2] I will use his terms. Each of these three models has been proposed by both policymakers and theorists as *the* approach to the development of the Third World.

The Mainstream Model

As Gellar summarizes this model,

For the most part, mainstream scholars in the U.S. define the process of Development as moving towards having more of those resources, attributes, and worldviews now found in the industrialized nations of the West; conversely, Underdevelopment is defined as a deficiency of those resources, attributes, and worldviews found in the West. Mainstream models tend to regard the "haves"— i.e., the dominant classes and nations—as the main generators of Development because of their superior efforts, skills, and virtues. Development occurs through a process of diffusion whereby the Haves transmit their resources, skills and virtues to the "Have-Nots" who are to use them in the manner prescribed by the "Haves." If Development is not readily achieved, failure is ascribed to some deficiency in resources, natural calamities, national vices, or the refusal or inability to follow the prescriptions recommended by the "Haves." The onus for Underdevelopment thus rests on the shoulders of the "Have-Nots."

This is the model of development with which most of us are familiar. What the Third World needs is more money, more technology, more education. Development is seen as a ladder. Some are already at or near the top. Others are near the bottom and need to catch up. However, some of the rungs in the middle are missing. If the First World would supply these rungs (money, technology, expertise) and if the Third World would concentrate on climbing the ladder and make it easy for the First World to install the missing rungs, then Third World countries could "take off" and begin to catch up. Nurse Ratched, in the metaphor of *One Flew Over the Cuckoo's Nest* (pages 246-253), represents this model. She is the First World supplying what her Third World patients need to become normal (developed).

In the Mainstream model, these missing rungs in the ladder should be supplied to the most economically advanced sectors of Third World countries—industry, business, and large-scale agriculture. If these sectors expand, then more jobs are created and more people get money. Thus more goods are bought and so more jobs are created, etc., etc. In this way, concentrating on the "progressive" sectors of Third World countries is supposed to set up a spiral through which the benefits of development trickle down to those at the bottom.

This was the primary approach taken during the UN's first two Decades of Development and it continues to be pursued by the newly rich oil-producing countries and other "middle developed countries" such as Brazil, South Korea, and Taiwan. Perhaps the best example of this Mainstream model is Brazil. As the largest and potentially richest of all Third

World countries, Brazil has staked its economic future on the market economy. Export cropping (see pages 101, 106-108), capital-intensive technology, urban-centered industrialization, and an extremely high degree of multinational corporation involvement are its major features. The annual economic rate of growth from the mid-1960s to the mid-1970s was a spectacular 10%. Many people have referred to Brazil as an economic miracle. But one has to examine what the "Brazilian miracle" has meant to the bottom 40% of Brazilian society before accepting it as the model for any Third World country interested in a new internal economic order based on bread and justice.

The Marxist Model

Again, in Gellar's words:

Although they (Marxist models) may incorporate many of the quantitative indicators of Development found in mainstream models—e.g., per capita income, literacy, mortality rates, etc.—their very definition of Development implies a rejection of the existing power relationships obtaining between "Have" and "Have-Not" classes and nations, a reordering of these power relationships in favor of the Have-Nots, and a different configuration of institutions and economic structures. Thus, Marxist and Neo-Marxist models, for example, regard Third World Development as movement towards the destruction and transformation of feudal and capitalist class structures and the establishment of a classless society based on collective ownership of the means of production. Conversely, Underdevelopment is defined not as diverse deficiencies of resources and skills found in the West which can be remedied through diffusion [export to the Third World] but a state of exploitation and poverty caused by capitalist expropriation of the resources and economic surplus generated by the proletarian classes and nations of the world. The onus for Underdevelopment thus lies not with the exploited "Have-Nots" but with the "Haves" who are, in fact, oppressors rather than the benefactors and "donors" depicted in the mainstream Development litera-

ture. Since the continued domination of the world by the
"Haves" blocks the path to Development, then Development can be achieved only by smashing and overthrowing
the status quo, by revolutionary violence if necessary.

There is a clear contrast between Mainstream and Marx-
ist models. Recalling the image of the ladder, those at the top
get there because they climb on the backs of those below them.
For instance, Spain developed because it enslaved the Bolivian
Indians and stole their wealth (Potosi silver, Ch. 2, pp. 29-31).
Today, for Marxists, the answer to Bolivian underdevelopment is not First World money, technology, and expertise.
Rather, the First World countries (and their few Bolivian
allies) that continue to enjoy development at the expense of
Bolivian workers and peasants have to be pulled down from
the top rungs of the ladder. The wealth they enjoy at the top
and the resources that got them there are really created by
the labor of the workers and peasants far beneath them on the
ladder. Thus, these resources should be owned and managed
by those to whom they really belong—"the proletarian classes
and nations of the world."

There are a number of examples of Third World countries
pursuing a new internal economic order along these Marxist
lines. Cuba and the former Portuguese colonies of Angola,
Mozambique and Guinea-Bissau are four good case-studies.
The Peoples Republic of China is probably the most thorough
and successful example of the Marxist model.

Chile under Marxist President Salvadore Allende (1970–
1973) also represents an interesting case for further study.
Since 1964, Chileans have experienced three clearly distinct
models of development. The Eduardo Frei years (1964–1970)
meant a largely Mainstream model, with some concern for
social justice. The present military regime is a combination of
free enterprise and repression. In between, Chile tried to build
a new internal economic order based on Marxist (and Moralist-Idealist) principles. Some wealth and a little power were
redistributed to the poor and powerless. Workers and peasants

gained some control over their lives and workplaces. The multinational corporations were nationalized. Land reform became more of a reality and less of a plan on paper. The odds were greatly against this experiment, however. First World opposition to such a new internal economic order was strong, and Allende refused to disarm the Chilean military. And it was these two forces that ended this experiment, at least for the present.

The Moralist-Idealist Model

As Gellar describes it:

Unlike many mainstream and Marxist models and theories of Development which purport to be scientific and value-free in their analysis, Moralist-Idealist models are primarily and explicitly normative [moral] in orientation and content. Thus, Development, i.e., the Good Society, is defined *primarily* in terms of Justice, Freedom, and Liberation rather than in terms of higher Gross National Product, industrialization, or public ownership over the means of production. Moralist-Idealist models remain utopian in nature because they clearly identify with the concerns of the people at the bottom and see the status quo as intolerable because of its harmful effects on people . . . . Underdevelopment is a moral as well as social fact. The persistence of Underdevelopment and the suffering which it entails is a scandal and an outrage, particularly when viewed alongside the affluence and conspicuous consumption of the wealthy. Moralist-Idealist models empathize with the plight of the poor while exhorting the dominant classes to change their unjust and callous ways just as the Hebrew prophets chided Israel's rulers in biblical times for violating God's commandments in oppressing the weaker and more vulnerable elements in society. Generally more attuned to the traditional cultural values and traditions of the Third World than their mainstream or Marxist counterparts, Moralist-Idealist thinkers also often criticize the "Haves" for systematically deprecating the culture and values of the "Have-Not" classes and nations and imposing their own definition of Development, interpretation of reality, and prescriptions for change on the world.

Often socialist in orientation, the Moralist-Idealist model is similar to the Marxist model in many ways. It rejects the mainstream image of the development of the Third World as a matter of supplying missing rungs in a ladder. It generally agrees with the Marxist position that the cause of underdevelopment in the Third World lies in the development of the First World.

But the moralist-idealist model differs from the Marxist model in its emphasis on a moral, rather than a scientific, analysis and approach to the problem. The Marxist sees underdevelopment rooted in some kind of historical necessity. The solution is equally necessary or scientific—class warfare in which the capitalist class is overthrown by the working class which it exploited. On the other hand, while recognizing the deep conflict between capitalist and working classes, the Moralist-Idealist tends to confront the capitalist class with the immorality of their actions and challenges them to stop their oppression of the poor. Thus, there is more of a commitment to nonviolence in the Moralist-Idealist model. It also has greater concern for the culture and values of Third World societies and for the non-material aspects of development. The Moralist-Idealist model is clearly ethical-religious in orientation and is reflected in the work of theorists like Denis Goulet, Paulo Freire, and Gustavo Gutierrez.

Third World examples of the Moralist-Idealist model in use are more difficult to identify. Rarely do Moralist-Idealist movements take power. Instead, they stand in opposition to those in power, calling them to a greater commitment to justice. Probably the two countries coming closest to this model are Tanzania in East Africa and Jamaica. Because Tanzania was so highly colonized and so economically poor, it is highly dependent on export crops and had to generate its new internal economic order to some extent from the top down. Nevertheless, self-reliance is at the heart of President Nyerere's Moralist-Idealist model. His African socialism (also called "communitarian socialism" and "Christian socialism") is based on increasingly self-sufficient, community-oriented ("ujamaa") villages. An educational system based on cooperative effort and service has been an important instrument in counteracting elitism and promoting a community vision.

Jamaica, too, was a highly colonized country that neither experienced a violent revolution nor severed its ties with capitalism completely. Under President Manley, Jamaica has committed itself to achieve a new internal economic order on the basis of "democratic socialism." Rather than try to expel the multinational aluminum companies, Jamaica raised the levy (tax) on its bauxite 700% and renegotiated with the multinational corporations (see Ch. 9, p. 169) controlling this major source of its income. Manley's efforts at reversing Jamaica's heavy dependence on food imports include turning idle lands over to small or landless farmers and setting up some cooperative farms. It also means a five-point national nutrition plan promoting, among other things, universal breast-feeding and weaning to indigenous food stuffs.

A third example of the Moralist-Idealist model of development is the Gandhian movement in India. Although Gandhi was unable to see his model of development implemented throughout India after independence in 1947, beginnings were made. Today, a number of Indian villages, districts and regions continue to struggle to build their society along Gandhian (Moralist-Idealist) lines. One good example is the village of Patti Kalyana, whose story is told in detail in the next chapter.

Comparison and Evaluation

Gellar provides a fascinating analysis of these three models, based on the popular novel and movie, *One Flew Over the Cuckoo's Nest.* It represents a "view from the bottom," as he puts it—how Mainstream development looks to the oppressed.

He critiques the Mainstream model, which he identifies with
Nurse Ratched, through the resistance of the patient, R. P.
McMurphy (Jack Nicholson, in the movie).

The Ratched-McMurphy Model: A View From the Bottom

In the real world, the people at the top like to see
themselves as beneficent and have others see the world
the same way in which they do. They also like to see their
institutions run smoothly, whether it is the International
Economic Order, the World Bank, a state university, a
prison, or a mental institution. Dissident elements are not
easily tolerated because they threaten the established
order by challenging its legitimacy and right to impose its
rules on everybody connected with the institution. From
this perspective, order is a virtue and disruption an
abomination. With a little bit of imagination, Ken Kesey's
popular novel, *One Flew Over the Cuckoo's Nest*, which
inspired the recent award-winning movie of the same title
can be used metaphorically to depict the International
Economic Order from the utopian perspective of the people at the bottom.

Ratched and McMurphy: Ideology and Utopia

One Flew Over the Cuckoo's Nest revolves largely
around the political struggle between Nurse Ratched, the
upholder of the Established Order, and R. P. McMurphy,
a fiercely independent rebel who refuses to be domesticated by the powers that be. Most of the action takes place
in a mental institution which we assume is run by the
same people who run the International Economic Order.

Nurse Ratched manages a ward in the mental hospital. Backed by the full weight of her bosses, her institutional position gives her the power to define Develop-
ment/normalcy/sanity in a way compatible with her own
interests and those of her employers. She can also impose
this definition on the patients in her ward. There is only
one way for the patients to develop, and that is in accor-

dance with Nurse Ratched's way. Getting well (Development) means taking certain kinds of pills (private capital), listening to the right kind of soothing music (attending Western universities), and participating in therapy sessions (international institutions like the World Bank) led by Nurse Ratched. The prescriptions for mental health (Development) are standardized and disbursed to all patients regardless of their condition (level of Development) at regular intervals in order to insure the smooth and efficient functioning of the ward.

Nurse Ratched perceives herself and the institution which she serves as benevolent. She perceives her patients as inferior (Underdeveloped) and lacking the character traits and behavior patterns needed for proper adjustment to the real world (International Economic Order). Since her patients are insane (underdeveloped), they have to be watched and controlled very carefully so that they don't do any harm to themselves or the ward. Her mission is to guide her patients, if possible, along the path to sanity (Development).

To fulfill her mission, Nurse Ratched must act as both a teacher and a policeman. As a teacher, she must inculcate her patients with the norms needed to make them sane. She has several means at her disposition to help her achieve this goal, including the wisdom of medical science (technology) and the techniques of therapy (public administration).

Moreover, she has sufficient physical resources to meet the basic material needs of the patients in her ward and provide them with a measure of physical security. As a policeman, Nurse Ratched is charged with maintaining order which is indispensable to the patients' progress and enforcing the rules. She has several means for keeping her patients in line and discouraging violations of the rules—withdrawal of privileges (access to foreign aid), electric shock treatments (military intervention), and in extreme cases, lobotomies (destruction of the offending regime). In cases of serious disruption or violence in the ward, Nurse Ratched can also call upon several powerful orderlies to help her restore order.

The inmates of the ward are themselves a varied lot. Some are "Chronics" (Fourth World) who are given little or no hope for recovery and who are barely kept alive in vegetable form by the mental institution which, in some instances, put them in their helpless condition through unsuccessful therapy. Then there are the "Acutes" (Third World) who can be divided into those who were involuntarily committed (through colonialism) and those who willingly entered the mental hospital (nominally independent Third World countries) to seek a certain measure of psychic and material security because they could not cope with their problems (Underdevelopment). Some relate more easily to the norms and rules laid down by Nurse Ratched, like the college-educated Hardin who thinks that he is better than his fellow inmates because of his superior education. Others like Cheswick are less reconciled to their being in the ward and bear a lot of latent hostility towards Nurse Ratched.

For the most part, the "Acutes" are a fairly domesticated group who docilely accept and obey Nurse Ratched's regime. But all this changes when R. P. McMurphy enters the scene. McMurphy is a former war hero, chronic brawler, and rebel who winds up in Nurse Ratched's ward after being transferred from a prison farm to the mental institution because of his disruptive behavior. McMurphy soon upsets the order of the ward because of his refusal to accept Ratched's definition of normalcy (Development) and prescriptions for progress as valid. From McMurphy's utopian perspective, the mental hospital becomes an oppressive institution and Nurse Ratched's rules and regulations instruments of oppression designed to keep the inmates (Third World) docile and dependent. He scoffs at the ideological facade which portrays Nurse Ratched as a benevolent soul and competent professional seeking only the well-being of her patients. Instead, he sees her as an evil and oppressive monster who uses her power in a vicious and spiteful manner when crossed. Despite his limited resources and precarious position, McMurphy becomes the champion of the oppressed inmates of the ward and enters into combat with Nurse Ratched. In standing up for his own autonomy and human dignity and provoking his fellow inmates to rebellion through his example, McMurphy becomes the nemesis of Nurse Ratched and a threat to the smooth functioning of the institution (International Economic Order). As such he must be either domesticated or destroyed.

Administrative Discretion and the Facade of
Democracy

Much of the action in the movie revolves around the therapy sessions which are based on the notion of the "therapeutic community" whereby all the participants work out their problems together in democratic fashion. In theory, the therapy sessions are designed to facilitate healing and prepare the patients for their eventual participation in the outside world as healthy and well-adjusted people. There, the patients learn and practice the norms and virtues of good citizenship, self-help, and mutual cooperation. Although led by Nurse Ratched, in theory the therapy session is essentially a democratic institution in which all the actors are more or less equal "Partners in Progress". But, in practice, it is Nurse Ratched who controls the agenda for discussion, manipulates the patients' emotions to keep them psychologically dependent, and uses Divide and Rule tactics to divert their latent hostilities and resentment towards her and their situation towards each other.

One scene in the movie is particularly instructive in demonstrating how democratic facades are often used to mask naked authoritarianism. Thus, when McMurphy suggests that the patients in his therapy group be permitted to watch the World Series on television, he sets off a chain of events which reveals the professed democracy of the "therapeutic community" to be a farce. At first, Nurse Ratched smiles and patiently explains that changes in ward policy—*i.e.*, watching the World Series—must be, in democratic fashion, approved by the patients. Since most of the patients know that Nurse Ratched disapproves and are afraid to cross her, only a few support McMurphy. McMurphy is in the minority in the voting; Democracy triumphs. By the next therapy session, however, McMurphy has organized the members of his therapy group behind him (unity of the Third World) and calls for another vote. When the group votes unanimously to watch the World Series on television, Nurse Ratched rules that ward policy can't be changed without a majority of *all* the patients in the ward including the incapacitated "Chronics" who don't know what is going on most of the time. Frustrated and infuriated at this cynical manipulation of the rules, McMurphy frantically seeks to find the vote he needs to get his majority. After a frenzied effort, he succeeds in getting the vote of Chief Bromden, a giant Native American on the "Chronic" side of the ward who has feigned deafness and dumbness for several years. The Chief raises his hand in support. The majority has spoken; democracy triumphs. (UNCTAD will have its way.) But, alas, Nurse Ratched has ruled that the decisive vote came too late after the election had been closed. There will be no World Series for McMurphy and his friends. Ratched wins because she controls the mechanics of the election. More significantly, even though she has violated the spirit of the democratic principles which she initially invoked to defeat McMurphy, she is able to make her decision stick because she also has control over the television.

McMurphy, however, refuses to accept defeat without putting up a fight. He is going to assert his contempt for Nurse Ratched's violation of "fair play" and his defiance of Nurse Ratched and her rules. The other patients in the group rally to his banner. McMurphy pretends to watch the Series on TV. The other patients join him. Soon they are all shouting and pretending to be watching and enjoying a World Series game when, in fact, they are watching themselves on closed circuit television. Ratched is livid with fury at this open defiance on the part of the patients who feel a sense of their own potential for the first time in the movie.

Two important lessons emerge from the World Series incident: (1) that formal democratic structures often serve as an ideological face masking the arbitrariness and naked authoritarianism of the dominant classes; and (2) that alternative patterns of behavior which deviate from those laid down by the rulers must be rejected, especially when initiated by the oppressed.

Cheswick's Rebellion: The Struggle for Control Over One's Resources

Another stirring scene in the movie version of *One Flew Over the Cuckoo's Nest* underscores the realities of power relationships in Nurse Ratched's ward and the high costs of rebellion. Cheswick, one of the patients in the therapy group, complains bitterly about the fact that Nurse Ratched has rationed the ward's cigarettes. Emboldened by McMurphy's defiant example, the once meek and fearful Cheswick gets up enough nerve to insist that Nurse Ratched give him *his* cigarettes. Nurse Ratched refuses, explaining that the cigarettes were being withheld so that they would not be "misused" by the inmates who, under McMurphy's instigation, had used them for gambling chips, thus violating ward regulations forbidding gambling. This explanation does not appease Chewsick who now *demands* the right to have access to and control over his own resources. Cheswick is now in open revolt and screams for his cigarettes *now!* McMurphy takes up Cheswick's cause and breaks a window in Ratched's office to get a carton of cigarettes which he then tosses to Cheswick. With the rebellion getting out of hand, Nurse Ratched calls in the orderlies to subdue the hysterical Cheswick and to restore order. McMurphy starts battling with the orderlies when they attempt to seize Cheswick and put him in a straitjacket. Chief Bromden joins the fray when he sees his friend McMurphy in trouble. The three men are finally subdued in brutal fashion after reinforcements have been brought in to quell the rebellion. They are then sent to the Disturbed Ward for electric shock treatment as their punishment for challenging Nurse Ratched's authority and disrupting the order of the ward.

The lesson is clear. The oppressed classes and nations don't have the real claim on their own resources. When they insist upon controlling their own resources as they see fit, they are regarded as threats to the established order of the dominant classes and nations of the world. In Chile, Allende, like Cheswick, insisted upon Chile's right to control its own copper resources. The World Bank did not like this; ITT and other American companies did not like this; the CIA did not like this. So the orderlies were brought in to reestablish order. Like Cheswick, Allende had violated the rules by too forcefully pressing for nationalization and socialization of the Chilean economy.

Reolution, Reaction, and the Martyrdom of McMurphy

The movie reaches its climax in the last few scenes. McMurphy is preparing his escape. But before he goes, he engineers a wild party in the ward during the wee hours of the night which totally disrupts the carefully organized system set up by Ratched to domesticate the patients. Everyone starts doing whatever they feel like doing and are having a ball. The barriers between the "Chronics" and the "Acutes" crumble as the two groups fraternize and frolic together. The patients drink, dance, sing, make love, smash Nurse Ratched's office and transform the ward into a chaotic but happy liberated territory. And there are no Nurse Ratcheds around to stop them.

But then the morning comes, and Nurse Ratched returns to the ward with her orderlies to restore order. For some inexplicable reason, McMurphy has blown his chance to escape with his lady friend. Now comes the reaction. The patients are pushed around, herded together, and lined up as rebels. Billie Bibbit is singled out for immediate punishment for having made love to one of McMurphy's loose ladies on ward property. Through her bullying and torments, Ratched crushes Billie's spirit and drives him to suicide. After learning of Billie's death, McMurphy, in a wild rage, attempts to strangle Nurse Ratched to death but he is clubbed into unconsciousness before he can succeed. McMurphy is then sent off to get a lobotomy which renders him incapable of further resistance.

With the rebellion put down and its leaders punished, the ward returns to its regular routine, once again under the watchful eye and smile of Nurse Ratched. However, McMurphy's resistance and martyrdom have not been in vain. Although order has been reestablished, Nurse Ratched is no longer the same power she was before the arrival of McMurphy. She now has to wear a neck brace and the patients know that she is not omnipotent. Moreover, McMurphy's example has inspired the once moribund Chief Bromden to gain enough self-confidence, courage, and strength to attempt an escape. But before doing so, he smothers McMurphy, now reduced to a helpless vegetable, to death with a pillow because he cannot bear to see his friend in such a pitiful state. The movie ends with the Chief, a symbol of America's most oppressed and exploited people, smashing his way out of the ward by throwing a huge chrome fixture through a window (an act requiring a prodigious feat of strength) and then running off into the night to freedom.

Although *One Flew Over the Cuckoo's Nest* was clearly not written as a Utopian Moralist-Idealist critique of the present International Economic Order, it does examine the actual functioning of institutions from the perspective of the people at the bottom by encouraging the reader to empathize with the plight of the patients in the ward and to applaud McMurphy's refusal to be domesticated by the power structure. It rejects the mainstream definition of normalcy (Development) imposed by Ratched, the interpretation of reality which presents the mental hospital and the people who run them ("Have" classes and nations) as benevolent, and the prescriptions (corporate capitalism) proposed by Ratched as ill-suited to the real needs of the patients. Moreover, it denounces the ideological weapons and physical violence used by Ratched to maintain her dominant position and keep the patients in her ward in line. Finally, the Ratched-McMurphy model affirms the primacy of Liberation over Order (Domesticated Development) and asserts the rights of the inmates (oppressed classes and peoples of the world) to resist dehumanization and exploitation and to run their lives and manage their resources in conformance with their own rather than Nurse Ratched's worldviews and interests.

Discussion Questions

1. What are the main characteristics of Nurse Ratched's approach to dealing with people? Describe real life situations in which you have seen people act like Nurse Ratched or in which you yourself have been "Ratched-ed."
2. What are McMurphy's main characteristics? Have you ever seen a McMurphy in action? If so, what happened?
3. Describe some situations in your life when you have identified with or acted like Nurse Ratched, McMurphy, Chief Bromden, Cheswick, one of the orderlies.
4. What parallels to the present global situation did you find in the " Ratched-McMurphy Model"?
5. How important is it to be the *agent* as well as the *beneficiary* of one's own (personal and societal) development?

6. Which of the two models would provide a better chance for "bread and justice"? Do either of them really do the job? Explain.

Resources

On the Mainstream Model—Brazil
  —Donald E. Syvrud, *Foundations of Brazilian Economic Growth* (Stanford University: Hoover Institution Press, 1974) is the view of a former U.S. Treasury Department attaché in Rio, 1965–1969.
  —Georges-Andre Fiechter, *Brazil Since 1964: Modernization under a Military Regime* (New York: Halsted Press, 1975) is a second favorable description of the "Brazilian miracle".
  —*Focus on Brazil: A Case Study of Development* (Global Development Studies Institute, P.O. Box 522, Madison, N.J. 07940) is an excellent 135-page workbook for advanced high school students and others on economic and social development in Brazil.

China
  —Jan Myrdal, *Report from a Chinese Village* and his later *China: The Revolution Continued*, both Vintage paperbacks, present a view of China's village life, through extensive interviews with the people. *Report* focuses on the cultural, political, and social aspects of China's "progressive social construction" between 1959 and 1963. The second work (1973) studies the same village eight years later and is also valuable in terms of its pictures.
  —"Shanghai: The New China" is a 33-minute, 16mm, color film (S. F. Newsreel, 630 Natoma St., San Francisco, CA 94101)—a CBS 1974 News Documentary—that presents a balanced report on the transformation of the Chinese port city from a decadent center of poverty and foreign domination to the modern Shanghai of today. Thus, it provides a view of the Revolution in an urban setting.

—The Washington Office on Latin America (110 Maryland Ave NE, Washington, DC 20002) and its monthly "Legislative Update".

On the Moralist-Idealist Model—
Tanzania

—*Self-Reliant Tanzania* (from Third World Publications, 15 Dovey Rd., Birmingham B13 9NT, England) is a comprehensive sourcebook on Tanzania, well-illustrated with photos and charts. It contains six essays by Nyerere, including "Education for Self-Reliance", "The Arusha Declaration", and "*Ujamaa*—The Basis of African Socialism."

—"Of People and a Vision" is a 20-minute, 16mm (Maryknoll Films) film offering a view of self-reliance through the lives of five Tanzanians helping to promote communitarian socialism in their country. The supportive presence of Maryknoll missionaries is quite evident in the film.

On Capitalism vs. Socialism

—Richard Taylor, *Economics and the Gospel* (Philadelphia: United Church of Christ Press, 1975). This book outlines the basic biblical principles that relate to economic issues. Then, in light of these principles, it evaluates and compares the U.S. economic system as it operates domestically and overseas with socialist examples. In addition, each chapter identifies changes that need to take place in the U.S. economic system, ways in which we can be part of such changes, and questions for discussion and further study.

—*This Land Is Home to Me*, the 1975 pastoral letter of the Catholic bishops of Appalachia, contains an almost poetic presentation and reflection on the economic realities of Appalachia. It focuses on the urgent need for fundamental changes in the capitalist model of development and bases this analysis on Scripture and Catholic social teaching.

—American Christians Toward Socialism (ACTS) is the U.S. branch of Christians for Socialism (ACTS National Office,

3540 14th St., Detroit, MI 48208). It has chapters in a number of U.S. cities (Chicago, Detroit, New York, Washington, DC, Berkeley, and elsewhere). Among its publications are *Option for Struggle: Three Documents of Christians for Socialism* and a series of working papers produced by various chapters of ACTS.

Chapter Fourteen

SELF-RELIANT DEVELOPMENT

This chapter outlines the basic components of a new internal economic order based on a self-reliant model of development and uses the village of Patti Kalyana to illustrate this model.

The kind of new internal economic order needed to ensure that a New International Economic Order is beneficial to the majorities, rather than the elites, of Third World countries is one based on principles of self-reliant development. Bread and justice, as defined in this book, are most fully realized in societies committed to self-reliance. Before examining what self-reliant development is, let's first see what it is not. Clearly it is not the Mainstream model of development presented in Chapter 13.

What Self-Reliance Is Not

Not a Ladder

Almost by definition, self-reliant development rejects the Mainstream notion of development as catching up with the First World. Besides the element of imitation implied in the notion of trying to climb faster up a single ladder of development, such an image ignores the real cause of why countries are at the bottom. As was pointed out in the last chapter, those at the top are there partially because they climbed up on the backs of those beneath them. The example of Potosi silver (Ch. 2, pp. 29-31) illustrates graphically the link between the underdevelopment of the Third World and the development of the First World.

Instead of acknowledging such a link, Mainstream theorists continue to offer technological solutions to what are basically social or political problems. What is needed are more money, technology and expertise, they claim. Technological revolutions like the Green Revolution are hailed as the answer, when in fact it is deeper social or political changes that are needed. Underdevelopment is a social or political problem requiring far-reaching changes in the economic institutions and arrangements whereby the First World continues to dominate the Third World. But most people refuse to face this fact. We still hear the familiar melody of "why don't they pick themselves up by their own bootstraps?" and "we did it, so why can't they do it?" Tolstoy's insight is quite appropriate here: "I sit on a man's back, choking him and making him carry me, and yet assure myself and others that I am very sorry for him and wish to ease his lot by any means possible, except getting off his back."[1]

Not a Bigger Piece of Pie

The Mainstream model offers a quantitative vision of development. In measuring development in terms of Gross National Product, per capita income, etc., it overlooks some important qualitative aspects of the use of resources. Economic growth almost becomes an end in itself. The Mainstream model projects an ever bigger pie, rather than a redistribution of the present pie. One concise statement of this view appears in a recent high school social studies text. James Calderwood, the economist author of *The Developing World: Poverty, Growth and Rising Expectations*, writes that "there is no future in arguing over who gets the largest slices of a pie of a fixed size. Instead, what must be done is to *bake a larger pie so that all can have more*. That means pushing ahead with economic growth in the world" (italics mine).[2] In this way, a bigger slice for the impoverished Third World would not require a smaller slice for the First World.

First of all, self-reliant models of development reject the image of an ever expanding pie. The emphasis on greater self-sufficiency and respect for the earth's limits is characteristic not only of Gandhian self-reliance but other Moralist-Idealist and Marxist versions of self-reliant development as well.

But self-reliance goes a step further. Besides rejecting an ever bigger pie, it projects a different set of bakers and ingredients. Using ingredients that they control—capital, technology, and the media (see Ch. 9)—the multinational corporations currently bake a pie that feeds them quite well. Until these bakers and ingredients are changed, the pie will not be distributed any differently. Thus, self-reliant models of development envision local communities and participatory Third World governments as at least co-bakers with the corporations. The new ingredients would be drawn much more heavily from the resources, skills, and technology available locally. And they would produce a very different pie—one tasty to the simple palates of the majorities of Third World peoples, and not just to the delicate palates of the few.

Not a Trickling Down

According to Mainstream models, Third World industrialists, bankers, large export farmers, etc. are the logical choices for a larger slice of pie. They can set in motion a process (see Ch. 13, pp. 240-41) that will enable additional bites of pie to trickle down to the masses below. This "trickle down" theory has been repeatedly challenged. Chapter 6 on export cropping revealed how investing agricultural technology, credit, and extension services in large scale agriculture resulted in fewer days a year worked, less income, and less food for the majority of farmers and farm workers. That wealth did not trickle down to the many. Rather, it was siphoned off by the few. Visually, it might look like this:

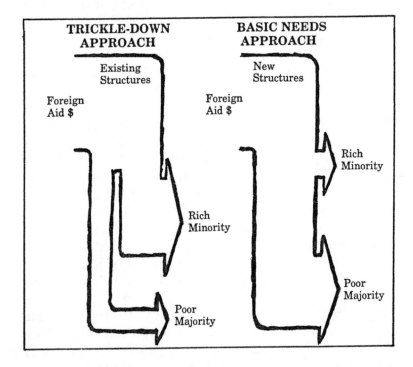

Let's return for a moment to the "Brazilian miracle" mentioned in Chap. 13 (p. 241). During the so-called miracle years, when Brazil's annual economic rate of growth averaged about 10%, the top 1% of the population increased its share of the national income from 12% to 17%. The bottom 50% of the population saw its share drop from 17.6% to 13.7%. The real value of the minimum wage dropped 55% during this same decade. What this means concretely is this. In 1966, it took a person working at the minimum wage 25½ hours to earn enough to buy a family monthly ration of 12 pounds of meat. Nine years later, according to Sao Paulo trade union statistics, that person had to work 66 hours for the same amount of meat.[3] If anything then, it would be more accurate to speak of a "trickle up" effect!

Thus, self-reliant development rejects concentrating national resources on the rich in the hope that something might trickle down. Instead, self-reliant development concentrates directly on those at the bottom and on their basic needs.

What Self-Reliance Is

Having explored what self-reliant development is not, let's see more of what it is. The definition offered in the Introduction to Part IV (p. 236)—

a model of development that emphasizes meeting the basic human needs of the masses of people in a country through strategies geared to the particular human and natural resources, values, and traditions of the country, and through strategies maximizing the collective efforts of people within each country and among Third World Countries—

focuses on four elements, the four basic components of justice.

1. Basic Human Needs

As previously stated, this means attacking poverty directly, rather than waiting for something eventually to trickle down. This direct attack would mean a priority in public expenditures on housing, health care, education and jobs. Land reform and other measures to redistribute the means of producing food are equally important.

In terms of "food self-reliance,"[4] this principle would imply that land and other agricultural resources would be concentrated on producing nutritious local staples. Only after that had been satisfied would industrial crops, livestock feed crops, and luxury vegetables and fruits be planted. Likewise, once local self-sufficiency in food has been achieved, trade can be beneficial in supplying those productive goods for further development that cannot be produced locally.

2. Building on Local/National Resources and Values

Here the stress is on creating educational systems, technology and jobs that are appropriate to the conditions, needs, resources and values of the people. Development involves the development of individuals as well as nations. Thus, genuine national development has to make full use of its peoples' strengths, creativity, resources, and its cultural and natural heritage. This aspect of self-reliance is beautifully expressed by Mahbub ul Haq:

> ... Not self-reliance in the sense of cutting our links completely from the world, but self-reliance in the sense of being so self-confident as a nation as to base our development on our own cultural values. Self-reliance is a very comprehensive concept which cuts across all walks of life. It implies not only reliance on our own industry or agriculture, or on our own domestic resources or technology. It is relying on our own thinking and our own value systems, without being defensive or apologetic.[5]

Perhaps the clearest example of this aspect of self-reliance is the notion of "intermediate" and "appropriate" technology, mentioned in Chapter 9 on multinational corporations (pp. 162-3). "Intermediate" denotes technology that is midway between advanced First World models and local, traditional methods. "Appropriate" refers to technology that makes the best use of the human, financial and natural resources available in a given situation. A good example is provided by Lisa

Leghorn and Mary Roodkowsky in *Who Really Starves: Women and World Hunger*:

> Women need small-scale machinery for food processing, for instance. A manual grinder can process 20 pounds of grain per hour, replacing the mortar and pestle, which in the same time can pound a maximum of only three pounds.... What technology is appropriate for use varies from situation to situation, however. In some of the rice mills of Asia where large-scale commercial machinery has been introduced, malnutrition has increased because the engine-powered mills discard the vitamin-laden husk. Such operations are costly, and they are owned and operated entirely by men. Hence the manual grinders, which seem less efficient, are not only more nutritionally sound but cost less. They also mean that the women will not become dependent upon distant mills to hull their rice.[6]

3. *Maximum Participation of the People*

First, this means participatory decision-making models throughout the institutions and systems of a country. Thus, self-reliant development clearly opts for the "McMurphy model" rather than the "Ratched model" of development. By its very definition, self-reliance implies people becoming the agents and not just the beneficiaries of development.

Secondly, this principle means increasing the productive capacities of the people. It does not mean welfare doles and slower growth rates. Chapter 6 on export cropping and Chapter 9 on multinational corporations both demonstrated how inefficient inequality is. That is, concentrating scarce national resources on the few large farmers or industrialists, rather than on the majority of smaller producers, does not mean greater production and wider distribution. In fact, the experience of small farmers in the U.S. as well as in many parts of the Third World points to the opposite conclusion.

Small farmers turn out to be more efficient producers, per unit of land, in most cases than large farmers. According to World Bank studies cited in *Food First*, the value of output per acre in India is more than one-third higher on the smallest farms. In Argentina, Brazil, Chile, Colombia, Ecuador and Guatemala, small farmers are three to fourteen times more productive per acre than large farmers. Where large farmers are factually more productive, the reason generally turns out to be their much greater access to credit, subsidies, land, guaranteed prices, etc.[7]

Why are small farmers—in the U.S. as well as in the Third World—more efficient? Collins and Lappe point out how small farmers plant more closely than machines do. They mix and rotate complementary crops and use their quite limited resources to the fullest. "Farming for the peasant family," as they put it, "is not an abstract calculation of profit to be weighed against other investments. It is a matter of life and death."[8] Thus, the emphasis on maximum participation of the people makes economic sense as well as social and moral sense.

4. Interdependence—Collective Self-Reliance

The collective or cooperative efforts of the masses of people within Third World countries need to be supplemented by joint efforts with the peoples of other Third World countries. This has been stressed several times, especially with regard to negotiating with the multinational corporations (Ch. 10, pp. 188-9) and to increasing trade markets (Ch. 5, p. 88). Thus, self-reliance is far different from the notion of total self-sufficiency and isolation that the term implies to some people. This element of interdependence in self-reliance will be explored more fully in Part V, especially Ch. 16, pp. 299-301.

To stimulate your reflection on the advantages of self-reliant models of development, read the following assessment provided in *Reshaping the International Order* and try to answer the questions below:

It enables nations to assume fuller responsibility for their own development within a framework of enlarged political and economic independence. It builds development around individuals and groups rather than people around development and it attempts to achieve this through the deployment of local resources and indigenous efforts. The mobilization of the creative energies of the people themselves—a resource neglected in many previous efforts at development—*contributes directly to the formation of new value systems, to the direct attack of poverty, alienation and frustration,* and to the more creative utilization of productive factors. Self-reliant development, with its reliance on local rather than imported institutions and technologies, is a means whereby a nation can *reduce its vulnerability* to decisions and events which fall outside its control: a self-reliant community will be *more resilient in times of crisis.* And since it is a style of development predicated upon a recognition of cultural diversity, it is an instrument against the excessive homogenization of cultures.[9] (italics mine)

(1) What advantages and disadvantages do you see in self-reliant models of development?

(2) How would self-reliant development specifically contribute, as the quotation states, "to the direct attack on poverty, alienation and frustration"?

(3) How would self-reliant development specifically make societies less "vulnerable" and "more resilient in times of crisis", as the statement claims?

Patti Kalyana as a Case-Study of Self-Reliant Development

Introduction

With the advent of the Green Revolution in India in the 1950s and 1960s, there has been a movement away from the kind of self-reliant development outlined above and championed by Mahatma Gandhi. Nevertheless, within India the Gandhian movement has remained committed to the principles and policies of self-reliant development. The village of Patti Kalyana in northern India represents one attempt of the Gandhian movement to implement such a model. Interestingly enough, in this same part of India, it is not uncommon for only half of the small farmers to be able to provide for their families' food needs for more than six months each year. Thus, the results of this self-reliant model are quite important for the rest of the area and country as a whole.

While national examples of self-reliant development are available—Chapter 13 mentioned Tanzania, China, Jamaica, Chile under Allende, and others—Patti Kalyana was chosen for detailed examination for several reasons. First, it is an example of a Moralist-Idealist model of development that is clearly different from both the Mainstream and the Marxist models summarized in Chapter 13. Secondly, it raises the serious question of whether and to what extent self-reliant development can succeed within a country where it is not a national policy. In its failures as well as in its successes, Patti Kalyana highlights the essential ingredients of self-reliance. Finally, Patti Kalyana is an effort to which I am personally related and with which I feel a real sense of solidarity.

General Description of Patti Kalyana[10]

The village is located in the state of Haryana, 40 miles north of New Delhi. It consists of three residential clusters and one uninhabited area and covers 3,529 acres. Its 1970 population was 4,901 (808 families). Village decisions—like the running of the village primary school, village sanitation, and care of village roads—are made by the *panchayat*, a group of ten adults elected by all the adult villagers.

Agriculturally, there are 1,300 owner-farmers, very few tenant farmers, and only 80 landless farm laborers. The 2,944 acres they farm are divided into 987 separate holdings. Two-acre plots are the rule, with a very few big farms. With family labor the common pattern in Patti Kalyana, it is not surprising that 490 of the 1,380 persons in agriculture are women. This is about double the proportion of women in agriculture in other parts of the region and the country. 80% of the farm land is irrigated, which is much higher than most Indian villages. Nevertheless, in 1970, mostly because of the limited agricultural workforce, about 65% of the land grew only one crop. Generally this crop was wheat.

Outside the agricultural sector, in 1970, another 820 villagers were employed in household and simple manufacturing industries, in trade and commerce, in teaching, and other occupations. Among the simple industries in the village, I observed in 1972 a *khadi* (hand-spun and hand-woven cloth) production and training center, rope-making and rope-making machine assembly operations, and the production of paper for greeting cards and documents. Finally, at least 75 residents, generally graduates of the government high school in the village, leave each year in search of opportunities in neighboring towns and cities.

Patti Kalyana's "Integrated Development Programme"

1. *The Vision.* According to the opening paragraph of "A Programme of Development for Village Patti Kalyana", this program was informed by the following vision:

> Over two decades of planned effort at development has incontrovertibly demonstrated that for development to be a continuous, self-sustaining process, rather than coming in sporadic spurts, it should be initiated at the grassroots; that those whose development is sought to be initiated, should be fully involved in the various stages of the process; that while external change-agencies can be made to serve an initial function of acting as catalysts of the change process, leadership should come up from within and that the sooner this happens the better; and that the process of development should be firmly based on the existing realities of the given situation, the preferences, the skills and even the traditions, but that it should be conceived in such a way that the movement towards modernity, in the best sense of the term, will obtain gradually and by stages. This would mean that each of our 500,000 villages must have a distinct role of its own in the development panorama, a role that should at the same time be in consonance with the total movement.

This vision clearly incorporates the four ingredients of self-reliant development. In particular, it emphasizes maximum participation of the people and building on local resources and values.

2. *The Framework.* On the basis of an extensive socio-economic survey conducted by the Gandhian movement, in close cooperation with the villagers in 1970, it was concluded that Patti Kalyana had apparently progressed as far as it could through individualistic efforts. The time seemed right for a collective or cooperative approach. The Haryana Gandhi Centenary Committee decided that it could only come about through some external catalyst. Thus, in 1971, this Committee and the village *panchayat* agreed to the establishment of *Swarajya Bharati*, an institution consisting of a team of Gandhian workers. Their task was to help carry out an action program based on a framework outlined the year before. This framework was agreed to by the village *panchayat* and was based on the following thirteen premises:

(1) Patti Kalyana's agriculture had vast potential;

(2) This potential was not being utilized because only family labor was available;

(3) It was desirable to continue to develop agriculture only as a family occupation. This seemed to be the best arrangement, for both social and economic reasons;

(4) More family labor, especially from women, would be available, if agriculture was made more attractive;

(5) This could be done by a school program for young children, designed for the convenience of women intending to work on the farms;

(6) Some children working on farms would be kept away by the school program, but women could replace them, thus raising the total labor input available;

(7) The other way to make farming attractive would be to offer training facilities in modern agriculture for women as well as men;

(8) Even with spectacular success in (5) and (7), there would be a shortage of labor for the best use of the agricultural resources of the village. Thus, some interme-

diate technology would have to be introduced. A modern equipment and training program should be started, including a small tractor and a small soil-testing laboratory;

(9) There should be a revolving fund to enable the small farmers to use modern techniques;

(10) There should be demonstrations of the proper techniques on the village common land;

(11) Since some 75 persons migrate each year, a 3-year program to create some 225 jobs within the rural industry sector should be begun;

(12) Since it was not envisioned that non-family labor would move into agriculture, some 175 jobs in the rural sector should be made more remunerative.

(13) The total cost of such a program would come to about 450,000 rupees, which is equivalent to about $54,000 in 1978 exchange rates.

3. Planning and Implementing the "Integrated Development Programme"

(a) *Agricultural Development.* The first step toward a cooperative approach to agriculture was the leasing for ten years of 140 acres of grazing land owned by 350 families of the village. This land was to serve as a training center for cooperative farming for young persons of small and marginal landholding families. It was on part of this land that multiple cropping patterns and methods would be tested and demonstrated. Interestingly, the lease agreement designated the money (10,000 rupees per year) for meeting the basic needs of the village. These specific needs were identified by the villagers themselves, as a way of furthering collective thinking and programming.

The second step was the development of a "farmers service center" designed to overcome the three biggest problems of small farmers—large landowners, money lenders, and middle men. The center coordinated the use of the village tractor and provided extension services, fertilizer and seeds, and credit. It directed the exploration for tubewells and served as a cooperative marketing organization for the cash crops produced.

(b) *Rural Industries.* Next, the Gandhian team and the villagers worked out a long-range plan for building the development of small industries on the agricultural base of the community. An important aspect of self-reliance, this plan provides an excellent model for small-scale agro-industrial development, as it is called. The land provided by the villagers was to serve as the nucleus around which various village industries would revolve. The focus was a combination of self-sufficiency and better nutrition in food production, of greater self-sufficiency in other basic needs, and of increased participation in local trading opportunities. In graphic form, the plan looked like this: ⟶

The first priorities went to setting up a dairy with ten buffalos and a brick-kiln, along with cane-crushing and sugar-making operations. Improving the village oil *ghani*, a simple machine for extracting oil from oil seeds like mustard seeds, was also done at the beginning. The raising of sheep and goats was rated as a promising future prospect because Patti Kalyana is situated only twelve miles from one of the biggest wool markets in India.

(c) *Educational and Social Development.* Corresponding to the agro-industrial program based on cooperative agriculture was an educational plan. It was designed to promote greater self-reliance through cooperative efforts and through the integration of theory and practice. First, for pre-school children, the villagers and the Gandhian team established the first of what would be ten *balwadis*. These are similar to "Head Start" programs in the U.S. This first *balwadi* served as a teacher-training center where young women were also taught how to make hosiery. Economic self-sufficiency was clearly an important goal.

VILLAGE-SCALE AGRO-INDUSTRIAL DEVELOPMENT

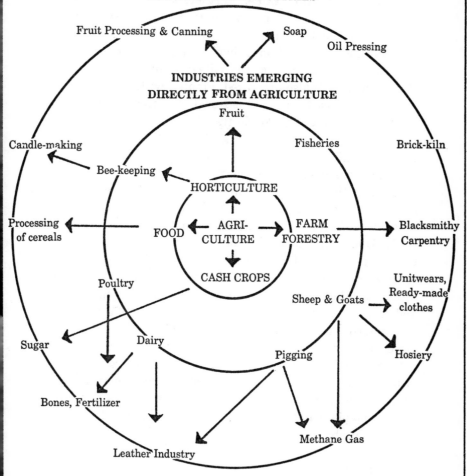

INDUSTRIES EMERGING FROM INTERMEDIATE INDUSTRIES

Fruit Processing & Canning   Soap   Oil Pressing

INDUSTRIES EMERGING DIRECTLY FROM AGRICULTURE

Fruit   Fisheries   Brick-kiln

Candle-making   Bee-keeping   HORTICULTURE

Processing of cereals   FOOD   AGRI-CULTURE   FARM FORESTRY   Blacksmithy Carpentry

CASH CROPS

Poultry   Sheep & Goats   Unitwears, Ready-made clothes

Sugar   Dairy   Pigging   Hosiery

Bones, Fertilizer   Methane Gas

Leather Industry

Methane Gas: from manure
Leather Industry: hides from dead animals
Bones, Fertilizer: from dead animals
Soap: oils from fruit
Candle-making: wax from bees
Blacksmithy & Carpentry: iron & wood from nearby

Secondly, adult education efforts were begun. One-day to three-day camps were organized for adult leaders. These sessions would focus on principles of cooperative farming, dialogue skills (for conducting meetings, consensus decision-making), and accounting skills. Further, the village set up a recreation room and a room for information on current events and technological developments. An emphasis was placed on disseminating information through charts, posters, wall maps, etc. Tours, for instance, of the village sanitation demonstration center, were also organized. Finally, with Patti Kalyana within the telecast range of the New Delhi television station, a proposal was made to provide transistorized radio and television support for the various agricultural, educational and other scientific newscasts.

Thirdly, a camp for college students and other volunteers working with the villagers during the summer was established. Lastly, a "Basic Education" middle school and high school would eventually be set up to complement the existing Basic Education primary school and to offer an alternative to the government high school. Gandhian Basic Education schools are committed to the development of heart and body, as well as mind. The program involves an integration of study and service—theory and practice. The teaching of a craft and an emphasis on artistic and other forms of creative expression are designed to develop creative, self-reliant persons who are able to stand up for what they believe. Through growing their own vegetables, the students not only learn to care for the environment, but also help to make the school as self-sufficient as possible. In fact, students do the cooking and cleaning tasks themselves.

4. The Results

In addition to the activities and services already mentioned, by July 1975, the cooperative farm—land previously unable to grow crops—had been cleared and fully irrigated and was yielding crops worth more than 100,000 rupees. Already by 1972, 236 additional part-time and some full-time jobs had been created, mostly in agricultural activities on the cooperative farm and at the brick-kiln. By 1975, full-time employment had been generated for more than 40 families. More than a dozen young women had completed the six-month training program at the *balwadi*, where well over one hundred children had participated. Several hundred farmers had benefitted from the "farmers' service center."

Moreover, a number of community services were undertaken by the villagers. These included the socio-economic survey, a village sanitation program, the hosiery training program, the laying of bricks in the village lanes, the extension of the boys' high school building, the construction of a small hospital, demonstration camps on water management technology and land levelling, the planting of 1200 trees by summer youth camp participants, and training in the village oil industry.

Lastly, at least a partial basis had been laid for the implementation of the bulk of the agro-industrial and educational aspects of the program. Whether the Gandhian team would be able to disengage themselves from their role as catalyst within the projected five to ten years was a question that would remain unanswered. On June 26, 1975, Mrs. Indira Gandhi, Prime Minister of India, declared a state of emergency.

It took only a week for the repressive repercussions to reach Patti Kalyana. As the leader of the Gandhian team described it in a recent letter, the project and the village became:

a victim of a political vendetta. Standing crops in about 50 acres were destroyed by driving cattle onto the fields, and preparations for the monsoon crop in the rest of the fields were set at naught. More than 1200 trees, which were planted only a week before by the boys and girls during the youth camp, were all uprooted and destroyed. Nevertheless, in spite of the political victimization, it was because of the peaceful perseverance of the villagers and the

panchayat that the land was ultimately transferred to the
panchayat . . . .

Following repeated requests from the *panchayat* and
with their assurances, when we again tried to take up the
work in full earnest, our fields were again devastated and
grazed by the same lawless element. When the *panchayat*
took up the matter with the authorities, the authorities
attached the property, with the result that the state machinery also became a party to seeing that our huge
investments, in the name of the public good, were brought
to ruin and our institution is in a state of bankruptcy.
Repeated requests and representations brought by the
villagers and the institution alike bore no results, as everyone tried to turn a deaf ear, seeing the mood of the
political bosses.

Despite the election of Morarji Desai, a long-time Gandhian, as Prime Minister in the spring of 1977, and his personal commitment to village industries and rural development, the financial loss was so great that the Gandhian
institution felt it had to pull out. But that was not the last
chapter in Patti Kalyana's experiment with self-reliant development.

First, the whole matter went to court in late 1977, with a
favorable verdict still anticipated. If the verdict is favorable,
then the village *panchayat* will probably take up the responsibility for managing the cooperative farm. The transition from
Gandhian leadership to village leadership will have taken a
giant step forward.

Secondly, the Gandhian team has regrouped and broad-
ened its focus. In mid-1978, it began a program of "Integrated
Development of the Area," directed primarily at the rural
poor. In addition to Patti Kalyana, 119 other villages in the
area (about 190,000 people) would be covered. The first step in
this program lay in setting up a "Rural Development and
Youth Training Center," with several sub-centers in different
parts of the area. Viewed as "growth centers," they would
provide both training for poor and undereducated rural youth
and the agricultural services provided by the "farmers' service

center" in Patti Kalyana (see pages 269-270). The Center is concerned with three main goals:

(1) economic development, by organizing training facilities in the various aspects of agriculture, animal husbandry and village handicrafts and industries;

(2) personal development through a non-formal educational process, by involving rural youth and adults in various training extension services;

(3) cultural change in fundamental values toward life, by involving the various educational and scientific institutions of the area in a cooperative approach.

And so the struggle continues. Will self-reliant development in Patti Kalyana and the surrounding area be successful in the long run? Let's consider how successful it has been so far.

Evaluation of Self-Reliant Development in Patti Kalyana

In trying to assess how well Patti Kalyana succeeded in establishing a self-reliant model of development, we should ask the following questions:

(1) In what specific ways did Patti Kalyana's "Integrated Development Programme" focus its efforts and resources on the basic human needs of all villagers? How well do you think it was/is doing in this regard?

(2) In what specific ways did it rely on the natural and human resources of the village and build on the culture, values, and traditions of the villagers? How well do you think it was/is doing in this regard?

(3) In what specific ways did it spread leadership among the villagers and incorporate them into decision-making? How successful do you think the Gandhian team was in promoting maximum participation in a development process that would no longer need them?

(4) In what specific ways did it foster interdependence?

(5) In what specific ways did it achieve the advantages of self-reliant development that were identified in the *Reshaping the International Order* statement on pp. 264-265 above?

Other basic questions raised by this case study are important for understanding the ingredients of successful self-reliant models of development. They include:

(1) To what extent can a program partially or largely planned and financed by outside sources survive major adversity?

(2) How far can self-reliant development proceed in a country where there is no national policy of self-reliance?

I asked some of these questions of the leader of the Gandhian team in Patti Kalyana. His answers provide further insight into both the possibilities and the difficulties of achieving self-reliant development. I quote two of them as the conclusion to this chapter:

Question: To what extent was the village involved in developing the framework for the "Integrated Development Programme" and in the planning of the various stages?

Answer: At the village farm, all those who were working at the farm were participating in program formulation as well as in the management. In the beginning, an effort was made to involve others not directly related to the farm, but this proved to be an unhealthy blockade. This was perhaps because they were never before exposed to such situations and hence the human weakness of jealousy could be seen in some of them. As a result, the village leaders and people in general decided to ask us to pursue the cooperative farm program in consultation with those who were involved in the actual working and to keep the rest of the villagers informed from time to time.

In the second place, the villagers in general, through their own meetings, were the ones to decide how to use the funds provided to the village from the leasing of the 140 acres. They made their own decisions on these matters.

Further, when we had our troubles during the Emergency, it was again the villagers who formulated the strategy and fought the situation. Nine of ten members of the village *panchayat* repeatedly passed resolutions at their meetings praising our efforts and spelling out the unjust loss inflicted on us. This was done in spite of threats from political quarters.

Question: In what ways would you say that your "Integrated Development Programme" achieved the principles of self-reliant development as outlined in this chapter?

Answer: If the villagers as a whole could have taken up the responsibilities, then self-reliant development would have been more fully achieved. The village *panchayat* can today be said to be the most resourceful *panchayat* in the State. But the irony is that politics will not allow the growth of such resources. If such resources are generated, they are bound to be washed away for unethical ends.

Regarding "food self-reliance", again, though vast stretches of waste land were brought under cultivation, food self-reliance can only be achieved when the small and marginal farmers are individually involved in the process. In this respect, we made considerable progress. The "farmers service center" reached 696 small farmers from about thirty different villages. But a more comprehensive program is needed.

Resources

1. On "What Self-Reliance Is Not"

a. Three especially effective critiques of the "trickle-down" theory are

—Susan George, *How the Other Half Dies*, p. 71.

—Andre Gunder Frank, "The Development of Underdevelopment," in Robert Rhodes, ed., *Imperialism and Underdevelopment: A Reader* (New York: Monthly Review Press, 1970).

—The vision of "another development" in the Dag Hammarskjold Foundation report, *What Now*, especially pp. 28–43.

b. For a critique of the "Brazilian miracle," there are numerous items, including

—Michael Harrington, *The Vast Majority: A Journey to the World's Poor* (New York: Simon & Schuster, 1978) uses the Brazilian miracle as his test case for demonstrating the causal link between First World development and Third World underdevelopment. An excerpt containing a 2-page analysis of the Brazilian miracle is presented in "The Development of Underdevelopment," *Christianity and Crisis*, October 3, 1977.

—*Child of the Dark: The Diary of Carolina Maria de Jesus* (Signet, 1962), is a simple, powerful, first-hand account of Brazilian life from the underneath—in one of Sao Paulo's worst slums. The diary details Carolina's struggle to retain her humanity in the midst of incredible poverty and the relative powerlessness of the poor to change their situation.

2. On "What Self-Reliance Is"

On the general theory of self-reliant development, three books are helpful:

—Dag Hammarskjold Foundation, *What Now*, especially pp. 28–43.

—*Reshaping the International Order*, especially Chapter 5.

—World Employment Conference of the International Labor Organization, *Employment, Growth and Basic Needs: A One-World Problem*, especially Part I. For a concise statement of self-reliant development, with an analysis of the different historical circumstances of Third World development efforts compared to First World Development, read Barbara Ward, *A "People" Strategy of Development*, Communiqué #23 (Washington, DC: Overseas Development Council, 1975; 10¢).

3. On Self-Reliance and Women

Much of the discussion and planning around the New International Economic Order has overlooked this important aspect of development. Besides the two items listed in footnote #6 above, there are a couple of other items that would be helpful:

—Mary Burke, "Women and World Economics: Some Suggestions for a More Creative Role for Women in World Development," NIEO Memorandum #6 (Washington, DC: Center of Concern, November 1976).

—The entire issue of *The New Internationalist*, October 1977.

4. *On Patti Kalyana*

"Third World Development: India, A Case Study," is a 30-minute slide presentation I produced in 1974. It uses Patti Kalyana as one example of self-reliant development, thus offering a visual translation. It is available for rentals only, from the Institute for Education in Peace and Justice in St. Louis.

Chapter Fifteen

WHAT CAN I DO?

This chapter suggests a variety of ways we can promote self-reliant development in the Third World and asks each person to decide which action makes the most sense for him or her to do.

Before asking what we can do to promote a new internal economic order based on self-reliance, let's examine how we are already involved in the issue. This involvement is two-fold. First, there are a number of ways in which we and our communities are unintentionally part of the problem. Secondly, there are other ways in which we are touched ourselves by the lack of bread and justice within many Third World countries. In each case, it is important to keep in mind that we as individuals are not the real problem, nor are we the primary victims. Nevertheless, we are much more involved than most of us probably realize.

How Are We Part of the Problem?
Remembering that our individual decisions affect Third World people infinitely less than corporate and government

policies do, let's look at the ways in which we unintentionally contribute to injustice in the Third World.

1. Buying

The products we buy can help finance cruel dictatorships. We saw this with regard to General Food's (Maxwell House) and Nestlé's (Tasters' Choice/Nescafe) purchases of Ugandan coffee (Chap. 7, p. 118). The products we buy can encourage multinational corporations to take over more Third World land for export cropping. We saw this with regard to Del Monte fruits and vegetables, Third World beef exports, and Nestlé's cocoa (Chs. 6, 7 and 12). As the largest buyer of Ghana's cocoa beans, with a vested interest in an abundant cocoa crop, Nestlé exercises considerable influence in economic decisions in Ghana.

While mass campaigns to end such purchases are not always the most appropriate response, we need to begin to examine our purchases. The reflections and action suggestions in Chapters 7, 11 and 12 should help us figure out the most appropriate response in each case.

2. Banking

Of special concern here is our possible unintentional support of apartheid in South Africa. The multinational banks and corporations like to think of themselves as promoting social change in South Africa by raising the wages of black workers and by improving working and living conditions for them. But these measures do not get near the redistribution of power and wealth called for in the notion of a new internal economic order committed to bread and justice. Chapter 11 suggests how we might respond to these banks.

3. Taxes

Our tax dollars finance much of the training and weapons used by many military dictatorships to control or eliminate movements to create a new internal economic order. Each year our representatives vote for military aid to some of the most repressive governments in the world—Nicaragua, Brazil, South Korea, the Philippines, Iran, and dozens of others. While it is not our fault that our tax dollars are used for such purposes, we contribute to the problem by our silence.

4. Church

Many Churches and church people in the Third World are suffering greatly because of their encouragement and/or involvement in self-reliant development efforts. Some of us, however, may belong to a Church that is intentionally or unintentionally supporting governments that are opposed to a new internal economic order. Generally, though, it is more a case of some Churches refusing to actively support groups struggling for such an order. Again, we are not to blame. But once we become aware of a problem, our silence becomes complicity. As a way of breaking our silence, we might begin to ask questions about how money collected for the "missions" is used and what kinds of projects it is supporting.

How Are We Touched by the Problem?

We, too, are victimized by the same forces that frustrate the building of a new internal economic order committed to bread and justice. Three ways come to mind.

1. Jobs

We saw in Chapters 9 and 11 how the expansion of multinational corporations into the cheap labor areas of the Third World hurts workers here as well as there. These "runaway shops", as they are often called, cost many First World workers their jobs. Directly or indirectly, millions in this country are affected.

2. Church

As just mentioned, many of our fellow Church people in the Third World are paying the price for their commitment to

a Gospel of justice and love. Whether we know them personally or not, if bonds of faith and love are real, then we suffer
too.

3. *Exiles*

Many communities in the First World have been touched
the past few years by refugees from places like Chile and
Argentina. These people, many of them former prisoners because of their political or religious convictions, remind us that
repression is not far away. In our efforts to help resettle them
in our communities, we are moved and angered by their situation.

What Can Be Done?

Action has been viewed throughout this book as a matter
of the works of justice, the works of mercy, and life-style
changes. The suggestions that follow involve all three, though,
again, the main concern is the works of justice. We need to
find ways of changing the situations and structures that prevent the necessary redistribution of power and wealth in the
Third World. There are four directions our actions might go
in: direct support of Third World efforts, human rights, multinational corporations, and working for a new internal economic order in our own country.

Support of Local Third World Efforts

One way to support and empower Third World peoples in
their struggles to build a new internal economic order is
through direct contact. Correspondence with Third World
groups—churches/missions, unions, cooperatives, etc.—is definitely a consciousness-raising experience for us. And it is an
especially helpful way of deepening our concern and commitment to justice. Such action is available to individuals as well
as groups like congregations, study/action groups, classes or
whole schools, prayer groups, and others.

The first step is to make contact with a representative of a
Third World effort. After describing who we are, we should

ask for a description of their effort(s) and particularly for ways in which *they* think we can be of some help (see the Sandoval letter below, as a caution here). Continued correspondence with this person or group could provide at least five things:

(1) encouragement—sharing our own efforts to promote bread and justice, acknowledging the inspiration we are getting from them, and pledging our continued support all have a positive effect.

(2) personalizing our concern—exchanging pictures and other items about ourselves can help build a personal relationship that concretizes and helps to sustain our mutual efforts.

(3) channels—Third World efforts need wider awareness and support and we can be that channel of information to others.

(4) resources—there are times when we can help provide material resources necessary for Third World efforts (see Sandoval letter below, for a caution).

(5) possible visits—if the relationship is sustained, there may well be some opportunities for visiting one another.

1. *The Churches*

The Churches are often the only institution in many Third World countries that is capable of challenging the governments of countries most in need of a new internal economic order without being eliminated. Thus, it might be wise to make contact with a Third World group through Church resources and work with local Church supported efforts. Among such Church resources are:

(a) *Maryknoll Missioners (Maryknoll, NY 10545)*. Maryknoll's monthly magazine, with its good pictures and stories on specific people and struggles for justice in the Third World, is an outstanding resource for personalizing the issue. Its framework is explicitly Christian. Because of this and because of Maryknoll's reputation over the years, the magazine is usually well-received by those people not readily disposed to these issues. Because of the cautions identified in the letter

from Maryknoll below (p. 286) it might be good to write them
first about a particular person or project you thought about
contacting from an article in the magazine.

(b) Jesuit Project for Third World Awareness (1846 W.
17th, Chicago, IL 60608). This is a group of Christians who
have worked in the Third World and whose vision and commitment embraces both a New International Economic Order
and a new internal economic order. They publish a fine
monthly newsletter, *Liberation*, that focuses on human rights
and economic justice struggles, particularly in Latin America
and South Korea. Because of its action orientation, this group
could provide direction for supportive involvement with Third
World groups.

(c) The overseas mission offices or departments of the
various denominations might be a source of leads and guid-
ance. Several have indicated a willingness to help in this
regard:

James Mayer
Partners in Mission
Association of Evangelical Lutheran Churches
P.O. Box 3786
St. Louis, Missouri 63122

Russell E. Brown
The Board of International Ministries
American Baptist Churches, USA
Valley Forge, PA 19481

2. Non-Church Resources

(a) *The Gandhi Peace Foundation (221 Deen Dayal
Upadhyaya Marg, New Delhi, India).* The Gandhian movement in India is comprised of several national organizations
working closely together. The Gandhi Peace Foundation is one
of these groups, with its main office in New Delhi. It has about
fifty smaller centers (as in Patti Kalyana) around the country

where Gandhian workers are involved in direct service as well as social change efforts. Mr. K. S. Radhakrishna would be the person to contact at the Foundation.

(b) There are a variety of Third World support groups in this country that could suggest points of contact with the Third World. See the *Human Rights Action Guide, 1978* (below), and/or contact the Washington Office for Latin America (110 Maryland Ave NE, Washington, DC 20002).

3. *Alternate Celebrations Catalogue*

As mentioned in Chapter 7 (pp. 120-21) one small step in the direction of supporting Third World efforts at self-reliance is through the purchase of the handicrafts of Third World peoples. Many of these are distributed through outlets described in the *Catalogue*. What such an action lacks in terms of attacking root causes it partially makes up for in meeting an existing need—gift-giving—that is both helpful and enjoyable.

As concrete and satisfying as these actions can be, they need to be more carefully considered. As works of mercy primarily, they do not address the causes of injustice. Further, they may involve some risk. In answer to a letter I wrote Maryknoll about these action suggestions, I received the following response from Maryknoll editor Moises Sandoval:

> The primary effort of Americans working for a redistribution of power in the Third World has to be right here in the United States. The causes of the misuse of power in Third World countries and the rise of repressive governments can often be traced to policies in the developed countries; sometimes to the United States .... Therefore, to fight against a violation of human rights in Latin America, for instance, one of the most effective things we can do is to try to change the policies of our government, because it is our support which usually brings these governments to power and keeps them there, as in Chile, Brazil and Nicaragua.
>
> As to sending letters to missioners, ... I suggest a cautious and discreet approach to the missioner who

might be involved in activities which might be threatening to the government of that country. Everyone needs encouragement and support and the missioner is no exception, but letters should be worded in such a way that they do not jeopardize the missioner.

As to sending financial support to the missioner, the risk is that the money might not reach him. That is why Maryknoll urges contributors to send their offerings to Maryknoll, New York, with instructions for transmission of the funds to the specific missioner or project the donor wants to aid. Maryknoll then transmits the funds through banking channels.

The best way to make the initial approach might be to ask the missioner for suggestions on how one could help advance his work.

Promoting Human Rights

Sandoval's letter makes it clear that the works of mercy need to be combined with the works of justice. And the works of justice need to address the institutions and policies of First World countries, as much as they do the institutions and policies of Third World countries. One specific area of focus is human rights.

Human rights and economic development are not unrelated. *How* they are related depends on the economic model being pursued in a particular country. An economic model or system that favors the few at the expense of the many violates human rights in at least two ways. First, it is denying the basic economic rights of people—sufficient life-goods. Secondly, such societies eventually lead to a denial of civil or political rights. Repression—from censureship to imprisonment, torture, exile and murder—is the only way such an unjust system can be imposed on a people awakened to their rights. Thus, human rights violations need to be seen as the symptom of much greater forms of economic injustice. It is this underlying economic injustice that this book has examined to this point.

Yet, it is still important to promote human rights. Most people are critical of gross violations of human rights. Thus, it is possible to mobilize public opinion at least against those governments most flagrantly violating these rights. In so doing, we may be able to reduce the extent of these violations. The result is hopefully fewer restrictions on those individuals and groups within Third World countries that are struggling to create a new internal economic order based on bread and justice. We can help in at least two ways.

1. Promoting a U.S. Foreign Policy Based on Human Rights

Economic and military aid from the U.S. (and other countries) provides both financial support and legitimization to Third World countries. The more repressive the government, the less support it has among its people. Thus, the more it needs both dollars and recognition from abroad. A military and economic boycott by even part of the world community would unmask the nature of governments that had little, if any, support at home. This would help free up the forces for change within that country.

Since 1975, what are referred to as "human rights amendments" have been attached to U.S. foreign aid legislation. These amendments state that military and economic aid will be cut off from countries that engage in consistent patterns of gross violations of basic human rights, unless it can be shown that the aid directly benefits people. Each year then, the U.S. Congress decides whether to apply these amendments to specific countries. The President's position on whether to apply the amendments in particular cases is also important.

Here is where we come in. We can write to the President and to the chairpersons of the Senate and House Foreign Relations Committees and to our own representatives in favor of applying the amendments to those countries where human rights are systematically being denied. To know which countries and when and how to act, here are four suggestions:

(1) The Washington Office on Latin America publishes a monthly (free) *Legislative Update* that provides facts on hu-

man rights concerns in Latin America and appropriate legislative action suggestions.

(2) The Coalition for a New Foreign and Military Policy publishes a *Human Rights Action Guide* each year. The 1978 *Guide* is an excellent source for legislative information, for how to lobby effectively, and for a list of publications and organizations for further information on specific geographic areas.

(3) *Action Guide on Southern Africa* is an issues and action resource published by the American Friends Service Committee (1501 Cherry St., Philadelphia, PA 19102).

(4) There are other action possibilities besides letters and visits to political representatives. Public education actions ranging from letters to editors of school, church and local newspapers; presentations to church and school groups; radio talk shows; leafleting local shopping centers; and public vigils are all important means for generating concern and promoting legislative efforts. A helpful resource here might be the *Human Rights Education Project* (1322 18th St. NW, Washington, DC 20036). It is a mobile exhibit designed to provide educational resources on human rights to local organizations. Equipped with multi-media programs, speakers, action workshops and a large, free-standing photographic exhibit focusing on Chile, Argentina and Uruguay, the Project travels to communities throughout the U.S. Write for schedule and rate information.

2. *Supporting International Human Rights Efforts of Other Groups*

The second way to promote human rights is by joining the efforts of other groups. Again, remembering that most human rights violations are symptoms of much deeper and more subtle forms of injustice, we should still consider the following possibilities:

(a) Amnesty International (2112 Broadway, New York, NY 10021). Amnesty International is a world-wide organization working for the release of political prisoners. There are more than 150 chapters in the U.S. alone—in almost every major city. If you do not know whether your city has a chapter or whom to contact, write the national office. It is much better to work as part of a group effort if possible.

Nevertheless, individuals can help. Using Amnesty International's quarterly newsletter, *Matchbox*, you can adopt a political prisoner for whom you will become an advocate. Amnesty International can provide further information on the prisoners they publicize. Amnesty International-USA has started a special "Campus Network" program for college students and faculty to act on urgent cases, to educate the community on human rights issues, and to publicize gross violations of human rights in particular countries as part of national and international AI campaigns. For details, write AI-USA's Western Regional Office, 3618 Sacramento St., San Francisco, CA 94118. Writing your Congresspersons and the U.S. Department of State on behalf of your prisoner and asking them to inquire about his/her well-being and to keep you informed is a next step. Writing the Embassy of the country involved and to the head of state in that country on behalf of your prisoner is important also. Ask about the health of the prisoner, about why he/she was imprisoned, and whether there was a trial with due process. Inquire also about when release is expected and about the condition of other members of the family. Amnesty International has documented time and time again the effectiveness of such letters. It is harder for a government to continue its repressive practices when it knows others are watching, caring, and perhaps also influencing the policies of their country toward that government.

(b) Chilean, Nicaraguan, South Korean, Iranian, Philippine and dozens of other human rights support groups provide information on the situation in their countries and how we can help. Maryknoll priest Miguel d'Escoto, himself a Nicaraguan, publishes an excellent information/action guide six times a year. Write him for a free subscription to *Nicaraguan Update*, at Maryknoll, NY 10545. Again, the *Human Rights Action Guide, 1978* would be helpful.

3. Challenging the Multinational Corporations and Banks

Sandoval's letter above (pp. 286-7) challenges us to examine how these multinational operations create obstacles to building a new internal economic order in many Third World countries. Despite disclaimers to the contrary, the continued presence of these corporations and banks in repressive Third World countries supports this repression in two ways. It provides the cash (investments and loans) that is often desperately needed and, in some cases, even the equipment needed for repression. And it provides the aura of legitimacy mentioned above. As former Prime Minister John Vorster of South Africa put it candidly a few years ago: "Every time a South African product is bought, it is another brick in the wall of our continued existence."[1] The more heavily the corporations and the banks are involved in a country, the more they feel they stand to lose from any redistribution of power and wealth. They have a vested interest in the status quo.

In terms of action possibilities, the resources and action suggestions described in Chapter 11 provide extensive direction with regard to these multinational corporations and banks.

Promoting a New Internal Economic Order in the U.S.

There are numerous efforts at building a new internal economic order in this country. Many of them offer possibilities for action for ourselves. As Dom Helder Camara, the Brazilian archbishop and fighter for social justice, keeps repeating, a revolution in values and institutions has to take place in the First World before it can be fully realized in the

Third World. Such a revolution will not happen overnight or
maybe even in our lifetime. But we know that we have to take
those first, second, and third steps, so that others will be able
to take the eighth, ninth and tenth steps.

1. Working with Local or National Groups
    —Union struggles are one possibility. The United Farm
Workers (P.O. Box 62, Keene, CA 93531), the J. P. Stevens
campaign (ACTW Union, 15 Union Sq., New York 10003), and
groups like the Rusk County Citizens Action Group that challenged Kennecott in northern Wisconsin (see Ch. 11, pp. 206-
07) are three campaigns we might consider.
    —Native American self-determination efforts need urgent
and constant support. Contact the national office of the Native
American Solidarity Committee (P.O. Box 3426, St. Paul, MN
55165) for how to help and the location of local and regional
offices.
    —Among the many groups working for the economic and
political rights of racial minority groups is the National Alliance Against Racist and Political Repression (national office:
150 Fifth Ave., Room 804, New York, NY 10012). Contact with
(writing and/or visiting) a political prisoner in the U.S. is a
way of supporting a person in need, as well as getting in touch
with injustice and deepening one's vision and commitment.
    —Clergy and Laity Concerned (CALC), the American
Friends Service Committee, and others are working on "peace
conversion", that is, converting from military priorities and
production to meeting basic human needs. Many local peace
conversion efforts try hard to link up with labor groups to
promote greater participation of workers in decisions about
what the company is producing and how.
    —As described in Chapter 7, National Land for People
and CALC's task force on the politics of food are focusing on
local communities and regions becoming more self-sufficient
in terms of food production.

2. Community Self-Reliance

The Institute for Local Self-Reliance (1717 18th St. NW, Washington, DC 20009) is a research and education organization exploring the possibilities of urban communities becoming productive, increasingly self-reliant systems. Among its concerns are communities raising their own food, generating their own energy, utilizing their "wastes", and directing their own affairs. The Institute investigates the technological, economic, and legal tools needed to make those possibilities real. Among other things, it publishes a "Community Self-Reliance Series" of booklets like *Energy, Agriculture and Neighborhood Food Systems* (1975; 16 pages) and provides consultation to urban groups interested in community self-reliance.

3. Strategy for a Living Revolution

Two excellent guides for promoting a new internal economic order are the Movement for a New Society's new publication, *Resource Manual for a Living Revolution*—an action guide for implementing the strategies contained in an earlier MNS effort, George Lakey's *Strategy for a Living Revolution* (San Francisco: W. H. Freeman, 1973). The *Resource Manual* is divided into ten parts—the theoretical basis for change, skills for working in groups, ways of developing communities of support, methods of personal growth, strategies for consciousness raising, ways of conducting training and education, organizing strategies, exercises and other tools for nonviolent resistance, other practical skills (fund raising, mass communication, cooking in large groups, etc.), and a list of groups to contact.

What Do I Do?

As we have done in previous chapters, let's examine a series of questions that will help us evaluate all the possibilities suggested in this chapter.

(1) Which action(s) have the best chance of succeeding?

(2) Which actions are important enough to do, whether or not they succeed?

(3) Which actions mobilize (or have the potential to mobilize) the broadest number of people?

(4) Which actions put us (or come closest to putting us) in direct contact with the victims?

(5) Which actions do the victims say they want people to do?

(6) Which actions involve the victims themselves in leadership positions?

(7) Which actions have the greatest potential for long-term change in the practices and policies of the institution(s) involved?

(8) Which actions have actual groups working on them?

(9) Which actions have the best potential for surfacing local-global linkages?

Having sorted through these possible actions, try to answer the following questions to help you decide which one of the actions makes the most sense for you at this time in your life:

(1) Which action seems to fit best with your own concerns, knowledge, skills, time?

(2) Which action is most likely to deepen and sustain your commitment to bread and justice?

(3) Which action would have the best potential for generating the support of others that you feel you would need to carry it off?

Resources

On Human Rights
—"Last Grave at Dimbaza," is a 16mm, color film (from the American Friends Service Committee and CALC) that is a powerful indictment of apartheid in South Africa and perhaps the clearest statement of the need for a new internal economic order in any country.

—"Institutional Violence" is a 30-minute slide/cassette presentation (from the Institute for Education in Peace and

Justice) that examines several important components of a new internal economic order (racial justice and sexual equality). Part II is especially helpful in illustrating the link between human rights violations and economic injustice. It offers action suggestions for each of the problem areas it examines and is based on Dom Helder Camara's notion of "the spiral of violence."

—*If you Want Peace . . . Defend Life* (Division of International Justice and Peace, U.S. Catholic Conference, November 1976) is an excellent resource for Christians. It presents liturgical and Scriptural resources to accompany information on repression, case studies of Argentina, Czechoslovakia, Indonesia, Iran and South Africa, and action and resource suggestions.

—"Structures of Injustice and Struggles for Liberation," sections #79–88, presents the reflections of the 5th Assembly of the World Council of Churches (in *Breaking Barriers, Nairobi 1975*) on human rights and a variety of action suggestions.

—"Collision Course" (see Chapter 9, "Resources").

On a New Internal Economic Order in the U.S. as well as Third World
—Newsreel (630 Natoma St., San Francisco, CA 94101) is an excellent source of films (in Spanish as well as English) on the struggles of labor, women, Blacks, Asians, Latinos, Native American, and prisoners in the US, as well as efforts in the Mideast, Africa, Cuba, Europe, Latin America (including Puerto Rico), Chile, Vietnam, Korea, and China.

Part V

GLOBAL INTERDEPENDENCE

Introduction

In previous chapters we have examined how a society, making use of its own resources and values, and promoting full participation by its people, can provide for basic human needs. Such a society should not then exist as an isolated entity. The next step in the society's development is interdependence. True interdependence is based on mutual respect, freedom and equality. It is not the result of the domination of one society by another. As citizens of the same world, we need each other. Nations enrich each other, whether by exchanging goods and services or sharing the unique aspects of their cultures.

Chapter 16 analyzes three different views of "interdependence" and finds one most consistent with a commitment to bread and justice. Chapter 17 provides a variety of ways in which each of us can live interdependently as citizens of what might be called a "global city."

Chapter Sixteen

LIFE-BOAT ETHICS OR SPACESHIP EARTH?

This chapter compares and helps us evaluate three differ-ent views of interdependence and leads to a decision about the kind of interdependence necessary to achieve bread and justice.

Introduction

In Part IV, the stress was on self-reliance. But as we saw with regard to trade, self-reliance is not the end in itself.[1] Once a society is providing for its basic human needs by utilizing its own resources and values and maximizing the participation of its people, then interdependence is the next step in its development. Under these conditions, increased interdependence through increased trade need not lead to greater inequities of power and wealth (see Ch. 6, pp. 110-3). Self-reliance for third world countries, then, might be seen as the essential transition from dependence to interdependence.

It is an absolutely essential step if the interdependence to follow is to be based on justice and not a more subtle form of dependence and exploitation.

This seems to be as true for nations as it is for individuals. Growth requires breaking out of the dependency of childhood, by going through a stage of what is often defiant independence. Once young adults have been able to "make it on their own," a whole new relationship with their parents often develops. This more cooperative relationship is rooted in the freedom and the equality of the people involved.

Similarly, nations need to exchange goods and services and be enriched by one another's diversity of perspective and culture. The nations of the world need one another. But we need one another on the basis of freedom, equality, and mutual respect, not on the basis of dependence and domination.

Chapter 3 (p. 51) made it clear that there are in fact two forms of interdependence. There is what was termed "horizontal interdependence," in which there is genuine cooperation. The relationship or interaction is mutually and equally beneficial to all involved. In contrast, there is "vertical interdependence." Those at the top of such relationships—whether they are a Nurse Ratched, a multinational corporation, or a First or Second World government—would like to think of the relationship with their patients or Third World countries as mutually beneficial. Those at the bottom, however, would have a much different view. They would oppose any strengthening or expanding of the relationship as strengthening the grip of those on the top. In all dealings between two groups, those on the top gain much more than those on the bottom. Why? Because those on top have much more power and that power ensures that decisions will benefit themselves first.

Let's apply this analysis to the preceding chapters. If Third World countries could break out of the colonial pattern forced on them—of being exporters of cheap raw materials and importers of more expensive manufactured goods—and follow the lead of the oil-producing countries, then maybe increased interdependence through increased trade would be mutually and equally beneficial. If a strict and effective code of conduct for multinational corporations would be put into effect and if a unified stance of Third World countries bargaining with the corporations would develop, then maybe there could be some kind of horizontal interdependence between the two. As it stands now, however, the interdependence in both cases is more vertical than horizontal. Exploitation still predominates over cooperation. This is why many people, especially in the Third World, are skeptical and even fearful about calls for greater interdependence. The last quarter of the 20th Century has supposedly ushered in the "era of interdependence." But which kind is it?

Three Perspectives on Interdependence

There are three main perspectives on interdependence. First, Garrett Hardin, originator of what has been called "lifeboat ethics," rejects the notion of interdependence. It will be our ruin, he contends, if we give in to the temptation "to try to live by the Christian ideal of being 'our brother's keeper . . .' " Henry Kissinger, former US Secretary of State, and others advocate the approach of enlightened self-interest for US foreign policy. This means interdependence, but an interdependence that is still more vertical than horizontal. The third perspective speaks of "spaceship earth" and a "global city," implying a horizontal interdependence. In outline form, the 3 perspectives line up as follows:

"Life-Boat Ethics"—No Interdependence
1. Interdependence is the problem!
2. Redistribution of goods will mean that no one will have enough.
3. With Third World population control, no redistribution of goods will be needed.
4. Self-reliance means meeting a nation's own needs within the present distribution of global resources.

Kissinger—Vertical Interdependence
1. Interdependence is in U.S. self-interest.
2. It means only a redistribution of goods.
3. It does not mean a redistribution of power.
4. Genuine self-reliance is to be resisted.

"Spaceship Earth"—Horizontal Interdependence
1. Interdependence presupposes self-reliance and means mutual and equal benefit.
2. It requires a redistribution of power . . .
3. . . . as well as a redistribution of goods.
4. We have an affluence problem more than a population problem.

1. Life-Boat Ethics

Garrett Hardin's concern is the population explosion. First, he challenges the irresponsibility of Third World countries for not controlling their population growth rate. Then, he criticizes First World "do-gooders" who pour more and more foreign aid into the Third World. This only encourages the poor to have more children. Soon there will not be enough for them or us. He uses the image of a lifeboat to describe this situation—too many people for the space and resources of our limited world. In his own words:

> Environmentalists use the metaphor of the earth as a "spaceship" in trying to persuade countries, industries and people to stop wasting and polluting our natural resources . . . . But does everyone on earth have an equal right to an equal share of its resources? The spaceship metaphor can be dangerous when used by misguided idealists to justify suicidal policies for sharing our resources through uncontrolled immigration and foreign aid. In their enthusiastic but unrealistic generosity, they confuse the ethics of a spaceship with those of a lifeboat.
>
> A true spaceship would have to be under the control of a captain, since no ship could possibly survive if its course were determined by committee. Spaceship Earth certainly has no captain; the United Nations is merely a toothless tiger, with little power to enforce any policy upon its bickering members.

... Metaphorically, each rich nation can be seen as a lifeboat full of comparatively rich people. In the ocean outside each lifeboat swim the poor of the world, who would like to get in, or at least to share some of the wealth. What should the lifeboat passengers do?

First, we must recognize the limited capacity of any lifeboat. For example, a nation's land has a limited capacity to support a population and as the current energy crisis has shown us, in some ways we have already exceeded the carrying capacity of our land.

So here we sit, say 50 people in our lifeboat. To be generous, let us assume it has room for 10 more, making a total capacity of 60. Suppose the 50 of us in the lifeboat see 100 others swimming in the water outside, begging for admission to our boat or for handouts. We have several options: we may be tempted to try to live by the Christian ideal of being "our brother's keeper," or by the Marxist ideal of "to each according to his needs." Since the needs of all in the water are the same, and since they can all be seen as "our brothers," we could take them all into our boat, making a total of 150 in a boat designed for 60. The boat swamps, everyone drowns. Complete justice, complete catastrophe .... [2]

2. Henry Kissinger's "Era of Interdependence"

Kissinger is not the only advocate of a modified vertical interdependence. This view has prevailed in US foreign policy ever since his historic speech was read at the UN by US Ambassador Daniel Moynihan. It was at the opening of the 7th Special Session of the UN of September 1, 1975, that the US declared that its confrontation with the Third World over economic change was over. A spirit of interdependence—of negotiation and cooperation with the Third World for a new international economic order—would now characterize US policy. The global nature of problems like the arms race, inflation, population and the environment has forced us to look toward global cooperation. If the oil-producing nations (OPEC) wanted an all-out economic war, there would be no winner. OPEC must cooperate with the First World, for global economic stability was at stake. In the opening of this speech, Ambassador Moynihan declared:

> The global order to colonial power that lasted through centuries has now disappeared; the cold war division of the world into two rigid blocs has now also been broken down, and major changes have taken place in the international economy. We now live in a world of some 150 nations. We live in an environment of continuing conflicts, proliferating weapons, new ideological divisions, and economic rivalry. The developing nations have stated their claim for a greater role, for more control over their economic destiny, and for a just share in global prosperity. The economically advanced nations have stated their claim for reliable supplies of energy, raw materials, and other products, at a fair price; they seek stable economic relationships and expanding world trade, for these are important to the well-being of their own societies.[3]

Against this backdrop, Moynihan offered two options. Side by side, they read:

Option One

"We (could) enter an age of festering resentment, of increased resort to economic warfare, a hardening of new blocs, the undermining of cooperation, the erosion of international institutions and failed development."

Option Two

"We have proposed specific ways of giving special help to the development needs of the poorest countries.... We know that the world economy nourishes us all, we know that we live on a shrinking planet. Materially as well as morally, our destinies are intertwined."

U.S. policy clearly followed the second option. The specific proposals embodied in the policy statement spelled out a modest program to redistribute some goods. It called for increased trade and more stable prices for Third World commodities. It urged a more favorable climate of investment for multinational corporations in the Third World, so that they would be more willing to invest their capital there. The speech recommended additional funds for the International Monetary Fund for Third World countries with special balance-of-payments problems.

But while the speech mentioned some increased voting rights in the International Monetary Fund for Third World countries, it was clear that the U.S. did not envision and would not support any major redistribution of global economic power. The Third World had just succeeded in one attempt to redistribute power—OPEC. The oil-producing countries had changed the rules. Instead of being dictated to by the giant multinational oil companies, as they had for decades, OPEC turned the tables on the First World. Thus, the possibility emerged that other Third World countries might form effective producer associations in the other strategic minerals for which First World countries were dependent on them. If so, then First World control over the world's resources would be further eroded. Thus, the time for cooperation had arrived. It is clear from the first of the two policy options presented by Moynihan above, that OPEC's actions were frowned on by the U.S. The phrases "economic warfare," "hardening of new blocs," and "undermining of cooperation" are all meant to refer especially to OPEC. The U.S. would be willing to help redistribute some of the First World's goods, but none of its power. In other words, the interdependence desired by the U.S. remains primarily vertical.

Finally, while this speech does not explicitly address the notion of self-reliance, the U.S. was, and continues to be, consistently opposed to it. Self-reliance as described in Part IV means a reduction of export cropping, a redistribution of land, appropriate and labor-intensive technology, a diversity of development models, control over the activities of multinational corporations operating in one's country, and an independent foreign policy. When countries have attempted such policies, they have met strong resistance from the U.S. Chile and Jamaica in Latin America, the former Portuguese colonies in Africa—Angola and Mozambique—and Vietnam are striking examples from the 1970's.

3. "Spaceship Earth" and "Global City"

(a.) *Horizontal vs Vertical Interdependence.* The third perspective on interdependence accepts the view of societal and human development presented at the beginning of this chapter. Genuine interdependence presupposes self-reliance. And self-reliance requires a redistribution of power. The only way that Third World countries can bargain effectively with the First World and its multinational corporations is to band together as OPEC did. Producer associations are like trade unions. Workers are powerless against management unless they are organized. So too Third World countries have been powerless until they began to organize themselves. "Collective self-reliance" is the term that has been used throughout this book to describe such strategies as the formation of producer associations. Without "collective self-reliance," horizontal interdependence is a fairy tale. Dr. Kissinger's worldview represents a step above the colonial era and the blatant exploitation of places like Potosi, Bolivia (Ch. 2, pp. 29-31). But it is not an interdependence based on "sovereign equality" as called for in the NIEO. Visually, these positions could be illustrated like this:

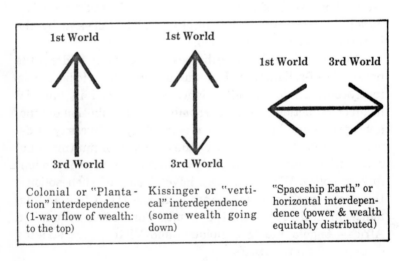

Colonial or "Plantation" interdependence (1-way flow of wealth: to the top)	Kissinger or "vertical" interdependence (some wealth going down)	"Spaceship Earth" or horizontal interdependence (power & wealth equitably distributed)

(b.) *Life-Boat or Luxury Liner?* But if the Kissinger perspective on interdependence is lacking, then Hardin's is even more lacking. First, the life-boat is a terribly misleading analogy. The image of billions of people scrambling to climb into an already filled lifeboat implies that each person fills roughly the same amount of space. In reality, if we want to use the lifeboat we should speak of about 15–20% of those in the boats weighing between 300 and 500 pounds, with the vast majority weighing 75 and 125 pounds. Paralleling Gandhi's often quoted statement that there is enough in the world for everyone's need but not enough for everyone's greed, we might point out the caution sign printed on the inside of the lifeboat: "made to hold a world of 150-pound persons." Hardin's ethic might be termed "survival of the fattest." In our weight-conscious, physical appearance oriented society, such figures might bring the point home effectively.

A more accurate image for the present reality might be that of a modified luxury-liner, where first-class passengers enjoy a luxurious cruise, while third-class passengers and the ship's crew struggle for survival. A variation of this image is that of a spaceship—"Spaceship Earth"—which Hardin rejects.

(c.) *"Spaceship Earth" and the Affluence Problem.* One description of "Spaceship Earth" is provided by David King in *International Education for Spaceship Earth:*[4]

Spaceship Earth: What Would You Do?

Just for a moment, imagine that you are a first-class passenger on a huge spaceship with thousands of passengers travelling through space at a speed of 66,000 mph. You discover that the craft's environment system is faulty. Passengers in some sections are actually dying due to the emission of poisonous gases into their oxygen supply. Furthermore, you learn that there is a serious shortage of provisions—food suplies are rapidly diminishing and the water supply, thought previously to be more than adequate, is rapidly becoming polluted due to fouling from breakdown in the craft's waste and propulsion systems.

To complicate matters even more, in the economy section where passengers are crowded together under the most difficult of situations it is reported that many are seriously ill. The ship's medical officers are able to help only a fraction of the sick and medicines are in short supply.

Mutinies have been reported, and although some of the crew and passengers are engaged in serious conflict in one of the compartments it is hoped that this conflict is being contained successfully; however, there is widespread fear as to what may happen if it cannot be contained or resolved within that compartment. The spacecraft has been designed with an overall destruct system, the controls of which have been carefully guarded. Unfortunately the number of technologists who have gained access to the destruct system has increased, and all of the crew and passengers have become uneasy due to evidence of mental instability in some of those gaining such access.

We could go on, but the point is: what would you do put in such a position?

Now that you have "imagined" this situation, you are ready to face reality. You are on such a spaceship right now—Spaceship Earth.

Hardin disagrees with this description of the world today. A spaceship, he says, implies a captain, but the world has none.

The UN, in his words, is a "toothless tiger." But apart from this one point, there is great similarity between the two descriptions of present global realities. The real difference lies in how we interpret and respond to these realities.

Hardin would point to the third class compartment of the spaceship, as he would to the swimming billions outside his life-boat, and say that there are too many of them for the spaceship. If they keep multiplying, then the spaceship's food and water supply, its space, its medical supplies, etc. will soon be exhausted. Who's to blame? Hardin would point to Third World countries that refuse to curb their population growth rate and First Worlders who insist on trying to feed these hordes.

There is no denying that the population growth rate is a problem. But it is not *the* problem. There is a two-fold *affluence* problem that threatens our world even more than the population problem. Overconsumption by the industrialized world is the first part of the affluence problem. Control of Third World agricultural resources, particularly land, by the few is the second part. First, overconsumption in the industrialized world.

There are too few resources for too many people only when a few of the many people consume many of the few resources. It is not the poor who are consuming these resources. Most of us are familiar with the food consumption comparisons—2000 pounds of grain consumed annually by the average citizen in many parts of the industrialized world, with much of that in the indirect forms of dairy and meat products.

Whereas, citizens of many Third World countries consume about 400 pounds of grain annually, most of which is consumed directly as grain. Taking into consideration the other resources consumed, especially by an industrial system committed to a wasteful economic growth, the difference in consumption is much greater than five to one. As Dr. Paul Ehrlich put it graphically:

The environmental impact of population is created by the interrelationship of population, consumption and technology. Developed countries are consuming energy and raw materials at five times their rate of population growth ... the addition of 75 million Americans (current population increase projections for the year 2000) in terms of consumption of ever-scarcer, non-renewable resources, is equal to that of 10 billion Nigerians or 22 billion Indonesians.[5]

But the consumption patterns of the industrialized world are only part of the affluence problem. The other half lies in the Third World itself, in control over land. As the Bread for

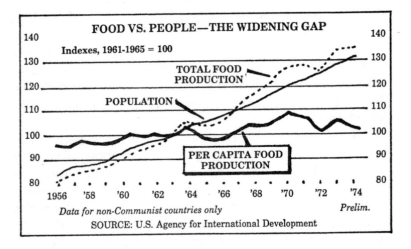

FOOD VS. PEOPLE—THE WIDENING GAP

Indexes, 1961-1965 = 100

TOTAL FOOD PRODUCTION

POPULATION

PER CAPITA FOOD PRODUCTION

1956 '58 '60 '62 '64 '66 '68 '70 '72 '74

Prelim.

Data for non-Communist countries only

SOURCE: U.S. Agency for International Development

the World position in the "Debate on Hunger" stresses, population growth rates decrease as poverty decreases. Adequate nutrition, health care, basic education and jobs are essential for reducing the poverty that breeds overpopulation. But land reform may be even more essential to this process.

There is a population problem which will only get worse if present patterns of land ownership in much of the Third

World are maintained. The Food and Agricultural Organization (FAO) world land census of 1960 revealed that "a mere 2.5% of landowners with holdings of more than 100 hectares (1 hectar = 2.5 acres) control nearly three-fourths of all the land in the world—with the top 0.23% controlling over half." That means that 1 out of every 400 landowners controls more land than the remaining 399 combined! And the concentration is worse two decades later because of increased export cropping (see Chapter 6) and the Green Revolution. Contrary to the Environmental Fund claim that "Population growth has pushed the peoples of Africa, Asia and Latin America onto lands which are only marginally suitable for agriculture," it is the multinational corporations and large locally controlled export cropping operations that have driven the small farmers to marginal lands.

As Susan George points out, "population could decrease and food production increase, but if the broad majority of the people still lacked the purchasing power to pay for their food or the means to produce it, hunger and malnutrition would still affect the same number . . . ."[6] Chapter 6 on export cropping demonstrated how increased control over agricultural resources by fewer people means less food purchasing power for the majority of people. Thus, the only workable answer in agricultural societies seems to be redistribution of the means of producing food (see Chapter 2, p. 25).

Horizontal interdependence, then, clearly requires both a redistribution of power and a redistribution of goods. Such redistributions are necessary both *between* the Third World and the First and Second Worlds and *within* each World. If the NIEO were to limit itself to a redistribution of goods only, then economically poor nations and economically poor people within nations will continue to be dependent and exploited. Hardin is right in one respect. The answer is not more surplus food shipments, except in emergencies. But he is wrong in his emphasis on birth control devices. The answer lies in a redistribution of the means of producing food, in self-reliant models of development, and in collective self-reliance. And it lies in a genuinely cooperative interdependence among the three Worlds.

A good example of this kind of interdependence is provided by the UN Law of the Seas Conference. Initially convened in 1958, this Conference continues to struggle with the notion of "common heritage." The seas and their riches belong to all humankind, say most of the participants. The seas should not be able to be controlled by those nations and corporations who have the technology to extract their mineral wealth. The resistance to this notion of the common heritage of humankind comes, obviously, from the US (and a couple of other First World nations) whose multinational corporations have been anxious to get at this wealth. "Common Heritage" includes five elements, all of which would help tilt vertical interdependence toward horizontal interdependence.[7]

1) What is part of the common heritage of humankind belongs to all. It cannot be appropriated by some.

2) It requires a system of joint management. In the case of the Law of the Seas, an International Seabed Authority has been proposed and generally accepted.

3) This management must be beneficial to the widest number possible. This includes shared control and decision-making as well as equitable distribution of resources.

4) These resources must be used for peaceful purposes only.

5) They must also be preserved for future generations.

Thus, the control or jurisdiction over the resources of the seas envisioned here is quite different from present international decision-making. Despite outcries to the contrary, real decision-making power in the UN and other international bodies is still a First World monopoly. And precisely because it is this distribution of decision-making power that would be changed in accepting the common heritage principle, we can expect that the distribution of the seas' resources would be much more equitable. An equitable redistribution of goods seems to follow, rather than precede, a redistribution of the power over these goods. As we saw in Chapter 1 (p. 14):

Redistribution of power ————————▷ Redistribution of goods

Unfortunately, those in power are very reluctant to see their power redistributed. Those on top generally prefer vertical interdependence to horizontal interdependence. They— we—have too much to lose. But Scripture raises a troubling question. It's a question that is also raised by many people on the bottom of vertical interdependence—"What does it profit a person if he/she gain the whole world but suffer the loss of their own soul?" This question might be asked of nations as well as individuals. What have we lost in getting to the top and fighting to stay there?

(d.) *The World as a Global City.* Before moving to the last chapter to examine what we can do to live and promote a horizontal interdependence, consider the image of a "Global City". It might look like this:

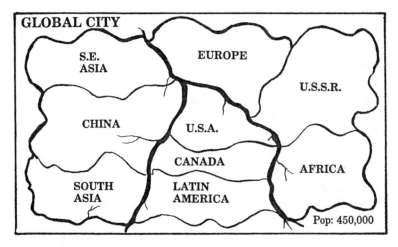

With a population between 450,000 and 500,000, Global City is composed of 11 neighborhoods divided chiefly by the city's two rivers, Pacific River and Atlantic River. At the confluence of the two rivers are situated the neighborhoods of

USA, Japan, and Western Europe—sometimes referred to as
First World neighborhoods. This is the commercial and recre-
ational center of the city. The southern half of the city contains a number of small farms that sell most of their food to
supermarkets located in the north. The fastest growing section of the city, number wise, is the south, where 70% of the
citizens currently reside. However, city services like schools,
hospitals, and transportation are concentrated in the north.
Redevelopment funds have likewise been spent in the north
for the most part. Along the eastern side of Atlantic River are
located the city's oil wells. They have been owned for years by
businesses based in the USA neighborhood. The two rivers
have served as the favorite recreation spot and an important
source of food for Global City-ites. But with the influx of new
industry, especially downtown, industrial pollution has become a serious problem. Both swimming and fishing have
been recently restricted. One of the problems confronting the
City Council is its limited budget. 40% of the budget goes to
the police department, which is expanding because of increasing violence in the city, particularly in the south.

About 20 years ago, dissatisfied residents in the south
began to form neighborhood organizations to demand better
services and an end to police harassment. Eventually these
neighborhood organizations united to form a Coalition of
Southern Neighborhood Organizations also known as
COSONO. COSONO's demands soon went beyond better services to a greater voice on the City Council, long dominated by
the First World neighborhoods. But it was not until the Middle East neighborhood took over the city's oil wells that the
City Council began to pay much attention. Then, when
COSONO demanded a new city charter based on the principle
of "1 neighborhood, 1 vote" and called for a new city budget
based on the principle that funds should be distributed equally
across all 11 neighborhoods, an emergency session of the
Council was called. Besides the 2 COSONO representatives on
the 8-person Council, other COSONO representatives have

been permitted to address the Council and remain as observers throughout the session. The emergency session is currently in its 7th week, but the outcome remains in doubt. The biggest stumbling block is the "1 neighborhood, 1 vote" principle. It would expand the Council to 11 members and give COSONO a majority of 6. But equal distribution of city funds is also in trouble because it would mean less for the northern neighborhoods. This is our "Global City."

If you were a member of the City Council of Global City—
—how would you describe the problems facing your city? What are their causes?
—what is your position on COSONO's demand for a new city charter based on the principle of "1 neighborhood, 1 vote"?
—how would you allocate city funds? what would be your priorities in a new budget?
—how would you like Global City to look in 20 years? Consider energy, transportation, industry, food production and distribution, recreation, education and health care, the police, communication, neighborhood relations, the city government.

Study Questions
1. Explain the major differences among the 3 perspectives on interdependence.
2. Which do you think is a more accurate image of today's world—Hardin's life-boat or a luxury liner—and why?
3. Which is a more serious problem—population or affluence—and why?
4. What would a world based on "horizontal interdependence" look like? How would it be different from today's world?

Resources

On the Relationship between Self-Reliance and Interdependence
    —Samuel L. Parmar, "Self-Reliant Development in an 'Interdependent' World," in *Beyond Dependency* (Washington,

DC: Overseas Development Council, 1975) is a perceptive 25-page essay on both self-reliance and interdependence.

On Interdependence on the Law of the Seas Conference

—The Oceans Education Project (245 Second St. NE, Washington, DC 20002) has produced excellent resources on this issue, including a 17-minute filmstrip entitled "A Common Heritage" and a monthly newsletter, *Soundings.*

On the "Lifeboat Ethic" Perspective and Population Control

—Garrett Hardin's two most famous essays are "Lifeboat Ethics: The Case Against Helping the Poor," *Psychology Today,* September 1974; and "The Tragedy of the Commons," *Science,* December 13, 1978.

—Two of the best refutations of Hardin's thesis are Daniel Callahan, "Life-Boat Ethics," The Hastings Report (Institute of Society, Ethics and the Life Sciences), December 1974; and

—"Bread and Life," a 27-minute, 16mm color film (from the Religious Broadcasting Commission, Washington Hotel Plaza, Seattle, WA 98101), features Garrett Hardin and two Seattle area professors in a visual point-counterpoint. Rental of the film is $22.50.

—Lester Brown's works, published through the Worldwatch Institute (1776 Massachusetts Ave. NW, Washington, DC 20036) of which he is the current director, present the best case for direct attack on population control.

—In contrast, more in line with the position taken in this chapter, are two quite helpful resources: the entire October 1974 issue of *The New Internationalist* and Barry Commoner, "How Poverty Breeds Overpopulation (and not the other way around)," in *Ramparts* magazine and available as a Bread for the World reprint.

On Vertical Interdependence

—The entire Kissinger-Moynihan statement is available from the U.S. Department of State, Bureau of Public Affairs, Washington, DC 20520.

—The positions and policy recommendations of the "Trilateral Commission"—the planning group of the political and economic leaders of the U.S., Japan and Western Europe that formed as a counter-response to growing Third World unity—would follow closely on the Kissinger-Moynihan view of interdependence.

—As a critique of the Trilateral Commission, members of the National Coalition for Development Action formed a "Trilateral Commission Working Group" and published a good collection of essays that is available from Earthwork (3410 19th St., San Francisco, CA 94110).

On Horizontal Interdependence and a "Global City"

—The World Order Models Project of the Institute for World Order (1140 Avenue of the Americas, New York, NY 10036) is an extensive transnational study of a world order based on horizontal interdependence. First, Second, and Third World perspectives on this new world order have been put together in a series of reports that are available from the Institute.

—"Bread, Justice and Global Interdependence," the 15-minute filmstrip accompanying this program, is an excellent visual presentation of this chapter and Chapter 17.

Chapter Seventeen

HOW CAN I LIVE AS A CITIZEN OF GLOBAL CITY?

This chapter offers both a vision of interdependence and a variety of ways we can promote interdependence—as a way of leading to personal decision and action.

Building a Global City based on principles of justice and equality would be an easier task if we had a City Council with both the vision and the power to do so. Unfortunately, at this point in history, we do not. The United Nations system seems to offer the best hope. The vision of horizontal interdependence is there, but it is certainly not shared by all members, especially those at the top. Changes are taking place in the international system. A New International Economic Order is no longer only a dream. But the UN has little power. Unless the US, and to a lesser extent the USSR and Western Europe, agree, little can be accomplished, especially in the areas of economic and military issues.

But we want to see a Global City develop and interdependence deepen. Most of us agree that interdependence means solidarity and solidarity means action, so we want to help build this City. But what can we do? How can we begin to live as citizens of Global City?

The Works of Justice and Changing Our Life-Style

Some people are concentrating their efforts on strengthening the City Council of Global City. Citizens who have joined the World Federalists, the United Nations Association (UNA), and other groups around the world are working hard to educate the public and influence national decision-makers on the need for a revision of the UN Charter. These same groups and others like the Oceans Education Project in Washington, DC, have been concentrating on the Law of the Seas Conference. If we can get the neighborhoods of Global City, especially the First World neighborhoods, to accept the notion of the seas and their resources as the "common heritage of humankind", then we have taken a giant stride toward building a horizontally interdependent Global City. Letters to our representatives on the City Council urging such acceptance would be at least a start.

Others of us have chosen to concentrate not so much on the City Council but on the practices of individual neighborhoods that are sustaining a vertical interdependence. This has been the focus of Parts II–IV of this book. You have been asked to consider a variety of actions and campaigns that are designed to change the policies of governments and corporations and to change the structure of national and international institutions. These works of justice have covered a wide range of issues and strategies:

—participating in a boycott of Nestlé and Del Monte products and notifying the corporations of our action and the reasons behind them;

—writing our political representatives to oppose military and economic assistance to governments engaged in gross violations of fundamental human rights;

—transferring our bank accounts from banks that refuse to cut back their support of apartheid in South Africa;

—buying jute products from Bangladesh, coffee from Tanzania, or one of the other products designed to make us more aware of economic injustice, and then telling others about the issue;

—challenging distorted advertising of the multinational corporations and making others aware of them;

—writing our political representatives in support of the enforcement of the Land Reclamation Act and buying food directly from small farmers as ways of getting "Safeway out of our stomachs".

Hopefully, other works of justice were suggested as you worked through this book. Hopefully, too, you have already investigated at least one of these action possibilities. Maybe you are already doing it.

One caution with regard to some of these and other works of justice is that they can become isolated actions. That is, they can often become "once-for-all" actions that do not engage or touch us regularly. Once some people have written their political letters, it's over for them. Once some people have decided to forego Nestlé, Del Monte, and General Foods products, they've done it. They might take another step, like trying to find friends to help them get Nestlé products out of their school. But again, once that project is over, they've done their part.

If that is the case, part of the problem seems to be a lack of internalization or commitment. The action or project can remain external to us. It can be "something to do." But it does not flow out of who we are inside and a deepening bond with and commitment to the victims of the policies or institutions we are challenging. This is one of the reasons why the works of mercy are important. As was mentioned in Chapter 1, working side by side with a victim often has a powerful way of moving us to resist the source of that victim's suffering.

Here, too, is where the third level of action identified in Chapter 1 plays a role. Changing our way of living can help in at least three ways.

(1) It is something we have to work at daily. We do not "simplify our lives" with one great act of letting go. This helps us develop a perseverance that can spread to our works of justice and make them more regular or sustaining.

(2) Such regular experimenting (Gandhi called them his "experiments with truth") with simplicity helps us on the inside. The small struggles we go through to change our lives deepen our commitment to change. As that commitment deepens, our actions flow more and more out of who we are and what we really want to be.

(3) These small struggles put us more in touch with the poor. We may choose to give away 10% or 20% of our income or choose a low-paying job that promotes justice. As we wrestle with how to pay bills, now that our income is reduced, we get a clearer sense of what poor people wrestle with all the time. Thus, there is a close relationship between the works of justice and changing our life-style.

Living Interdependently

Since the first four parts of this book have concentrated on the works of justice, it would be good to examine more closely a way of life that might undergird such works. How can we live interdependently on a daily basis? Again, this means more than identifying a whole series of actions we can do. Such actions are the external expression of an inner spirit, vision, and commitment. Thus, before looking at what we can do, let's spend some moments getting in touch with who we are on this planet earth.

One vision that has helped to open the eyes of many people to the interdependence of life and what that calls each of us to was voiced in 1854 by Chief Sealth (Seattle). This leader of the Suquamish tribe in the Washington territory delivered a prophetic speech to mark the transferral of ancestral Indian lands to the US Government. The following excerpts represent about one-third of his remarks and are based on an English translation by William Arrowsmith, unfortunately in heavily masculine terms.

The Great Chief in Washington sends word that he wishes to buy our land .... We will consider your offer. For we know that if we do not sell, the white man may come with guns and take our land .... We will consider your offer to buy our land. But it will not be easy. For this land is sacred to us.

This shining water that moves in the streams and rivers is not just water but the blood of our ancestors. If we sell you land, you must remember that it is sacred, and you must teach your children that it is sacred, and that each ghostly reflection in the clear water of the lakes tells of events and memories in the life of my people. The water's murmur is the voice of my father's father. The rivers are our brothers, they quench our thirst. The rivers carry our canoes, and feed our children. If we sell you our land, you must remember and teach your children that the rivers are our brothers, and yours; and you must henceforth give the rivers the kindness you would give any brother ....

We know that the white man does not understand our ways. One portion of land is the same to him as the next, for he is a stranger who comes in the night and takes from the land whatever he needs. The earth is not his brother, but his enemy, and when he has conquered it, he moves on .... He treats his mother, the earth, and his brother, the sky, as things to be bought, plundered, sold like sheep or bright beads. His appetite will devour the earth and leave behind only a desert.

.... You must teach your children that the ground beneath their feet is the ashes of our grandfathers. So that they will respect the land, tell your children that the earth is rich with the lives of our kin. Teach your children what we have taught our children, that the earth is our mother. Whatever befalls the earth, befalls the sons of the earth. If men spit upon the ground, they spit upon themselves. This we know. The earth does not belong to man; man belongs to the earth. This we know. All things are connected like the blood which unites one family. All things are connected. Whatever befalls the earth befalls the sons of the earth. Man did not weave the web of life; he is merely a strand in it. Whatever he does to the web, he does to himself . . . .

. . . Even the white man, whose God walks and talks with him as friend to friend, cannot be exempt from the common destiny. We may be brothers after all, we shall see. One thing we know, which the white man may one day discover—our God is the same God. You may think now that you own Him as you wish to own our land; but you cannot. He is the God of man, and His compassion is equal for the red man and the white. This earth is precious to Him, and to harm the earth is to heap contempt on its Creator. The whites too shall pass; perhaps sooner than all other tribes. Continue to contaminate your bed, and you will one night suffocate in your own waste.

. . . So if we sell you our land, love it as we have loved it. Care for it as we have cared for it. Hold in your mind the memory the land as it is when you take it. And with all your strength, with all your mind, with all your heart, preserve it for your children, and love it, as God loves us all. One thing know. Our God is the same God. This earth is precious to Him. Even the white man cannot be exempt from the common destiny. We may be brothers after all. We shall see.[1]

This speech expresses in graphic terms much of what is implied in the Biblical notion of "stewardship," discussed in Chapter 1 (pages 11-12). We have a responsibility to one another because we are sisters and brothers. We have a responsibility to the earth because we are mutually dependent—the earth on us and we on the earth. We have a responsibility to future generations because they too are our sisters and brothers. What we have—our life, our skills and insights, and our possessions—are gifts meant to be used for building up the human family, the Global City, and, many would add, the Kingdom of God. If we share this vision and want to live it out more fully, what can we do?

Shakertown Pledge

A group of people asked themselves this same question not many years ago. As individuals they had been "experimenting with truth", trying to live more interdependently. They decided to come together in a restored Shaker village near Harrodsburg, Kentucky. As they themselves describe it, "a number of us were personally moved by the global poverty/ecology crisis we saw all around us, and we covenanted [pledged] together to reduce our levels of consumption, to share our personal wealth with the world's poor, and to work for a new social order in which all people have equal access to the resources they need."[2]

Their covenant or pledge came to be known as the Shakertown Pledge. It has nine parts, each of which can be lived out in a variety of ways. Listed below are some of the ways different people have been trying to live this pledge—to live as citizens of Global City. The listing does not imply that any of us try to do all the suggestions. Rather, it is meant to open up possibilities for each of us. Hopefully, each of us will identify further possibilities.

In reflecting on these action possibilities, we should keep three things in mind. First, our beliefs and commitments need to be expressed in action. Secondly, our actions need to be right for us. That is, they should fit with our skills, interests, responsibilities, and shortcomings. What is right or appropriate for some of us may not be for others. Finally, most of us change our lives one step at a time. We should not let ourselves be overwhelmed by how much we are not doing. Rather, we should decide what is our next step, work out a plan for doing it, do it, reflect on the doing, and see where it leads us. If we are willing to persevere in a life of experimenting with truth, we will take many, many steps. But we do not have to take them all at once.

1. I Declare Myself to be a World Citizen

Some people are hesitant about interdependence and world citizenship. What happens to patriotism in all this, they ask. The view of patriotism underlying this whole book was perhaps best expressed in 1965:

> Citizens should develop a generous and loyal devotion to their country, but without any narrowing of mind. In other words, they must always look simultaneously to the welfare of the whole human family, which is tied together by the manifold bonds linking races, peoples and nations.[3]

We share a common humanity. And for those of us who believe in God as Source of all life, it is clear that we are all sisters and brothers.

We can express our world citizenship by addressing ourselves to the needs of people beyond our national borders. This book is all about such people and how we can challenge the injustices that keep them poor. More concretely,

—we can read as world citizens; *Maryknoll Magazine, The New Internationalist,* are all excellent resources;

—we can buy as world citizens; the *Alternate Celebrations Catalogue* is a good source for distribution outlets of Third World handicrafts (see page 120); Bangladesh jute products are also available through a variety of sources (see pages 123-125);

—we can write as world citizens: keeping in touch with at least one or two people in other parts of the world or with a whole village or community (see Ch. 15, page 283) is one way;

—we can pray as world citizens: putting the needs of people around the world before God and our community of faith deepens our sense of unity.

2. *I Commit Myself to Lead an Ecologically Sound Life.*

Chief Sealth's speech provides all the reasons why this is an essential expression of interdependence. It is also one of easiest expressions, since there is so much that needs to be and can be done. Concretely,

—we can recycle cans, bottles, and papers as daily opportunities for action;

—we can start a vegetable garden and experiment with organic farming; schools and churches might consider using some of their grass area for a community vegetable garden;

—we can conserve energy by biking, walking, and using public transportation more often;

—we can conserve energy by reducing the number of items we plug into our walls.

3. I Commit Myself to Lead a Life of Creative Simplicity and to Share My Personal Wealth With the World's Poor.

As Paul Ehrlich put it in the previous chapter (p. 310) the average US citizen "has roughly 50 times the negative impact on the earth's life-support system [resources] as the average citizen of India." The world cannot afford US consumption patterns. Those of us who live in at least relative affluence must cut back toward some kind of *just* standard of living, as difficult as that is to measure.

In simplifying our lives, we should discover a greater freedom. The kind of single-mindedness called for in a life committed to justice is often undermined by attachment to a lot of comforts. We can get too comfortable and have our commitment and passion dulled by having too many things. We are told that no one can serve two masters (Mt. 6:24). Concretely,

—we can simplify our eating by cutting back on liquor, meat, snacks, and expensive meals out;

—we can seek out inexpensive and creative forms of entertainment;

—we can pool and share some of our talents (as in a parish skills bank) and possessions (especially things like tools) with other individuals, families and groups;

—we can use the public library instead of always buying our books and records;

—we can share the money saved by such measures with people working to change policies and institutions that are doing injustice.

*4. I Commit Myself to Join With Others in Reshaping
Institutions in Order to Bring About a More Just Global
Society in Which Each Person Has Full Access to the
Needed Resources for His or Her Physical, Emotional,
Intellectual, and Spiritual Growth.*

This whole book is the rationale for working to change institutions that contribute to hunger and oppression. Dozens of action suggestions have been considered. Generally they fall into five categories:

—letters and visits to political representatives to pass, change, or enforce legislation, so as to promote horizontal interdependence;

—support of stockholder resolutions and other forms of voting, to change economic and political institutions;

—boycotts of products and companies/banks that promote injustice, and notifying them of our actions;

—educational efforts to make others aware of the issues;

—public demonstrations and other forms of "direct action" against the institutions and to educate the public.

*5. I Commit Myself to Occupational Accountability, and
In So Doing I Will Seek to Avoid the Creation of Products
Which Cause Harm to Others.*

The choice of a career is one of the biggest decisions of our lives. Some people get trapped into jobs they would like to leave but cannot, for economic reasons. Many others, however, have choices, but often do not think about the impact their job/career might have on themselves, on others, and on the larger society. Their chief criteria are salary, advancement, prestige. Stewardship, however, refers to our talents as well as to our possessions. Our talents are gifts meant for the service of others. Concretely,

—we can actively look for careers where we can be of service and promote social change;

—we can raise questions within our jobs about the helpfulness of the goods/services we are providing and about what changes we could help make;

—we can make sure that we are honestly portraying our goods/services to the public;

—we can support other workers and groups like Clergy and Laity Concerned who are challenging corporations to produce goods and services that meet peoples' basic needs.

6. I Affirm the Gift of my Body, and Commit Myself to its Proper Nourishment and Physical Well-Being.

People committed to promoting justice are generally quite active and busy. It can be a very demanding as well as deeply satisfying way of life. It takes its toll on our bodies as well as our spirits. To be capable of sustaining our commitment over long days and long years, we need to keep physically fit. Concretely,

—we can walk and bike, not only to conserve energy but also to stay in shape;

—we can eat and drink in ways that are healthy, inexpensive, and conserving of grain (Frances Moore Lappe's *Diet for a Small Planet* is an excellent guide to such eating);

—we can avoid a lot of junk food, especially candy and others having large amounts of refined sugar.

7. I Commit Myself to Examine Continually my Relations With Others, and to Attempt to Relate Honestly, Morally, and Lovingly to Those Around Me.

Some people committed to social change can become so immersed in it that it can affect their personal relationships. There is not time for people. Occasionally, over-involved parents have sacrificed their children to the cause. Sometimes we do not pay enough attention to the personal needs of ourselves and others in the groups to which we belong. Concretely,

—we can seek out actions or projects that can involve, rather than separate us from, our friends, spouse, children;

—we can avoid becoming too busy to be with people, especially when they are hurting;

—we can build people up, rather than always criticizing or, worse, ignoring them;

—we can learn to be honestly critical of others' actions, whether they are political or corporate representatives or co-workers and friends, without rejecting them as persons; and to accept constructive criticism from others as well.

8. I Commit Myself to Personal Renewal Through Prayer, Meditation, and Study.

As mentioned above (pp. 320-21) it is crucial that our actions are expressions of who we are and what we really want to be and do. This requires us to be in touch with our inner self. Regular meditation and prayer are ways of reflecting on our doings, our hopes, our fears, our calling. Study is equally important. While we do not need to know everything about an issue before we act, we should be able to express both what the basic issue is and why we are involved in it. Concretely,

—we can reflect daily on what we are doing and why;

—we can read regularly the newsletters from groups like Bread for the World and the Friends Committee on National Legislation that provide important legislative information and directives for our political action. If we can find a couple of friends to do this with us, then we can expand our knowledge and support one another at the same time;

—we can try to read regularly one or two magazines that provide some further background on the issues: besides those already listed, *The Food Monitor, The Interdependent, Development Forum, The Corporate Examiner, Creative Simplicity* are among best sources for the issues addressed in this book;

—we can join or form a study group like the "Macro-Analysis Seminar" of the Movement for a New Society, to go more deeply into the causes of global economic injustice and to move toward more creative strategies for confronting this injustice.

9. I Commit Myself to Responsible Participation in a Community of Faith.

Without a community of faith, many of us would not have the courage, inspiration, support, and the challenge we need to be creative and persevering in our response to injustice. Further, it is essential to live what it is we are striving for—to build as well as to resist. In other words, building a community of faith is part of living out in the present the kind of future we are struggling to promote. On the other hand, many of us are already part of faith communities that do not go beyond themselves. As Jim Douglass repeats throughout his excellent book, *Resistance and Contemplation*, contemplation without resistance is contemplation of one's navel. Resistance without contemplation is blind activism. Concretely,

—we can invite our communities of faith to be a source of challenge and support for action on behalf of justice;

—we can invite other members of our communities of faith to join us in such action;

—we can share the faith dimension of our commitment to justice with those with whom we are working;

—we can help make our worship services an experience of our oneness with the human family and an opportunity to grow in awareness of our sisters and brothers.

Conclusion

Many of these actions involve minimal risks. Others, however, are threatening. They challenge not only the economic and political institutions of our society, but many of its basic values as well. So, aware that each step may not be easy, we take courage from the lives of people like Dorothy Day, Martin Luther King, and Mahatma Gandhi. We act, believing that, in the words of Isaias:

> If you do away with the yoke, the clenched fist, the wicked word,
> if you give your bread to the hungry, and relief to the oppressed,
> your light will rise in the darkness, and your shadows become like noon.
> Yahweh will always guide you, giving you relief in desert places.

He will give strength to your bones and you shall be
like a watered garden,
like a spring of water whose waters never run dry.
(Isaias 58:10–11)

What Do I Do?

As in previous chapters, let's examine a series of questions that will help us evaluate all the possibilities suggested
in this chapter.

(1) Which actions have the best chance of succeeding?

(2) Which actions mobilize (or have the potential to mobilize) the broadest number of people?

(3) Which actions come closest to putting us in direct
contact with the victims?

(4) Which actions have actual groups working on them in
our area?

(5) Which actions have the best potential for surfacing
local-global linkages?

Having sorted through these possible actions, try to answer the following questions to help you decide which one of
the actions makes the most sense for you at this time in your
life:

(1) Which action seems to fit best with your concerns,
knowledge, skills, time?

(2) Which action is most likely to deepen and sustain your
commitment to bread and justice?

(3) Which action would have the best potential for generating the support of others that you feel you would need to
carry it off?

Resources

*On the Relationship between the Works of Justice and
Life-Style Changes*

—"Global Interdependence", the third filmstrip accompanying this book, focuses on the realities of interdependence

and how we can promote global interdependence. It concludes with the "Shakertown Pledge."

—"Gandhi As Peacemaker", produced by the Institute for Education in Peace and Justice, 1974, is a 20-minute filmstrip on Gandhi's integration of social change, non-violence, and simplicity of life.

—Eknath Easwaren, *Gandhi the Man* (Glide Publications, 330 Ellis St., San Francisco, CA 94102) is the best presentation (text and pictures) on Gandhi as a person and as a possible role-model for ourselves.

On Implementing the Shakertown Pledge

—*Taking Charge: A Process Packet for Simple Living, Personal and Social Change* (Simple Living Program of the American Friends Service Committee, 2160 Lake St., San Francisco, CA 94121) is probably the best guide to taking charge of the various aspects of our lives—asking the right questions, generating creative alternatives, and integrating personal and social change.

—*99 Ways to a Simple Lifestyle* (Center for Science in the Public Interest, 1757 "S" Street, NW, Washington, DC 20009, 1976) is a 316-page guide to alternative ways of living (heating and cooling, food, clothing, gardens, solid wastes, transportation, health).

—*Alternatives, An Alternate Lifestyle Newsletter*, is a quarterly update to the alternate lifestyle suggestions contained in the *Alternate Celebrations Catalogue*. Both are published by Alternatives, 1924 3rd, Bloomington, IN 47401.

—"Education for Liberation and Community", sections #33–36, presents the reflections of the 5th Assembly of the World Council of Churches (in *Breaking Barriers, Nairobi 1975*) on simplicity in Church life-style.

General Appendix

Organizations and Other Resources

Of the many organizations described or listed in the body of the manual, the following are the ones most directly involved with several or all of the NIEO issues. Some of them are research and/or education in orientation. Others are action-oriented. Most combine both orientations. Particular resources produced by and/or available through these organizations—resources that are of major interest to the themes in this manual—are highlighted in conjunction with the appropriate organization. In alphabetical order:

1. *Action Center* (formerly the Food Action Center)—1028 Connecticut Ave NW, #302, Washington, DC 20036. A group of people working to mobilize young people, especially college students, for food, justice and development. They publish action-oriented materials, including *Sustenance*, their monthly newsletter, and are a helpful guide especially for the annual Food Day actions. Especially helpful for college campus ministry and hunger study/action groups.

2. *Bread for the World*—207 E. 16th St., New York, NY 10003. An excellent guide for legislative action and hunger organizing, BFW has chapters throughout the country. Its monthly newsletter is a valuable resource on both legislation pending and short analyses of the NIEO issues as they relate to hunger.

3. *Center of Concern*—3700 13th St. NE, Washington, DC 20017. A group of theologically based economists and other social scientists who publish a *NIEO Memorandum Series*, a monthly newsletter (*Center Focus*) that examines global issues from a Christian perspective, and several larger pieces integrating justice and faith. They have done fine work on women and the NIEO.

4. *Clergy and Laity Concerned* (CALC)—198 Broadway, New York, NY 10038. A group of theologically based activists, with chapters throughout the country, whose concerns involve both NIEO and *nieo* issues—especially U.S. foreign policy, human rights and political repression, the politics of food, and the role of the U.S. military-industrial complex in all of this. Their monthly *CALC Report* offers good short action-oriented pieces on these issues.

5. *Development Education Center*—121 Avenue Road, Toronto, Ontario M5R 2G3, Canada. Publishers of a variety of material designed for high school and college teachers, including items which they developed with *Development and Peace* (67 Bond St., Suite 305, Toronto, Canada), publishers of development materials especially for Canadian Catholics. The Winter 1975 issue of Developpax is a fine 4-page collection of graphs, charts, and definitions that introduce the NIEO to beginners.

6. *GATT-Fly*—11 Madison Ave., Toronto, Ontario M5R 2S2, Canada. This project of Canadian Churches for Global Economic Justice publishes a variety of NIEO related materials, especially on commodities and MNCs, and is involved in public education. Write for a catalog of materials, many of which are cited in the footnotes of this manual.

7. *Institute for Education in Peace and Justice*—2747 Rutger, St. Louis, MO 63104. Producers of a variety of teacher materials on justice and peace issues. They are involved in extensive teacher-education on hunger, global awareness, racism, multicultural education, and mutuality in education. Of particular value is their comprehensive manual for teachers, *Educating For Peace and Justice* (5th Edition, 1976, $8.00).

8. *Institute for Food and Development Policy*—2588 Mission St., San Francisco, CA 94110. Producers of *Food First, World Hunger: Ten Myths,* and *Food Monitor* monthly, IFDP is involved in a "Rural Realities Project" designed to demonstrate and organize around the fact that hunger can be overcome (only) by national and global policies to redistribute the means of producing food.

9. *Interfaith Center for Corporate Responsibility* (ICCR)— 475 Riverside Drive, New York, NY 10027. A coalition of churches and regional coalitions within churches in the U.S. challenging corporations and banks to take social responsibility seriously. As is clear from this manual, ICCR is involved in a variety of actions dealing with public education and organizing as well. Their publications include the monthly 8-page *Corporate Examiner.*

10. Maryknoll/Orbis Press—Maryknoll, NY 10545. Producers of excellent books on justice and the Third World issues, of the fine monthly magazine *Maryknoll,* and the *Education for Justice: A Resource Book,* by Thomas Fenton—for high school and college educators, especially in a Christian context.

11. NARMIC/AFSC—1501 Cherry St., Philadelphia, PA 19102. NARMIC has been producing excellent research and research guides on the U.S. military-industrial complex for a number of years. Their finest effort is a slide presentation cited several times in this manual: "Sharing Global Resources"—a 45-minute slide/cassette presentation on the NIEO and a New Internal Economic Order. It focuses particularly on trade and the MNCs, with Chile, Jamaica, and Appalachia as case studies of MNC exploitation. Extensive documentation and a study/action guide accompany the presentation and enhance its value to educators especially.

12. *Overseas Development Council* (ODC)—1717 Massachusetts Ave NW, Washington, DC 20036. Highly influential in the Carter administration, ODC has published a number of fine pieces over the years. Their annual publication—*The U.S. and World Development: Agenda 1979* (updated each year)—

and their Communiqué series and other shorter pieces are excellent presentations of a more conventional perspective on the NIEO. Of special interest to high school and college educators is their *Focusing on Global Poverty and Development: A Resource Book for Educators*, by Jayne Millar Wood, a massive teachers' manual offering short essays, classroom activities, and a wealth of data and bibliographical information.

13. *SODEPAX* (Committee on Society, Development and Peace—of the Pontifical Commission on Justice and Peace of the Holy See and the Programme Unit on Justice and Service of the World Council of Churches)—150 Route de Ferney, 1211 Geneva 20, Switzerland. It established in 1976 a 3-year ecumenical program entitled "In Search of a New Society: Christian Participation in the Building of New Relations Among Peoples," for greater awareness of global injustices, of the Christian responsibility to help, and of what ecumenical groups can do. It focuses specifically on the broader vision of the NIEO developed here. Its bimonthly bulletin, *Church Alert*, presents fine essays on church teaching and global economic injustice. The best regular theological accompaniment to the other resources described in these pages.

14. *Transnational Institute* (part of the Institute for Policy Studies)—1901 Q St. NW, Washington, DC 20009. An outstanding group of researcher-activists several of whom have been cited a number of times in this manual—Richard Barnet, Orlando Letelier, Michael Moffitt, Howard Wachtel. Their focus is equally on a NIEO and a New Internal Economic Order and their 40–60 page studies make good student reading, primarily at the college level.

15. *World Development Movement*—Bedford Chambers, Covent Gardens, London WC2E 8HA. Another fine group of research-activists whose special focus is international trade issues, particularly commodity studies and action campaigns. Write for a list of their materials.

Glossary

Agribusiness: corporations involved in the manufacture and distribution of farm supplies, in farm production, and/or in the processing, packaging and distribution of farm commodities and products.

Balance-of-payments deficit: a situation in which a country is paying more money to other countries than it is receiving from them. Such "payments" include trade, foreign investment, salaries of government/military personnel overseas, etc.

Balance-of-trade deficit: a situation in which a country is paying more to other countries for imports than it is receiving from these countries for exports.

Buffer stocks: stockpiles of specific commodities accumulated by a commodity authority (like the current International Tin Council or the proposed Integrated Commodity Authority) and used to regulate supplies (buying in periods of over-supply and releasing some of the commodity in periods of undersupply), so as to stabilize prices.

Capital goods: equipment, machinery and goods used to produce other goods.

337

Capital-intensive technology: tools, machinery and processes that would require large outlays of money (capital) and generally require relatively few persons to operate, in contrast with *labor-intensive technology* (see below).

Cash crops: crops like coffee, bananas, cocoa, sugar and tea that are grown and sold primarily for export rather than as food for local consumption.

Collective self-reliance: joint efforts by countries in similar situations or geographic locations to increase economic activities (e.g., trade) among themselves and/or to bargain more effectively with other countries and groups (*producer associations* are one such example).

Commercial banks: what people normally think of as banks (lending primarily to individuals and corporations), in contrast with international banks like the World Bank, the Inter-American Bank, and others that lend primarily to governments.

Commodity agreement: an agreement between the producers and the consumers of a particular commodity to regulate the price and the supply of the particular commodity so as to benefit both producers and consumers.

Common Fund: a several billion dollar fund proposed to facilitate the establishment of the *Integrated Commodity Program* by creating and maintaining *buffer stocks* in the eighteen commodities, and supporting improved prices to the producers of these commodities.

Comparative advantage: the theory that each country has certain natural conditions (e.g., type of soil, terrain) that allow it to produce certain items (e.g., coffee or tea) more efficiently than all others.

Creditor: the lender.

Debt moratorium: a period of time during which the repayment of loans is suspended.

Debt renegotiation: negotiation between a lender (creditor) and a debtor over changing the interest rate on previous loan(s), or the time in which the loan(s) must be repaid, or other parts of the agreement.

Debt servicing payments: the payments of interest charges on loans from various lending institutions.

Debtor: the borrower.

Direct foreign investment: the establishment by a corporation of branches, affiliates (where the parent corporation controls less than 50% of the capital), or subsidiaries (where the parent corporation controls 50% or more of the capital) in foreign countries.

Dividends: money paid to the shareholders of a corporation out of corporation earnings.

Embargo: a government order prohibiting trade with a particular country or group of countries.

Empower: to enable another to develop abilities and take charge of his/her own life.

Expatriated earnings: see **Profits repatriated** below.

Export credits: loans to countries to permit them to buy exports from the lending country.

Export crops: see **cash crops** above.

Export platform: an overseas factory, generally in the *Third World*, that allows the multinational corporation controlling it to produce goods for export more cheaply than in countries in the First World.

Extension services: technical services provided to farmers by government, often through agricultural colleges or agencies.

Fluctuating currency: a situation, common to many *Third World* countries, in which the value of a country's currency (money) frequently rises and falls (generally falls) in relationship to the currencies of other countries.

Foreign exchange earnings: the income to countries from the export of their products.

Fourth World: a term used by some to designate the poorest of *Third World* countries.

Free trade: trade between countries in which there are no barriers or restrictions such as **tariffs** (see below).

Generalized System of Preferences: the United Nations' decision to grant preferential *tariff* treatment by all developed countries to certain manufactured goods originating in all *Third World* countries on a *non-reciprocal* basis.

Gross Annual Sales: the total value of the goods sold by a particular corporation in a particular year.

Gross National Product: the value of all the goods and services produced by a country in a given year.

Group of 77: another term for **Third World** countries as a whole, coined in the 1960's at a point when there were only 77 independent countries in Latin America, Asia and Africa.

Historical necessity: in Marxist theory, the inevitable movement from one form of economic organization of society to the next, that is, from feudalism through capitalism to socialism and then communism.

Home country: the country in which a particular multinational corporation has its international headquarters.

Horticulture: the art of cultivation of a garden.

Host country: a country in which a multinational corporation has an overseas branch or subsidiary.

Import quotas: a ceiling on the quantity of particular imports.

Indexation: a proposal to establish an automatic link between the price of manufactured goods and the price of raw materials, such that any increase in the prices of First World manufactured goods would automatically be matched by increases in the prices of *Third World* raw materials.

Inputs: items added in the production of a product, as in adding fertilizer and pesticides in the production of food.

Integrated Commodity Program: proposed by the *Third World* at UNCTAD IV as a way of dealing with eighteen commodities (including coffee, cocoa, sugar, bananas, cotton, rubber, tin, copper, bauxite) as a group rather than in separate **commodity agreements** (see above). Thus, this would involve the creation of one central International Commodity Authority.

International credit: the borrowing power that some countries have because of their contributions to the International Monetary Fund.

International Monetary System: the system set up by the Bretton Woods Agreement of 1944 that established the International Monetary Fund (IMF) and the World Bank (the International Bank for Reconstruction and Development). The IMF is supposed to promote stability in international monetary (money) matters by administering a world currency reserve which member countries can tap if they find themselves in balance of payments difficulties (see above). Secondly, the IMF formulates the rules of the monetary game which member governments are asked to follow and which, once they are accepted, the IMF is called upon to enforce.

Labor-intensive technology: tools, machinery, and processes that allow or require large numbers of persons to work, in contrast with *capital intensive technology*, which requires relatively few workers to operate.

La Raza: a Spanish term for "the race" or "the people," used by Latino and Chicano people in the U.S. as a sign of their dignity and determination to control their own lives.

Liberalism: a term sometimes used to refer to capitalism.

The market: a phrase referring to the basic operation of capitalism in which prices are supposedly set according to the law of supply and demand. For instance, if there is a scarcity of supply "in the market" and if demand for these goods remains firm, then the price should go up (and vice versa).

Marketing contracts: contracts generally between large companies and local land owners/producers that require these producers to grow their own crop(s) according to company specifications and to sell their crop(s) to the company which, in turn, markets the crop(s).

Neo-colonialism: the continuing though subtle economic (vs. political) control of the *Third World* by the First World.

Neo-Marxist: referring to theories and theorists that offer variations on the socialism/communism of Karl Marx.

Non-aligned Nations (also **Non-aligned Movement**): an organization of *Third World* countries that came together in the 1950's under the leadership of President Tito of Yugoslavia and Prime Minister Nehru of India to pursue a policy of independence in relationship to the U.S. and U.S.S.R. Still very active today and quite critical of Western capitalism.

Non-reciprocity: a preference granted *by* one or more parties in an agreement that is not granted *to* them.

Non-tariff barriers: other restrictions on imports, such as health regulations (tight limits can be set on insecticides or other preservatives in foodstuffs exported by countries), packaging (loose cargo is unacceptable to industrialized countries' mechanized transport handlers), **import quotas** (see above), and others.

Offshore production site: see **export platform** above. Both terms indicate a geographic closeness to the First World country in which the multinational corporation is headquartered, as in the case of the U.S. and Mexico, where a number of corporations have production facilities.

Oligopoly: similar to a monopoly (where a single corporation has control over a particular market), an **oligopoly** is a shared monopoly, that is, a situation where a few companies have control over a particular market, e.g., the "Big Three" auto makers.

Patent: a government grant to an inventor for a specific period of time (generally ten to twenty years), allowing that person or corporation the exclusive right to make, use and sell the invention or discovery.

Patented technology: equipment or processes that cannot be produced, used or sold other than by the owner of the patent.

Petrochemicals: chemical products made from petroleum.

Pharmaceuticals: drugs and products related to the drug industry.

Portfolio investments: owning stock in another corporation, in contrast with **direct foreign investments,** which means setting up or buying up an overseas corporation that thereby becomes a branch of the parent corporation.

Primary commodities: items in their original, raw or unprocessed state, such as foodstuffs and minerals before they are processed. Examples include coffee, beans, cocoa beans, tin, unrefined oil, fresh fruits and vegetables.

Profits repatriated: profits made in a foreign country by an investor and returned to the country where that investor is located or headquartered.

Producer associations: also known as cartels. These are organizations of businesses or countries that agree to regulate production, pricing, and marketing of specific goods. The Organization of Petroleum Exporting Countries (OPEC) is the most well-known example.

Public international enterprises: businesses owned and operated, not by private individuals, but by governments or agencies created by the governments of the world.

Raw material: see **primary commodities** above.

Reinvested earnings: corporate profits that are put back into corporate operations, in contrast with **repatriated profits,** which are taken out of the country where they are made and returned to the country where the multinational corporation is headquartered.

Royalties: payments to the owner of a right, such as a **patent,** for the use of it.

Semi-manufactured and **manufactured: primary commodities** or **raw materials** that have been processed to some extent. If cocoa beans are the primary commodity, then cocoa powder is the **semi-manufactured** state of the cocoa bean, and chocolate is the **manufactured** state.

Speculative commodity: an item that is bought and sold for profit, like stock in a corporation.

Stabilization: attempts, such as the use of **buffer stocks** (see above), to make the supply and price of particular goods more regular, constant and stable.

Stockholder resolution: a motion presented by a stockholder or group of stockholders in a particular corporation to the annual meeting of stockholders to have the management of the corporation either disclose or change some policy(s) of the corporation.

Subsistence farming: farming solely to provide food for one's own family, in contrast to **cash cropping**, which means producing crops for sale.

Synthetics: compounds formed by chemical reaction in a laboratory, in contrast to products of natural origin; for example, plastic bags are a synthetic substitute for jute (natural fiber) bags.

Tariff: an import tax or duty that people must pay to buy foreign products.

Technology-intensive manufacturing: like capital-intensive technology, this phrase means the processing of goods by sophisticated technology rather than by large numbers of workers.

Terms of trade: the relationship or balance between the income a country receives for its exports and the cost of its imports. For most *Third World* countries, the *terms of trade* are unfavorable because they receive less for their raw material exports than they pay for their imports of manufactured goods and oil.

Third World: the more than 120 countries of Latin America, Asia, and Africa, sometimes referred to as the "developing world." Within the term *Third World,* many people use terms such as "less developed countries" and even the "Fourth World" to designate those poorest of Third World countries, with "middle developed countries"referring to the newly rich oil-producing countries and rapidly industrializing countries like Brazil, South Korea, and Taiwan. *Third World* is also used to designate any group of people that is poor because it is dominated or exploited by other groups. Thus, racial minorities in the U.S. are sometimes referred to as "Third World peoples."

Transfer pricing: the accounting practice of some multinational corporations whereby they fix prices for their intracompany transactions (purchases and sales of items within the parent company and its subsidiaries or branches). These prices are rarely related to competitive market prices of those same items. Prices are fixed for the purpose of increased parent company profits, by means of showing on the books the highest costs (and thus the least profits) in areas where tax rates are the highest, and the lowest costs (and thus the highest profits) in areas where the tax rates are the lowest.

Notes

Chapter One

1. Synod of Catholic Bishops, *Justice in the World*, "Introduction." Available from the U.S. Catholic Conference, 1312 Massachusetts Ave NW, Washington, DC 20005.

2. Quoted in Pope Paul VI, *On the Development of Peoples*, #23, published by, among others, the Daughters of St. Paul, 50 St. Paul's Ave., Jamaica Plain, Boston, MA 02130.

3. *Policy Statement on Human Rights*, American Baptist Churches, USA (Valley Forge, PA 19481), p. 3.

4. Synod of Catholic Bishops, "Evangelization Statement", 1974. Available from the U.S. Catholic Conference.

5. *This Land Is Home to Me*, p. 7. Published by and available from the Catholic Committee of Appalachia, 31-A South Third Ave., Prestonsburg, KY 41653.

6. On the Development of Peoples, #17. The Committee on Society, Development and Peace (SODEPAX), an agency established jointly by the World Council of Churches and the Vatican, presents a summary of the statements of the World Council of Churches over the past ten years on this theme. See "In Search of a New Society: Christian Participation in the Building of New Relations Among Peoples," in *Church Alert*, May 1976, produced by SODEPAX (150 Route de Ferney, 1211 Geneva 20, Switzerland), pp. 13–14.

7. Dennis E. Shoemaker, *The Global Connection: Local Action for World Justice* (New York: Friendship Press, 1977), pp. 23ff, discusses this same point in some detail.

Chapter Two

1. Arthur Simon, *Bread for the World* (New York: Paulist Press, 1975), p. 39.

2. Rev. John McRaith, "Testimony to a Senate Ad Hoc Hearing on the World Food Conference," December 18, 1974 (National Catholic Rural Life Conference, 3801 Grand, Des Moines, Iowa). Official policy statements on hunger by U.S. Christian churches include the *American Baptist Policy Statement on Hunger*, June 24, 1975; *The United Church Confronts the World Food Crisis* (A Pronouncement of the 10th General Synod of the United Church of Christ), June 30, 1975; *Human Hunger and the World Food Crisis* (A Policy Statement of the National Council of the Churches of Christ in the USA), October 11, 1975.

3. Passed by the U.S. Congress in late September 1975. The full text is available from Bread for the World (207 E. 16th, New York, NY 10003).

4. These examples are more fully described in Joseph Collins and Frances Moore Lappe, *Food First* (Boston: Houghton-Mifflin, 1977), Parts VII–IX.

5. Published by Alternatives, 1924 E. Third St., Bloomington, IN 47401.

6. E. V. Walter, *Communities of the Poor* (London: Oxford University Press), quoted in *Creative Simplicity* (Newsletter of the Shakertown Pledge Group), January 1977, p. 19.

7. *Development Education Viewpoint #1* (Toronto: Development Education Centre, 1975), pp. 3–5.

Chapter Three

1. *Principles of a NIEO*, preamble. See document in the Appendix. Also, the *Programme of Action*, X.

2. Jeremiah Novak, "In Defense of the Third World," *America*, January 21, 1978, p. 36.

3. Among those whose vision and proposals for a NIEO go beyond the UN version are the 1976 World Employment Conference of the International Labor Organization; the Dag Hammarskjold Foundation report, *What Now*; and *Reshaping the International Order*, pp. 71–77.

4. *Principles*, "j". *Principles* "m", "n", and "t" also refer to changes in the redistribution of wealth through changes in trade mechanisms.

5. *Principles*, "l", also *Principles* "o" and "p".

6. *Principles*, "d"; also "k".

7. Mahbub ul Haq, *The Third World and the International Economic Council, 1976*, p. 11.

8. The quotations in this section are from the *Principles*, "e", "g", "e", "a", "f", "h", and "i".

9. The quotations in this section are from the *Principles*, "c", 2.

10. The *Principles* referred to in this section are "s" and "t".

11. ul Haq, *The Third World* . . ., p. 7.

12. The *Principles* quoted in this section are "3" and "b".

13. ul Haq, *The Third World* . . ., pp. 12–18; *Reshaping the International Order*, pp. 22–23, 47–48.

14. Denis Goulet, "Interdependence: Verbal Smokescreen or New Ethic?" (Washington, DC: Overseas Development Council, 1976), quoted in Orlando Letelier and Michael Moffitt, *The International Economic Order* (Washington, DC: Transnational Institute, 1977), p. 30.

Chapter Four

1. *Survey of Current Business* (Washington, DC: Bureau of Economic Analysis, US Department of Commerce, July 1973) and *The U.S. and the Developing World: Agenda for Action 1973* (Overseas Development Council), and contained in Jayne Millar Wood, *Focusing on Global Development and Poverty: A Resource Book for Educators* (Overseas Development Council, 1974), pp. 569–570.

2. This graph is drawn from many sources. *World Bank Annual Report, 1977*, pp. 108, 114–115; Howard M. Wachtel, *The New Gnomes: Multinational Banks in the Third World* (Washington, DC: Transnational Institute, 1977), p. 19; *Reshaping the International Order*, p. 36; *Agenda 1977* (Overseas Development Council), pp. 206–207; *Employment, Growth, and Basic Needs* (World Employment Conference), pp. 129–130.

3. Thomas Fenton, *Coffee: The Rules of the Game and You* (New York: The Christophers, 1974); and *Maryknoll Magazine*, March 1976, p. 53.

4. *Agenda 1977*, p. 223.

5. *Nestlé in the Developing Countries* (Vevey, Switzerland: Nestlé Alimentana, 1975), pp. 100, 227; *Nestlé Annual Report 1975*; Susan George, "Nestlé Alimentana S.A.: The Limits to Public Relations," Third World Institute (Minneapolis), pp. 25–27.

6. International Monetary Fund, *International Financial Statistics*, November 1977.

7. *1976 Commodities Yearbook* (New York: Commodity Research Bureau, 1976), pp. 105, 110; *Food First*, p. 185. "A New Approach to World Reserves," *Development Forum*, September 1978, p. 7.

8. George H. Dunne, *The Right to Development* (New York: Paulist Press, 1974), pp. 102–103.

9. *World Bank Annual Report 1977*, p. 109.

10. Tibor Mende, *De l'Aide à la Recolonisation* (Paris: Editions de Seuil, 1972), pp. 84ff, quoted in *The Right to Development*, pp. 134–135.

11. "Reflections on UNCTAD IV," (Toronto: GATT-Fly, 1977); Howard Wachtel, "Why the Banks Bailed Out Peru," *Business Week*, March 21, 1977; *The New Gnomes*, pp. 29–35.

12. Jeremiah Novak, "In Defense of the Third World," *America*, January 21, 1978, p. 34.

13. Mahbub ul Haq, *The Third World and the International Economic Order* (Washington, DC: Overseas Development Council, 1976), pp. 4–5.

14. *Teaching International Development: A Monday Morning Manual* (IDERA, 2524 Cypress St., Vancouver, British Columbia), p. 87.

15. Mahbub ul Haq, "What Happened to the North-South Dialogue?", *The Interdependent*, May 1978, p. 7.

16. "Chocolate with a Bite," from *Yes, But What Can I Do*, in *Study Action Pack on World Development* (New York: United Nations Development Program, 1976), p. 13.

17. Rudolf H. Strahm, "Jute, Not Plastic! A Campaign to Educate Swiss Consumers," *Ideas and Action* (Food and Agricultural Organization, November 1976), p. 10.

Chapter Five

1. "Jute, Not Plastic," *Ideas and Action*, p. 10. See *Principles for a NIEO*, "m", in the Appendix to Chapter 3.

2. *Food First*, pp. 216–226.

3. Much of the information in this section is taken from Tettah A. Kofi, "The International Cocoa Agreements," *Journal of World Trade Law*, Vol. 11, No. 1, January/February 1977, pp. 37–51.

4. *ICDA News* (International Coalition for Development Action), August 8, 1977, and all subsequent issues update developments in the NIEO negotiations.

5. *Agenda 1977*, pp. 97–103.

6. "A Compromise on LDC Debt," *The Interdependent*, Vol. 5, No. 4, April 1978, p. 4. *ICDA News* #8 (August 30, 1978).

7. Mahbub ul Haq, *Possible Effects of Trade Liberalization on Trade in Primary Commodities* (World Bank Staff Working Paper #193, January 1975), quoted in *United States Economic Relations with the Developing World* (A Commentary on the NIEO, prepared for the Committee on Social Development and World Peace of the U.S. Catholic Conference), June 28, 1976, p. 20. See *Principles for a NIEO*, "n", in Appendix to Chapter 3.

8. *Food First*, p. 193, where Collins and Lappe report that in 1967, the gross profit margin earned in chocolate production was 38% higher than the average margin for comparable food processing industries.

9. UNDP Paper #9, p. 8. Also Robert McNamara, "Address to the Board of Governors," September 26, 1977 (Washington, DC; The World Bank), pp. 15–17.

10. Among other sources, Pope Paul VI, *On the Development of Peoples*, #22–23.

11. Samuel L. Parmar, "Self-Reliant Development in an 'Interdependent' World," in *Beyond Dependency* (Washington, DC: Overseas Development Council, 1975), p. 4.

12. Frances Moore Lappe and Eleanor McCallie, *Informal, On-Site Report on the Banana Industry in the Philippines* (San Francisco; Institute for Food and Development Policy, 1977). Also, "Banana Hunger," *Food Monitor*, March-April 1978, p. 12.

13. Julius Nyerere, "The Economic Challenge: Dialogue or Confrontation?", p. 3.

14. Bread for the World, "Price Stabilization for Whom?", September 1977.

Chapter Six

1. "Commodity Price Stabilization and the Developing Countries: The Problem of Choice," World Bank Staff Working Paper #262, July 1977, p. 19.

2. *Food First*, p. 203; Peter Dorner, "Export Agriculture and Economic Development," statement presented to the Interfaith Center for Corporate Responsibility, 1976.

3. Susan George, *How the Other Half Dies* (Montclair, NJ: Allanheld, Osmun & Co., 1977), p. 19; and "A Profile of the Philippine Banana Industry," *Solidaridad II* (A Publication of the Resource Center for Philippine Concerns, No. 6, Jan/Feb 1978), p. 6.

4. "Agro-Exports: Curse of Cane," *Agribusiness Targets Latin America* (NACLA Report on the Americas, Vol. XII, No. 1, Jan-Feb 1978), p. 32.

5. *How the Other Half Dies*, p. 18; also *Agenda 1977*, p. 186; and *USCC Commentary*, p. 41 citing FAO statistics.

6. *Food First*, p. 170.

7. *Ibid.*, pp. 264–268.

8. "Agro-Exports," p. 32. See also "Colombia Connection," *Time*, January 29, 1979.

9. "Food Production for Whom?" (Bread for the World, 1976).

10. *How the Other Half Dies*, p. 69.

11. *Food First*, p. 266.

12. "What Is the New International Economic Order?" (Toronto: GATT-Fly, 1975), p. 8.

13. *Food First*, pp. 186–187.

14. *Ibid.*, p. 181.

15. *Ibid.*, pp. 181–182.

16. *Ibid.*, pp. 98–101.

17. *Ibid.*, pp. 47–61.

18. *Ibid.*, pp. 103–104.

19. "Bitter Fruits," *Latin America & Empire Report* (NACLA, Vol. X, No. 7, September 1976), p. 13.

20. Fr. Vince Cullen, "Sour Pineapples," *America*, November 6, 1976, pp. 300–301.

21. "Agro-Exports," p. 26.

22. Correspondence from Fr. Ed Gerlock to Ms. Chris Henderson, September 21, 1977.

23. John Dillon, "The Limitations of the Trade Issue" (Toronto: GATT-Fly, 1973), p. 1.

24. *Food First*, pp. 198, 200.

25. "Export Agriculture and Economic Development," pp. 6–7.

26. *Food First*, pp. 75–90.

27. United Nations Economic and Social Council, Preparatory Committee for the Special Session of the General Assembly Devoted to Development and International Cooperation, Second Session, June 16–27, 1975 (E/AC. 621/8, May 5, 1975), p. 8, quoted in *Food First*, p. 202.

28. *Food First*, p. 206.

29. "Agro-Exports," p. 32.

Chapter Seven

1. "McNamara on The Largest Issue: World Economy," *The New York Times*, April 2, 1978.

2. Jack Nelson, "U.S. Beef Imports: A Proposal," *CALC Report*, November-December 1977, p. 10.

3. Fr. Frank Quinlivan, personal correspondence with the author, April 1978.

4. *Yes, But What Can I Do?*, in A Study/Action Packet on World Development, United Nations Development Program (United Nations Plaza, New York, 1976), is the source of the chocolate bar campaign, as well as a number of others not described in this chapter. The tea campaign comes from the World Development Movement.

5. Rudolf H. Strahm, "Jute, Not Plastic," *Ideas and Action* (Food and Agricultural Organization, Freedom from Hunger Campaign/Action for Development Program, 00100 Rome, Italy), November 1976, pp. 9–12.

6. National Land for People, "NLP's Legislative Program," p. 2.

7. Jack Nelson, "U.S. Beef Imports: A Proposal," *CALC Report*, November-December 1977, pp. 9–18; and personal correspondence with the author, May 1978.

Chapter Eight

1. Norman Girvan, *Economic Nationalists versus Multinational Corporations: Revolutionary or Evolutionary Change?* (Toronto:

Development Education Centre, 1975), p. 34; and William F. Ryan, S.J., "Multinational Corporations and the NIEO," Memorandum #4 (Washington, DC; Center of Concern, August 1976), p. 2.

2. Richard Barnet and Ronald Muller, *Global Reach: The Power of the Multinational Corporations* (New York: Simon and Shuster, 1974), p. 18.

3. North American Congress on Latin America, "Bitter Fruits," *Latin America and Empire Report*, Vol. X, No. 7, September 1976, p. 19; and Robin Jurs, *Background Paper on the Del Monte Resolution* (San Francisco: Northern California Interfaith Committee on Corporate Responsibility, 1977), p. 13.

4. *Global Reach*, pp. 16–17, 258–260.

5. *Survey of Current Business*, Vol. 53, No. 9, Sept. 1973 for 1972 data; see Aug. 1977 for 1977 data.

6. "Transnational Corporations and the UN," *Development Issue Paper #3* (New York: United National Development Program, 1976); also *Reshaping the International Order*, p. 39.

7. UNDP Paper #3, p. 4; *Global Reach*, p. 16.

8. *New Gnomes*, pp. 8–9.

9. *Fortune*, August 1977; *National Basic Intelligence Fact Book*, July 1977 (Government Printing Office: Washington, DC 20402).

10. UNDP Paper #3, p. 3.

11. Girvan, *Economic Nationalists versus Multinational Corporations*, p. 30.

Chapter Nine

1. *Global Reach*, p. 297.

2. *Ibid.*, p. 161.

3. *Ibid.*, pp. 153–154, 140–142.

4. Raymond Vernon, *Sovereignty at Bay: The Multinational Spread of US Enterprises* (New York, 1973), cited in Ryan, "Multinational Corporations and the NIEO," p. 5.

5. *Global Reach*, pp. 153–154.

6. *Ibid.*, pp. 155, 139.

7. *Ibid.*, p. 135.

8. Girvan, *Economic Nationalists versus Multinational Corporations*, p. 31.

9. "Less Expensive and More Appropriate Technologies in the Developing Countries," Development Issue Paper #11 (United Nations Development Program, April 1976), p. 3; and "Transfers of Technology to the Developing Countries: Removing the Barriers," Development Issue Paper #10 (United Nations Development Program, February 1976), p. 3. The figure of $1.5 billion for 1970 is more conservative than the figure of $1.8 billion that the UN estimates for Third World payments to multinational corporations in 1968 for its technology, in UNDP Paper #3, p. 5.

354 NotesNOTES

10. UNDP Paper #11, p. 3.

11. *Reshaping the International Order*, p. 279. 80% means 317 of 409 agreements between the Andean countries and multinational corporations.

12. "Women of the World: The Facts," *The New Internationalist*, October 1977, p. 8. Also Lisa Leghorn and Mary Roodkowsky, *Who Really Starves: Women and World Hunger* (New York: Friendship Press, 1977).

13. *Global Reach*, p. 136.

14. *Ibid.*, p. 143.

15. *Ibid.*, pp. 144–145.

16. *Ibid.*, p. 146.

17. *Food First*, pp. 130–131.

18. *Shield: Winter 1975* (San Francisco: Del Monte Corporation, Vol. 27, no. 3), pp. 2–3.

19. Jack Nelson, "Del Monte in the Philippines," *CALC Report*, 1977, p. 10.

20. Correspondence from Fr. Ed Gerlock to Chris Henderson, September 20, 1977.

21. Northern California Interfaith Committee on Corporate Responsibility, "Analysis of the Del Monte Corporation Annual Meeting, September 27, 1977," pp. 7–8.

22. "Sharing Global Resources," *Documentation* (National Action Research on the Military Industrial Complex and the American Friends Service Committee, 1977), p. 52. The map is reprinted with the permission of NARMIC and is taken from one of the slides in "Sharing Global Resources."

23. *Global Reach*, p. 183.

24. *Ibid.*

25. *Food First*, pp. 307–309.

26. *Ibid.*, p. 305.

27. *Ibid.*, p. 309, quoting the *Columbia Journal of World Business*, Winter 1974.

Chapter Ten

1. *Global Reach*, p. 19.

2. "Canada: A Modest Response," *Time*, May 15, 1972.

3. Dale L. Johnson, ed., *The Chilean Road to Socialism* (Garden City, NY: Anchor Press, 1973), pp. 12–18, cited in *Sharing Global Resources: Documentation for NARMIC Slideshow* (Philadelphia: American Friends Service Committee, 1977), p. 61.

4. "The Latin America Banana Crisis," Development Issue Paper #1 (United Nations Development Program), cited in *Documentation for NARMIC Slideshow*, p. 46–47.

5. *Principles for the NIEO*, "e".

6. UNDP Paper #3, pp. 6–7.

7. This whole section is based on the slide show "Sharing Global Resources" and the excellent documentation accompanying it, especially pp. 61–91.

8. This is the text of her statement in the slideshow. Currently working with the Committee for Human Rights in Chile, Isabel Letelier is also the widow of Orlando Letelier, former Chilean Ambassador to the U.S. who was assassinated in Washington, DC, September 1976.

9. Norman Girvan, *Copper in Chile* (Mona, Jamaica: University of the West Indies, Institute of Social and Economic Research, 1972), p. 60, cited in *Documentation for NARMIC Slideshow*, p. 66.

10. *Anaconda Annual Report for 1972*, cited in *Documentation for NARMIC Slideshow*, p. 67.

11. The complete sources of these two Senate reports is the U.S. Senate, Staff Report of the Select Committee to Study Governmental Operations with respect to Intelligence Activities. Both are published by the Government Printing Office and available from Congress. The memo quoted in the text is from the report entitled *Alleged Assassination Involving Foreign Leaders* (1975), p. 231.

12. UNDP Paper #3, UN document E/AC.62.8, issued May 5, 1975.

13. *Ibid.*, p. 1.

14. Interfaith Center for Corporate Responsibility has copies of the 6 principles and extensive analysis of them.

Chapter Eleven

1. *Global Reach*, p. 305.
2. *Ibid.*, pp. 380-382.
3. CALA Newsletter, December 1976, p. 1.

Chapter Twelve

1. Robert Ball, "Nestlé Revs Up Its U.S. Campaign," *Fortune*, February 13, 1978, pp. 80–90; and Susan George, "Nestlé Alimentana S.A.: The Limits to Public Relations," INFACT, June 1977; and *Nestlé 1977* (The Annual Report) are the sources of most of the information in this "Introduction."

2. *Nestlé in the Developing Countries* (Nestlé, Avenue Nestlé, 1800 Vevey, Switzerland, 1975), cover.

3. J. E. Post, "The Infant Formula Industry: Strategy, Structure and Performance," unpublished research findings; and Ann Crittendon, "Baby Formula Sales in Third World Criticized," *The New York Times*, September 11, 1975.

4. M.E. Smith, R.N., and R.N. Doan, M.D., of the Child Development and Mental Retardation Center, University of Washington in Seattle.

5. *Protein Advisory Group Manual on Feeding Infants and Young Children* (PAG Document 1.14/26, December 1971).

6. Robert Ledogar, *Hungry for Profits* (U.S. Food and Drug Multinationals in Latin America), IDOC-North America (235 E. 49th St., New York, NY 10017), p. 130; and Alan Berg, *The Nutrition Factor: Its Role in National Development* (Washington, DC: The Brookings Institute, 1973), p. 95.

7. Cited in Mike Muller, *The Baby Killer* (London, 1974), p. 13.

8. *Supermercado Moderno*, February 1977, cited in Leah Margulies, "A Critical Essay on the Role of Promotion in Bottle Feeding," *PAG Bulletin*, Vol. VII, No. 3–4, September-December 1977, p. 77.

9. Alan Berg, "The Economics of Breast-Feeding," *Saturday Review of the Sciences*, May 1973, pp. 29–32.

10. "What Are Third World Governments Doing About the Infant Formula Scandal?", INFACT, 1978, pp. 1–2.

11. Fatima Patel, letter to Richard Huston, Director, Nutrition Information, Ross Laboratories, August 20, 1977, and available from INFACT as part of a series of letters on the whole issue.

12. "Formula for Malnutrition", CIC Brief, Interfaith Center for Corporate Responsibility, New York, April 1975, p. 3A, cites several studies.

13. Nestlé, *A Life Begins*, quoted in CIC Brief, p. 3B.

14. Dr. Benjamin Spock, *The Common Sense Book of Baby and Child Care* (New York: Duell, Sloan & Pierce, 1945), pp. 36, 39, 42; Dr. Derrick Jelliffe's testimony at the Berne (Nestlé vs. Third World Action) trial, cited in Susan George, "Nestlé Alimentana S.A.: The Limits to Public Relations," pp. 15–16.

15. See also *Food First*, p. 315.

16. Fatima Patel letter to Richard Huston.

17. INFACT Newsletter, September 1977, p. 3.

18. *Food First*, p. 316; Jane O'Reilly, "Especially in the Third World: Mother's Milk Is Best," *The Washington Star*, June 14, 1976.

19. Quoted in *Food First*, p. 316.

20. CIC Brief, pp. 3C–3D.

21. *Ibid.*

22. Reprinted in "What Are Third World Governments Doing About the Infant Formula Scandal?", p. 1.

23. International Pediatrics Association, "IPA Seminar on Nutrition," *Bulletin of the International Pediatrics Association*, Vol. 4 (October 1975), p. 21.

24. "Code of Ethics and Professional Standards for Advertising, Product Information and Advisory Services for Breast-Milk Substitutes," (November 19, 1975), p. 1; Nestlé statement quoted in *The Baby Killer*, p. 13; Arthur Furer (Nestlé President), quoted in "The Formula Flap," *Time*, February 16, 1976, p. 57.

25. Available from Nestlé in Vevey, Switzerland, or White Plains, NY.

26. Drs. Thompson and Black, World Health Organization *Bulletin*, 52, 2, 1975, quoted in Susan George, "Nestlé Alimentana S.A.: The Limits to Public Relations," pp. 11–12.

27. "PAG Comments on Objectives of International Council of Infant Industries (ICIFI) and Its Proposed Code of Ethics," PAG Letter No. 83/76, January 23, 1976, pp. 1–2.

Chapter Thirteen
1. *The Third World and the International Economic Order*, p. 1.
2. All material by Sheldon Gellar is taken from "Development Models, Development Administration, and the Ratched-McMurphy Model: A View from the Bottom," in *Administration for Development: A Comparative Perspective on the Middle East and Latin America*, Occasional Paper (School of Public and Environmental Affairs, Indiana University, Bloomington, IN, September 1976), pp. 11–25.

Chapter Fourteen
1. From a graphic poster contained in *A Study & Action Pack for World Development* (United National Development Program Informational Division, UN Plaza, New York, NY 10017).
2. James D. Calderwood, *The Developing World: Poverty, Growth and Rising Expectations* (Glenview, IL: Scott Foresman & Co., 1976), p. 103.
3. Leonard Greenwood, "Brazil Bishops Rap 'Economic Miracle,'" *Washington Post*, May 20, 1973; Marvin Howe, *New York Times*, December 14, 1974.
4. *Food First*, pp. 373–81, 168, elaborates on principles of "food self-reliance," most of which have been incorporated into this analysis of self-reliant development.
5. *The Third World and the International Economic Order*, p. 51; also *Reshaping the International Order*, pp. 65–66.
6. Elizabeth O'Kelly, "Appropriate Technology for Women," quoted in Lisa Leghorn and Mary Roodkowsky, *Who Really Starves: Women and World Hunger* (New York: Friendship Press, 1977), p. 25.
7. *Food First*, pp. 156–62.
8. *Ibid.*, p. 157.
9. *Reshaping the International Order*, pp. 66–67.
10. The information on Patti Kalyana is from two reports—*A Programme of Development for Village Patti Kalyana* and *Integrated Development Project*, both produced by the Swarajya Bharati (Ashram, Patti Kalyana, India, 1972)—and from an on-site visit in the summer of 1972, and from correspondence with Akumar Kumar, director of the Gandhian team.

Chapter Fifteen

1. John Vorster, *The Johannesburg Star*, August 26, 1972, quoted in "U.S. Corporate Expansion in South Africa," CIC Brief, *The Corporate Examiner* (New York: Interfaith Center for Corporate Responsibility, April 1976), p. 3A.

Chapter Sixteen

1. George Kent, "Varieties of Interdependence," *Prioritas* (The Peace Laboratory, 438 N. Skinker, St. Louis, MO 63130), January 31, 1977, pp. 12–17, is the source of several of these points.

2. Garrett Hardin, "Lifeboat Ethics: The Case Against Helping the Poor," *Psychology Today*, September 1974.

3. Daniel Moynihan/Henry Kissinger, "Global Consensus and Economic Development," United Nations, September 1, 1975 (U.S. Department of State, Bureau of Public Affairs), pp. 1, 16.

4. David C. King, *International Education for Spaceship Earth*, New Dimensions Series #4, 1970 (New York: Foreign Policy Association), p. 73.

5. Paul Erlich, *New York Times*, November 4, 1970.

6. Susan George, *How the Other Half Dies*, pp. 35, 290.

7. *Reshaping the International Order*, pp. 82–84.

Chapter Seventeen

1. Among other places, the full text of Chief Sealth's speech is printed in the December 1976 issue of *Fellowship* magazine (write the Fellowship of Reconciliation, P.O. Box 271, Nyack, NY 10960).

2. "Shakertown Pledge" (The Shakertown Pledge Group, 3104 16th Ave South, Minneapolis, MN 55407), p. 2.

3. *The Church in the Modern World* (Documents of Vatican Council II, 1965), #75.